W9-DJG-999

Art *of the* Brooklyn Bridge

A VISUAL HISTORY

Art *of the* Brooklyn Bridge

A VISUAL HISTORY

Richard Haw

Routledge
Taylor & Francis Group

Dedication

For Pippa and Charlie, for when they grow up,
and as always for Erica.

Frontispiece: Joseph Stella, *Bridge* (detail)

First published 2008
by Routledge
270 Madison Ave, New York, NY 10016

Simultaneously published in the UK
by Routledge
2 Park Square, Milton Park, Abingdon, Oxon OX14 4RN

Routledge is an imprint of the Taylor & Francis Group, an informa business

© 2008 Taylor & Francis

Designed and typeset in Perpetua by Alex Lazarou, Surbiton, England
Printed and bound in the United States of America on acid-free paper by Sheridan Books, Inc.

Library of Congress Cataloging in Publication Data
A catalog record has been requested for this book

ISBN10: 0-415-95386-3 (hbk)
ISBN13: 978-0-415-95386-3 (hbk)

Contents

Acknowledgments

While my name may stand as the sole author of this work, art books are the most collective efforts in publishing. In putting this one together I have racked up countless debts and it is my great pleasure to acknowledge just a few of them here.

My first and greatest debt is to the scores of archivists, librarians and registrars whose generous help and endless patience made this book possible. For numerous acts of kindness and understanding, I would like to thank everyone with whom I have corresponded over the past two years, and especially (in no particular order) Sue Grinols at the San Francisco Museums of Fine Art, Amy Rupert at Rensselaer Polytechnic Institute's Folsom Library, Jill Reichenbach and Kristine Paulus at the New-York Historical Society, Uri Kolodney and Susan Rittereiser at the University of Texas Libraries, Carol Jones at Yale University Library, Erin Schleigh at the Museum of Fine Arts, Boston, Marguerite Lavin and Melanie Bower at the Museum of the City of New York, Thomas Lisanti at the New York Public Library, Fiona Patrick at the Cornell University Library, Julie May at the Brooklyn Historical Society, Barbara Brand at the Stony Brook University Library, Polly Armstrong at the Stanford University Library, Lisa DeBoer and all the staff at the Brooklyn Public Library's wonderful Brooklyn Collection, Beth Moore at the Telfair Museum of Arts and Sciences, Mickey Koch at the Des Moines Art Center, Sue Nurse at the University of Rochester's Memorial Art Gallery, David Kencik at the San Diego Museum of Art, AnnaLee Pauls at the Princeton University Library, Kathleen Kornell at the Cleveland Museum of Art, Joan Anne Maxham at the Metropolitan Museum of Art, Ruth Janson at the Brooklyn Museum of Art, Merry Armata at the Sterling and Francine Clark Art Institute, Heather Scanlan at the Walker Art Center, Juliana Driever at the Queens Public Library Gallery, Rivka Weinstock at the Art Commission of New York, Jonathan Friedlander at the Bonni Benrubi Gallery, Eva Waters and Sandi Knakal at the studio of Ellsworth Kelly, Delinda Buie at the University of Louisville, Michael Shulman at Magnum Photos, Linda McCurdy at the Duke University Library, Mara Linskey at the Charles H. MacNider Museum, Trisha Murray at the Berry-Hill Galleries, Joan Gonsalez at the office of Barney Ebsworth, and Robin Dettre and Andrew Thomas at the Smithsonian American Art Museum.

In addition to the above, dozens more people lent their time, answered questions and helped locate images, especially: Joseph Allerhand, Silverio Bracaglia, Jean Bubley, Andreas Bühler, Jeffrey Coven, Sally Forbes, Mick Gidley, Suzanne Julig, Lionel Kelly, Dong Kingman Jr., Becky Lawton, Li-lan, Gene-Manuel, Pam Mendelsohn, George Miles, Sarah Morthland, David Nye, John Solum, Yael Reinharz, Daniel Treiman, Phyllis Wrynn, and Bonnie Yochelson. Thank you all so much.

I would also like to extend my deepest thanks to all the artists who agreed to be in the book: Rose Alber, Tom Baril, Bascove, Michel Bayard, Jonathan Blum, Jen Ferguson, Stanley Greenberg, Horst Hamman, Robin Holland, Mike Iacovone, Thomas Kellner, Ellsworth Kelly, Arthur Leipzig, Dona MacAdams, Trish Mayo, Peter de Sève, Charlie Samuels, Kenneth Snelson, Jerry Spagnoli, Hank Virgona, and Milford Zornes. I am, of course, honored.

Numerous friends at John Jay College helped keep me sane and smiling throughout. For warm encouragement and the occasional pint, I would like to thank: Priscilla Acuna, Valerie Allen, Michael Aman, Andrea Balis, Michael Blitz, Bettina Carbonell, Ed Davenport, Betsy Gitter, Don Goodman, Carol Groneman, Ann Huse, Pat Licklider, Mark McBeth, MaryAnn McClure, Adam McKible, Jerry Markowitz, John Matteson, Ed Paulino, Allison Pease, Shirley Sarna, Dennis Sherman, Chris Suggs, Marny Tabb, Anya Taylor, Sam Thomas, Darryl Westcott-Marshall, and Richard Zeikowitz. While it might be a cliché, it is also very true: I couldn't ask for finer comrades.

A PSC-CUNY Research Award and a grant from John Jay's Office for the Advancement of Research were crucial in securing images and permissions, and I would like to thank Jacob Marini and James Levine for all their help.

This project got going thanks to two Routledge alumni: my friends Rob Tempio and Dave McBride. Rob listened to my ideas, told Dave and after a few drinks in Park Slope, a contract was signed. From the off, and from within and without, their belief and enthusiasm have helped drive this book. Steve Rutter came on board as I was finishing up and proved himself a fine editor, a loyal supporter and valuable ally. Anne Horowitz kept my spirits up while slogging through all the images, Beatrice Schraa worked feverishly in the final, crucial stages, and Alex Lazarou did an incredible job designing and laying out the book. To you all: it's been a real joy and an absolute pleasure.

This book is dedicated to Pippa and Charlie, my niece and nephew, and to Erica Brody, whose presence lights my world and guides my thoughts. Without Erica, this book would have been much worse, as would my life.

Crank, Crackpot, and Creative Genius: Plans to Bridge the East River (1800–1867)

New York is a fantastic incongruity: at once a centralized metropolis through which the wealth of a nation flows and an isolated island community cut off from its neighbors and the rest of the country. For much of its long and storied history, the entire region has been dominated and defined by what the Commissioner's Plan of 1811 described as "those large arms of the seas which embrace New-York Island": the Hudson and the East rivers.[1]

The need for sure and steady passage across the East River is as old as the Lenape tribes that populated the region in the years before European settlement. With the establishment of New Netherlands, the issue took on more urgency. From the beginning, Long Island was for agriculture and New York was for commerce, and, as any good farmer knows, no amount of expert husbandry will pay the bills if you can't get your wares to market. Unfortunately for those on Long Island, their only sizable market lay over the East River. Even more unfortunately, what passed for a ferry service was neither sure nor steady.

The East River was a total mess for much of the seventeenth and eighteenth centuries. With strong winds and erratic currents, the journey across was arduous and wildly unpredictable. Rowboats were forced to endure the vagaries of strong shifting tides; often, sailboats would catch a stiff breeze and, within the blink of an eye, fetch up on either Governor's or Blackwell's Island. Not only were skiffs and scows yo-yoing frantically up and down the water, they were neither shipshape nor Bristol fashion. Often overloaded and understaffed, they were in fact downright lethal. Spooked livestock could upset even the stoutest vessel, and at night collisions were standard fare.[2]

By 1800, oars and sails could no longer be trusted with the city's commercial future. Clearly, New Yorkers needed to get busy. And get busy they did. A bridge was a financial imperative, and in New York calls for economic improvement are always answered by

William Burgis, *The South Prospect of the City of New York,
in North America*, 1717 (published 1761).
Engraving 17.3 × 52.7 cm. Courtesy of the Miriam and Ira D. Wallach
Division, The New York Public Library/Art Resource, NY.

a thousand different voices, many of which emanate from the shaded region between
crank, crackpot, and creative genius.

Opening the Debate, 1800–1802

The nineteenth century is littered with myriad schemes to bridge the East River. Some
are intriguing, most are harebrained, and it all began at the very beginning of the century
when talk of a bridge began to swirl around the drawing rooms of New York and Brooklyn. As Jeremiah Johnson noted in 1800 in his private notebook:

> It has been suggested that a bridge should be constructed from this village across the
> East River to New York. This idea has been treated as chimerical, from the magnitude
> of the design; but whosoever takes it into their serious consideration, will find more
> weight in the practicability of the scheme than at first view is imagined. This would
> be the means of raising the value of the lands on the east side of the river. It has been
> observed that every objection to the building of this bridge could be refuted and that
> it only wanted a combination of opinion to favor the attempt. A plan has already been
> laid down on paper, and a gentleman of acknowledged abilities and good sense has
> observed that he would engage to erect it in two years' time.[3]

Who exactly was doing the suggesting was a mystery—as was the "gentleman of acknowledged abilities"—but, right on cue, "in two years' time," they banded together, called themselves the "Subscribers, Inhabitants of the City of New-York and Long Island," and issued the first formal bridge proposal in an open letter to the "Honorable ... Representatives of the People of the State of New-York." "Actuated only by motives which embrace public utility," the group declared that with "intercourse between" the two "insular" regions "at all times uncertain, and sometimes impracticable," a bridge was "indispensable" if the "great and increasing population of the city of New-York" were to enjoy "a daily supply" of the "necessaries of life."[4] The lobbyists and their intentions must have been well-known locally: their proposal touched a nerve and caused a firestorm of debate. Like conflicting obituaries waiting for a death, it forced proponents and opponents to leap into action.

One correspondent, who, in the fashion of the times, went by the *nom de plume* "Hydraulicus," also worried about the "deprivations" likely to affect the growing, yet "insular" city. More important, however, were military concerns and, oddly, noxious gases. Should a foreign fleet land below the city's fortifications on Long Island, what would prevent them from marching straight up to Brooklyn, where "they may command the city, and lay it under contribution, or burn it?" A bridge, apparently; although one need hardly mention that if a foreign army could lay waste to New York from Brooklyn Heights they could probably lay waste to a bridge also. The East River's "tempestuous" currents also worried Hydraulicus. Not only did the tides carry boats precariously up and down the East River, they also carried "a species of air or gas, which is extremely detrimental to animal life." Produced by the "decomposition [of] animal or vegetable matter" (dumped daily into the East River) this miasma was carried over the whole region by the rapacious tides. However, his solution went beyond mere bridging. To calm the tides and cure disease, New York would have to dam the entire river.[5]

As Hydraulicus was greeting readers of the *Daily Advertiser*, a gentleman styling himself "Common Sense" was appealing to the *Mercantile Advertiser*. A dam would have the opposite effect to that envisioned by Hydraulicus, he claimed. Tides were beneficial, not detrimental. They carried the "the street-water and filth" away from the city, not around it, all the while supplying "a pleasant and refreshing breeze" in summer. "Salutary and cooling gales" actually seemed to fascinate Common Sense more than bridges, yet after spending several paragraphs on the subject he finally got to the crux of the opposition: "The 'port and harbor,' have made the city ... what it is," he remarked, and "the latter can never be benefited by an injury done to the former." New York's prosperity was enabled and sustained by shipping. To compromise this was madness, especially as a bridge would only join "two islands" and neither to the "*main land*."[6]

Opposition to the bridge proposal mounted in the following days. An unnamed correspondent allowed that, while a bridge was worthy of the "most serious consideration,"

Common Sense must prevail. A bridge would naturally impede river traffic and was therefore unthinkable. Another allowed that if "we could reasonably expect such great benefits from the purposed [sic] bridge, no time ought to be lost in carrying the proposal of Hydraulicus into effect," before going on in great detail to rubbish each and every aspect of the scheme. The debate drifted towards parody with the entry of "Caligula"— "would it not be a greater convenience," he wondered, "to erect a bridge from the Battery to Elizabethtown" where New Yorkers could do a little strawberry picking?—and was put to bed, at least for the time being, in the most direct and succinct manner by the ironically named Philo-Hydraulicus: "the events of the last year have afforded convincing testimony, that the most sublime theory, and the most absurd practice, when united, form the perfection of human virtue and talents."[7]

Thomas Pope and John Stevens, 1807–1812

John Stevens—an engineer, inventor, and railroad pioneer—revived the bridge debate in early 1807 and spent much of the next few months refining his ideas and lobbying the state Senate. Somewhat obviously, he then spent several weeks reading assorted attacks on his proposal in the newspapers before abandoning the bridge idea and moving on. To tunnels, as it turns out.[8]

Stevens brought a more comprehensive approach to the bridge question. If piers in the river were a major objection, then he would build no piers. Instead, he would construct a *floating* bridge, complete with draw-bridges to accommodate river traffic. And if bridging the East River merely joined two islands, and neither to the mainland, then clearly both the Hudson and the East River needed bridging simultaneously. Stevens's proposal was read in front of the New York State Senate on February 28, 1807, where the issue was referred to committee. Stevens met with the members who, on March 6, reported back that the "proposed bridges … may be applied to purposes highly beneficial to the public," yet no full endorsement was forthcoming. Instead, the issue was thrown back on the city: "as this project involves considerations of the highest importance, and as objections may be made against the same, by persons concerned in navigation," the committee instructed Stevens to test his ideas before the public—by reprinting them in newspapers in New York and Albany—before resubmitting his petition at the next legislative session.[9]

Stevens's petition finally appeared in December 1807, and shortly afterwards all hell broke loose in the press. The response was entirely predictable, but Stevens didn't help his own cause either. Between his first and second petitions, Stevens ditched his floating draw-bridge plan and opted for the *bête noire* of the shipping industry: a permanent arch bridge. The assault was begun by "A Citizen": "among the number of plans proposed to obstruct the navigation, and ruin the harbor of New-York, none were more ruinous in its consequences to this city than" Stevens's. Writing in the *American Citizen,* "A Merchant" went further, wondering whether "it is not a plan of foreign projection, to aid in injuring the welfare of the city?" After all, "an inimical government could not by any intrigue adopt a more secure plan to interrupt the commercial importance of New York, than by forwarding this plan." Suspicious on all fronts, the Merchant also worried about real estate speculation, as did others. Why "the necessity of a junction between Long Island and New York," he asked, "unless to gratify the avarice of a few opulent landholders at the expense of public prosperity?" The debate continued to rage but the issue had been defined: the commercial lifeblood of the city was about to be sacrificed to the whims of real estate speculation. By the middle of February 1808 the issue was effectively dead and Stevens's petition was never again mentioned in Albany.[10]

VIEW OF THE FULTON FERRY BUILDINGS, BROOKLYN, LONG ISLAND.

"View of the Fulton Ferry Buildings, Brooklyn"
Ballou's Pictorial Drawing-Room Companion, January 3, 1857. From the author's collection.

Stevens was hamstrung by the legislature and attacked by the public, but a larger adversary lurked a mile or so up the East River from his intended site. On August 16, 1807, a bizarre floating contraption was launched from a factory at Corlears Hook on the East Side of Manhattan and, to the surprise of almost everyone, proceeded to motor around the Battery and up to Albany. All belching smoke, flying sparks, and whirring cogs and levers, Robert Fulton's "queer-looking craft" (as one eye-witness described it) made the round-trip in record time.[11] Much tinkering still remained, but the writing was on the wall: the era of the steam boat was about to begin.

Steamboats meant nothing to Thomas Pope, an obscure inventor and landscape gardener, and neither, as it happens, did the East River. Yet, over the years his name and his bridge—the grandiloquently named "Flying Pendent Lever Bridge," the inspiration behind Emily Barton's successful recent novel, *Brookland* (2006)—have become intrinsically linked to the history of the East River. Pope is often cited as the first person to draw up plans to span the river. Unfortunately, nothing could be further from the truth.

In 1807, Pope made his first public appearance in an open letter to the *Evening Post*— in which he attacked the "*inconsistent, expensive, delusive, destructive, deformed, weak and unmeaning* structure[s]" that passed for modern bridges—and, two years later, on June 26, 1809, he invited the Common Council of New York "to visit a Model of a Bridge

View of Brooklyn, L.I. from U.S. Hotel, New York, 1846.
Hand-colored lithograph by David William Moody. Print 39.6 × 93.6 cm.
Courtesy of the New York Public Library/Art Resource, NY.

which has been constructed consisting of one Arch only & which might be thrown over the widest rivers." Whether any Council members came is anyone's guess, but Pope was determined, and in 1811 he published his now-famous *A Treatise on Bridge Architecture*—the work on which his reputation is based.[12]

Actually, Pope's reputation rests on a single small aspect of his *Treatise*. The book itself is an odd combination: it begins with a rather rude and belligerent rant, continues voluminously through the history of bridge building (all of which is copied directly from other books), and concludes with a truly terrible 210-line poem of heroic couplets. In between, Pope pauses to explicate the theory, design, and construction of his own bridge. Consisting of two thin wooden arms cantilevered on either shore by massive stone abutments, and designed to meet halfway to form a long, flat arch, Pope's bridge was a disaster waiting to happen. Wood has neither the rigidity nor the tensile strength to support a span of any appreciable length, and, if attempted, Pope's bridge could have spanned no more than 50 feet of the river before snapping under its own weight.[13]

At no point in the book does Pope mention the East River. Instead, his Flying Pendent Lever Bridge was meant to be generic, a standard design fit for any crossing. Yet Pope wasn't content to leave the question of location entirely unstated. The first thing one sees on opening the book is a wonderfully rendered engraving of his bridge in profile—the flat wooden arch bridge stretching with grace and ease from one shore to another—beneath which Pope reprints the first few lines of his poem: "Let the broad arc the spacious HUDSON stride, / And span COLUMBIA'S rivers far more wide." Upon closer inspection, the engraving itself is no generic location, but the banks of the Hudson River: to the left, the rural hills of New Jersey, to the right the commercial bustle of the New York harbor. The presence of a steamboat—just beginning to ply their trade on the Hudson—is further evidence.[14]

Pope's book was not the announcement of a proposal but the final act of a four-year project. His last hurrah came in Philadelphia a year later with the showing of "A Grand Model, of T. Pope's Flying, Pendent, Lever, Bridge" at the Mansion House Hotel, for the first and last time explicitly stated "suitable … for the East River at New York." To publicize his Philadelphia debut, Pope wrote to the *Aurora and General Advertiser*. Describing himself as "an artist engaged in the science of Architecture," Pope humbly begged leave to raise the question of bridge-building, and went on to hope that his views on this "important subject" would be picked up and reprinted throughout the city. Pope's hopes in this matter went the way of all his wishes. His letter appears to have had no impact whatsoever.[15]

With little talent as an architect or an engineer, Pope was an inconspicuous individual, roundly ignored during his lifetime. Yet in a marvelous twist of history, he has managed to survive, thanks in large part to his book's opening page. The continued fascination with his treatise stems from his beautiful drawings, and the bold

"View of Thomas Pope's Flying Lever Bridge"
Reprinted in *St. Nicholas Magazine*, July 1883.
From the author's collection.

vision they contain, not from any innate engineering aptitude. Had Pope's treatise appeared without illustrations, one imagines, his name would be lost to all but the most specialized antiquarians. Instead, his exquisitely rendered etchings have managed to captivate generation after generation. Given the beauty of his designs and the daring of his plans, we seem to want to hear stories of him. And mythmakers have obliged. From the farfetched reminiscences of an unnamed New Yorker published in *St. Nicholas* magazine in 1883 to Barton's *Brookland*, Pope's legend has grown to include more fancy than fact.[16] Yet, this is hardly the point. Although frustration and disappointment were his constant companions in life, Pope's name has managed to live on as a testament to how Americans can dream, though not to how they can build.

Tunneling Beneath the East River, 1825–1857

On May 10, 1814, the East River was finally conquered, not by bridges but by machines. Fulton's new steamboat—the *Nassau*—made the journey between Beekman Slip and Ferry Street in an astonishing six minutes, and in its wake all talk of connecting New York with Brooklyn dissipated.[17] The silence lasted eleven years and was broken by events in Europe, not by some essential need or defect in New York. On March 2, 1825, work began on Marc Isambard Brunel's stupendous 1,300-foot tunnel beneath the Thames in London, and by August 22 questions were being raised in New York.

Having read of Brunel's project, the editors of the *New-York American* were "at a loss which most to admire, the magnitude of the undertaking, or the folly of the projectors," before going on to wonder: "what would be thought here of a scheme to carry a *turnpike under the East River?*" Neither engineering skill nor will, they concluded, but sheer cost. "John Bull … is whimsical, and he has a right to his whims, as he can afford to indulge in them." Americans, they feared, could not.[18]

A gentleman calling himself "Aquarius" didn't agree. A "culvert or tunnel" from New York to Brooklyn was entirely feasible, he thought, especially if constructed "on the plan of that now forming at London under the Thames." Americans possessed no less ingenuity than their British cousins, especially for a project guaranteed to "benefit the public, and at the same time promote their own interests." Unmoved, the *Gazette* thought Aquarius just as whimsical as John Bull—his "speculations … wild and chimerical"—but refused to "laugh at him, or sneer at his lucubrations." After all, steamboats were once thought "visionary," and thousands had "ridiculed the idea of forming a canal from the Hudson to Erie," so they threw the issue to the consideration of their readers and elicited response. None arrived.[19]

The idea of an East River tunnel followed the fortunes of the Thames Tunnel. Silence reigned in New York from the late 1820s to the mid-1840s as Brunel's project floundered. His tunnel flooded twice during the first three years, killing at least six workers. And the river brought more than the fear of drowning into the underpass: it brought all the toxic filth of London. By the early nineteenth century, the Thames was effectively an open sewer, and as water leaked into the work site "tunnel sickness" began to spread among the laborers. Many fell ill—including Brunel and his extraordinary son Isambard—while

"Holcomb's Submarine Carriage Way, fig. 1"
Scientific American, June 6, 1857. From the author's collection.

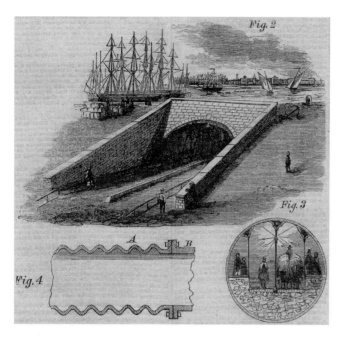

"Holcomb's Submarine Carriage Way, figs. 2–4"
Scientific American, June 6, 1857. From the author's collection.

others died or were struck blind. The project was eventually shut down for seven years, but was reopened in 1835. Perceptions changed, however, once the tunnel opened in 1843. Shortly after, the *Daily Advertiser* reported that some of Brooklyn's "wealthiest citizens" were "agitating the subject of a tunnel under the East River." If Londoners could do it, they reasoned, why couldn't New Yorkers? They could, of course; but the question was, would they want to? Although jubilation accompanied the tunnel's opening, it was a forbidding place and a financial failure. Even Nathaniel Hawthorne, no stranger to dark visions, was repulsed by its "tomb-like" appearance: "the damp plaster of the ceiling and walls, and the massive stone pavement, the crevices of which are oozy with moisture." Standing before the tunnel, he decided, was like gazing into "everlasting midnight."[20]

Although Hawthorne visited the tunnel in 1862, its shortcomings were known much earlier. When the *Tribune* began to lobby for a bridge in 1849, the *Long-Island Star* shot back: from "a pecuniary point of view ... the bridge would be a gigantic failure, like the Thames Tunnel. ... Its aerial galleries would be deserted, while the comfortable and well-warmed seats of the fine steam ferry boats would be filled to over flowing."[21] In the face of such criticism, the *Tribune* then went on, somewhat bizarrely, to switch horses and advocate a tunnel. Unsurprisingly, the *Star* again rubbished the proposal, and the tunnel issue promptly fell out of vogue.

The idea of subaqueous travel resurfaced in 1857 when *Scientific American* showcased two plans: Joseph Sendzimir's "Submarine Thoroughfare" and H.P. Holcomb's "Submarine Carriage Way." Both plans sought to lay vast iron tubes on the river bed to form a continuous roadway from New York to Brooklyn. Sendzimir's thoroughfare consisted of three tubes—one flat central section flanked by two inclined— covered by masonry; Holcomb's carriage way comprised thirty 50-foot tubes bolted together with flanges. Such plans had the advantages of cost (they would be cheaper than a bridge), uninterrupted navigation (the tubes would be laid at the deepest portion of the river), and access (neither would affect the commercial life of either waterfront).[22]

The Suspension Bridge Comes of Age, 1829–1855

While tunnel advocates were straining to gain attention, bridge proposals buzzed around at an increasing pace. In 1829, the *New-York Gazette and General Advertiser* announced that "a magnificent project, we hear, is now in agitation in this city ... that of erecting a bridge from the foot of Maiden Lane to Brooklyn, high enough to allow the largest ships to pass under it."[23] Despite receiving the now customary scorn of most of the press, the project—"yet in its crudest state"—was unique: it was the first to propose a *suspension* bridge across the East River, albeit on the chain model not the wire plan. With granite towers and two carriageways enclosing a central walkway, the 1829 plan prefigured that adopted in 1867. In other respects, it mirrored Thomas Telford's Menai Straits Bridge in Wales, completed just four years earlier. Stone arch abutments—projecting 300 feet into the East River—flanked a center span of 500 feet.

Telford's bridge was a remarkable success. It established the suspension principle as a viable way to span great distances while preserving navigation. It did not, of course, convince everybody, and neither did the 1829 proposal. The *New-York Mirror* railed against "the incalculable mischief" of such a "stupid project." "How distressing it would be to witness the shocking deformity, nay, the almost wanton destruction of so fine a haven" as the New York harbor, noted the *Mirror*, before concluding that all talk of a bridge must be silenced forthwith.[24] Nevertheless, further discussion came thick and fast.

Jeremiah Johnson re-entered the bridge debate in 1834 while running for mayor of Brooklyn, and this time his views on the subject were negative. The river that separated New York from Brooklyn was a fine thing, he declared: after all, the two cities held no common "object, interest, or feeling." Unfortunately, the Old General lost the election and, shortly afterwards, Brooklyn's Common Council commissioned a study "relative to the expediency and probable expense of erecting one or more bridges between the cities of Brooklyn and New York."[25]

The impetus for the council's study may have emanated, in part, from the pages of the *American Railroad Journal*, which, in January 1835, published a proposal by William Lake, a civil engineer with a home in Brooklyn and offices in New York. Having to commute daily across the East River, Lake had become "forcibly struck" by "the many inconveniences attending" the ferry service; equally, by the fact that an East River bridge was "not only practicable, but would be a profitable speculation for any company to be engaged in." Lake proposed a five-span bridge "on the suspension principle" with a central span of 545 feet adjoined to two spans of 315 feet on either side.[26] As with many previous and future projects, however, the proposal and subsequent dialogue came to naught. Engineers were clearly convinced by suspension bridges, yet politicians were not. Technical know-how is, after all, only the junior partner of construction; without sufficient money and political will, no project makes it off the drawing-board.

But the mid-nineteenth century was a time of drawing-boards, of new plans and new technologies. In 1836, General Joseph G. Smith proposed that a dike be built across the river, and, two years later, a Mr. Graves shifted the focus upriver when he published plans to erect an "iron hanging-bridge" over the east and west channels of the East River at Blackwell's Island. Rooted on solid ground, Graves' bridge—a three-span affair of 700 feet per span—had the look and feel of a modern suspension structure. Vaulting clear over the East River, the bridge appeared both elegant and unobtrusive.[27] But the purpose of a bridge was for sure and swift transportation from bustling Brooklyn to lower New York, not from one relatively unpopulated rural area to another. As Benjamin Latrobe, the country's foremost architect, understood in 1807, Blackwell's Island was an engineering tease and a geographical red herring: a great asset to bridge-builders placed right where no one yet needed a bridge.[28]

"Plan for a Suspension Bridge Across East River"
The Family Magazine, May 1, 1838. From the author's collection.

The 1830s proposals form a prologue to the first great age of American suspension bridges. In 1842, Charles Ellet built the country's first modern suspension structure over the Shuylkill River at Fairmont, and, shortly afterward, an obscure young engineer by the name of John Roebling got his start in Pittsburgh with a suspension aqueduct over the Allegheny (1845) and a suspension bridge over the Monongahela (1846). The engineering community held its breath while these bridges were built, opened, and tested by use. Doubters still remained, of course, but their number grew smaller and their opposition less vocal. With the completion of Ellet's 1,010-foot long suspension bridge over the Ohio River at Wheeling in 1845, and with work underway on a mighty *railway* suspension span—the first of its kind—across the Niagara Gorge, the wire suspension bridge came of age.

Word of Ellet's magnificent achievement at Wheeling helped to reignite the debate in New York. The *Tribune* led the charge, with editorial after editorial advocating a suspension bridge over the East River. Short on detail and long on rhetoric, the *Tribune* affirmed that "such a bridge would become instantly an immense and important thoroughfare,

Joachim Ferdinand Richardt (American, 1819–1895), *Fulton Ferry, Brooklyn*, 1859.
Graphite with pen and black ink. Sheet: 28.6 × 46.6 cm. Fine Arts Museums of San Francisco, Gift of Gustav Schneider, 51.19.7.

second scarcely to Broadway itself."[29] Such talk raised the ire of an obscure young Brooklyn journalist by the name of Walt Whitman who fired back at the *Tribune* from the pages of the *Sunday Dispatch*: "We notice there is much talk, just at present, of a Bridge to Brooklyn. Nonsense. There is no need of a bridge, while there are incessantly plying such boats as the New-York, the Wyandance, and the Montauk."[30] Shortly afterwards, in January 1850, Charles W. Burton held a public lecture at Clinton Hall in New York to advance the idea of a bridge linking New York and Brooklyn, and was ridiculed by the always curmudgeonly *Long-Island Star*: "New Yorkers are extremely anxious to take us into their embrace. We are old and strong enough to look out for ourselves, and so long as we can keep well regulated and expeditious ferries we are satisfied."[31]

Enter Roebling, 1855–1867

On March 16, 1855, a large crowd gathered at Niagara Falls to watch a train pull 20 double-loaded freight cars from Canada to the United States over a stupendous new suspension bridge. Most feared that the bridge—strung 230 feet high over the Niagara Gorge—would collapse, taking with it five years of effort and nearly half a million dollars. The span's supremely confident engineer, however, took the hubbub in his stride. John Roebling watched the trials "sitting upon a saddle on top of one of the towers" and reported feeling "less vibration than I do in my brick dwelling at Trenton during the passage of an Express Train."[32] His Niagara suspension bridge—the world's longest and the first to carry railroad traffic—was a huge success, making Roebling an overnight sensation, the foremost bridge engineer in a country desperate for bridges.

Roebling returned home in the wake of his triumph to find his mailbag overflowing. One short query by two New Yorkers—Archibald H. Lowry, a real estate speculator, and Henry Kneeland, a merchant who caused a small scandal five years later when he shot himself in the head—wondered whether Roebling could examine "the East River at Blackwell's Island with a view of bridging it." Sensing the big stage, Roebling rushed off to New York, and on June 13, 1856, reported back that "a first class structure, in point of convenience, strength, permanence & beauty" would cost $1,216,740. Roebling's plan called for a 500-foot central span over Blackwell's Island flanked by two spans of 800 feet each.[33]

Lowry and Kneeland baulked at Roebling's price tag, and on August 18, 1856, the engineer signed a contract to throw a bridge over the Ohio River between Covington and Cincinnati, an opportunity he had been lobbying for since 1846. The Ohio deal put Roebling's New York ambitions on hold. But not for long. Roebling continued to set his mind to the problem while in the Midwest (Roebling set his mind to problems like most people buy groceries). He began to sketch, to plot, to calculate. The project, he decided, would be his crowning glory. But he would not work up in the lonely reaches

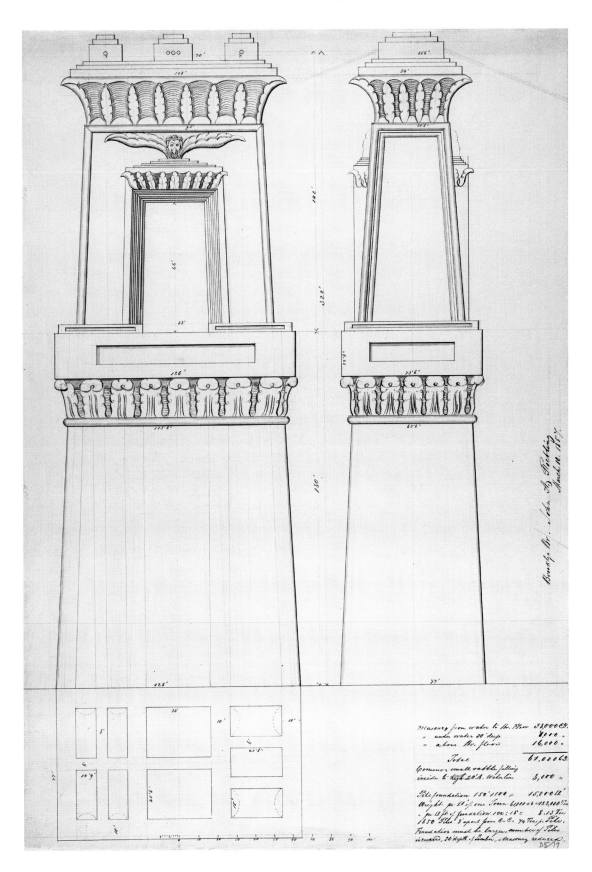

John Roebling, "Designs for a Bridge at Blackwell's Island," 1856.
Courtesy of the Institute Archives and Special Collections, Folsom Library, Rensselaer Polytechnic Institute.

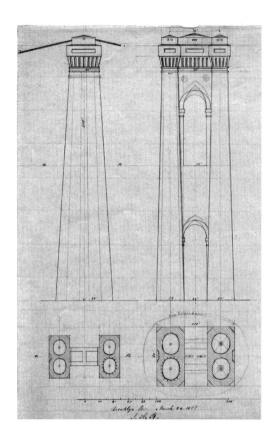

John Roebling, "Designs for a Bridge at Blackwell's Island," 1856.
Courtesy of the Institute Archives and Special Collections, Folsom Library, Rensselaer Polytechnic Institute.

of Blackwell's Island, but at the commercial and political heart of lower New York, where the need was greater and the challenge more demanding.

By March 1857, Roebling was ready to go public. With an itemized proposal in hand, he sought out influential industrialists and politicians, before announcing his intentions in a letter to Horace Greeley at the *Tribune*. Greeley was an obvious correspondent friendly to a permanent link between the two independent cities: "New York and Brooklyn," he proclaimed in 1849, "must be united."[34]

Roebling's letter was a model of practical promotion. He began with the future prospect, not with current conditions. Irrefutably, New York and Brooklyn faced a coming crisis. Both cities were growing rapidly and their populations could, within "fifty years," reach well into the "millions" on "both shores." This escalation would necessitate more and more ferries, eventually turning river traffic into a floating circus. "Delays and collisions" would rule the journey between New York and Brooklyn, creating gridlock and serious harm to commercial shipping. In essence, Roebling subtly turned all previous arguments on their head: far from ruining navigation, a bridge was actually the only practical way to maintain it. Without a single-span wire suspension bridge, the East River would become nothing more than a parking lot.

Roebling's initial designs replicated his work at Niagara. Running from City Hall Park to Brooklyn Heights, a lower floor would carry "all kinds of vehicles and passengers" while the upper floor would house two railroad tracks. The span

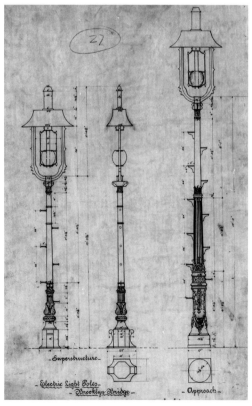

Anonymous, "Electric Light Poles," n.d.
Courtesy of the New York City Municipal Archives.

would also function as a destination: "strangers in the city will be induced to make a trip for the sole purpose of enjoying the grand sight." In equal measure, observatories placed at the top of the towers would further enhance the bridge's role as a tourist beacon.[35]

Roebling's letter generated a wealth of local chatter, but no contract. Under his influence, a bill to incorporate the "New York and Brooklyn Suspension Bridge Company" was introduced into the New York State legislature, but it failed to pass.[36] This, of course, did not stop the tenacious Roebling. It had taken him ten years to secure his Ohio contract, and if it took a further ten years to secure an East River commission, so be it. And, as things shook out, it did.

Roebling kept the idea of an East River bridge before the engineering community while in Ohio. In March 1860, Roebling published a lengthy article about his plans in the *Architects' and Mechanics' Journal*. He still intended a structure along the lines of his Niagara span, this time with "sidewalks on both floors" to attract sightseers, and again warned of the commercial implications of a crowded and congested East River. Roebling was leery of stating a fixed location, but had decided that any bridge must "bring the City Hall of New York within a five minute ride of the City Hall of Brooklyn." As far as local government was concerned, Roebling had also determined that for "the enterprise to be successful [it] must be conducted by individuals." "As to the corporations of Brooklyn and New York undertaking the job, no such hope need be entertained in our

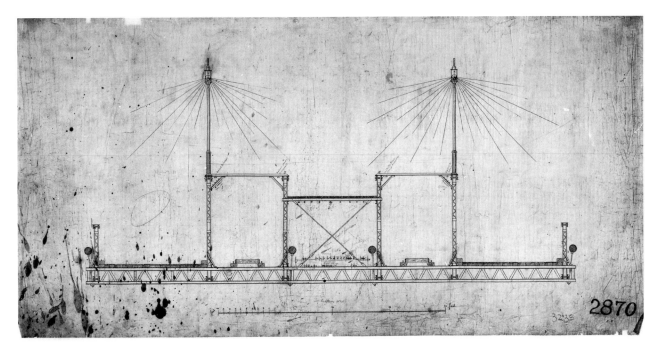

Anonymous, "Roadway Cross-section," n.d.
Courtesy of the New York City Municipal Archives.

time," he noted, before getting to the elephant in the room: "nor is it desirable to add to the complication and corruption of the governmental machinery of these cities." Few heeded Roebling's warning, but a year later work begun on the Tweed Courthouse and looting became the principal business of local government.[37]

Roebling pushed for his East River plan again in 1864 with a letter to *The Engineer*.[38] Once more, the project received favorable reviews, but it would take the intervention of Colonel Julius W. Adams—the designer of the nation's first modern sewerage system (in Brooklyn, coincidentally)—to give the project its first real burst of energy. Adams returned from the Civil War in 1865 and began to lobby around Brooklyn for a tubular suspension bridge of his own design. Through his work on the city's waterworks, Adams possessed the one thing Roebling lacked: direct access to Brooklyn's political and financial muscle. Composed of "elliptic tubes, placed side by side and supported by ribbons of steel," Adams's bridge was never a serious contender, but the idea roused the attention of local contractor and Democratic heavyweight William C. Kingsley. Sensing a contracting goldmine, or at least the commercial expansion of his adopted city, Kingsley became convinced about the benefits of a bridge and set out to make it happen. His first move was to enlist the old Brooklyn patriarch and state senator Henry C. Murphy.

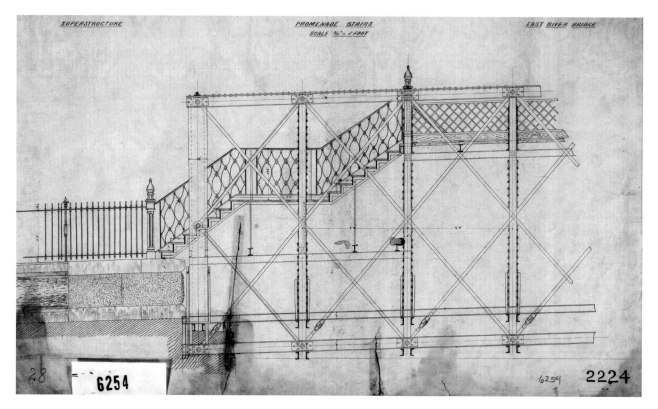

Anonymous, "Superstructure: Promenade Stairs," n.d.
Courtesy of the New York City Municipal Archives.

Once a great figure in the nation—he came within a single of vote of the Democratic presidential nomination in 1852—Murphy was an odd but astute choice. In the twilight of his career, and holed up in his mansion in far-flung Bay Ridge, his voice was no longer the city's most influential, but his newspaper was. As proprietor of the *Brooklyn Daily Eagle*, Murphy was able to direct and influence the bridge discussion in ways that Roebling and Kingsley could only dream of.[39]

While Adams, Kingsley, and Roebling plotted and planned, other proposals circulated. In December 1856, Sammuel Nowlan exhibited designs for a stone arch bridge of five successive 300-foot spans, described by *Scientific American* as "the most ingenious plan yet proposed for such a structure over the East River." Another five-span arch bridge—this time of cast-iron design—was exhibited at the offices of J.P. Stryker in lower New York eleven years later. The winter of 1867 was a particularly fertile time for bridge proposals. On January 23, the East River froze solid and, in a matter of days, bridge proposals were flooding into the local papers, "most all of which will tumble with their own weight," commented Alfred Boller (while proposing his own "suspension trussed girder bridge" at a meeting of the American Institute), "and fall still born to the ground." The most bizarre called for a giant X-shaped bridge—called "The Brooklyn Combination Bridge"—with two terminals in each city. In 1869, U.S. Navy engineer Edwin L. Brady began to lobby for what the *Brooklyn Daily Union* described as

Anonymous, "Brooklyn Bridge Approaches," n.d.
Courtesy of the New York City Municipal Archives.

BROOKLYN BRIDGE

the "virtual destruction of the vexatious East River." Brady wished to "run a dike, several hundred feet wide, with streets, houses and docks upon it, from the New York side of South Ferry clear across to Brooklyn."[40]

For Roebling, the great freeze of 1867 arrived like a blessing. Three weeks earlier, his Covington and Cincinnati Bridge opened to rave reviews and national fanfare. With a center span of over 1,000 feet, it effortlessly took its place as the world's longest suspension bridge, at the exact same time that the public was clamoring for someone to bridge the East River. It didn't take Kingsley and Murphy long to realize that it would be madness to entrust such a massive project to anyone but Roebling.

Everybody agreed, and on May 23, 1867, Roebling signed a contract that went far beyond anything he had hoped for. Contracted to act as chief engineer, he was also free to design and construct any type of bridge he desired. As David McCullough explains, "a man had been selected, rather than a particular plan."[41] Actually, Roebling's plans had hardly advanced since his initial proposal ten years earlier. But they would, and over the next three months, with his carte blanche in hand, he closeted himself in his office in Trenton and worked feverishly at his drawing-board. By September 1, 1867, he was ready to issue a full report:

> The contemplated work, when constructed in accordance with my designs, will not only be the greatest Bridge in existence, but it will be the greatest engineering work of this continent, and of the age. Its most conspicuous features, the great towers, will serve as landmarks to the adjoining cities, and they will be entitled to be ranked as national monuments. As a great work of art, and as a successful specimen of advanced Bridge engineering, this structure will forever testify to the energy, enterprise and wealth of the community, which shall secure its erection.[42]

Roebling's bridge would be bold, daring, and audacious; it would confer glory upon its sponsors and lead Brooklyn, New York, and the nation into a bright new future. Now, of course, all he had to do was build it. Unfortunately, the task would prove harder than even the most ardent skeptic had imagined.

FACING PAGE

Kathy Osborn, *Seeing the Need*, 1991.
Courtesy of the artist (www.kathyosborn.com).

PROPOSED SUSPENSION BRIDGE ACROSS THE EAST RIVER,

[SEE PAGE 90.]

"Proposed Suspension Bridge Across the East River, New York"
Scientific American, August 5, 1868.
From the author's collection.

CHAPTER ONE

Construction, Completion, and Panic (1867–1883)

If New York is a fantastic incongruity, then so is its most famous bridge. A modernist icon, the Brooklyn Bridge is very much a pre-modern creation. It was built without trucks, telephones, or any other now-standard modern technologies; it was built with an abacus and a slide-rule, with horses, wooden cranes, and whiskey as a medicinal cure-all. Quite literally, the bridge was hand-made: the foundations dug by hundreds of sandhogs, the granite towers manhandled into place, the cables hand-wrapped, and the roadway pieced together by a small army of craftsman and laborers.

The same elements that lend the bridge its essential heroism also gave it a dark and dangerous heart. Technologically, the span was a massive, messy leap into the future, plagued by uncertainty, miscalculation, and great physical danger. Built during an era clouded by scandal, greed, and corruption, the construction was driven by dishonesty, unbridled ambition, and personal mania. More accurately, the construction of the Brooklyn Bridge was, in equal parts, heroic epic (a seemingly impossible task achieved against great odds), juicy Gilded Age soap opera (all pulsing melodrama, bickering stock characters, and overwrought sentimentality), and eighteenth-century Gothic horror (replete with corpses, dark caverns, sinister intrigue, and rampant deception). It is little wonder then that storytellers have been drawn to the bridge since it opened. Looking back, however, one wishes that Mark Twain or Herman Melville had been among them. Twain knew that great undertakings often follow a path marked by absurdity and human weakness. And Melville understood the mania of outsized dreams and the dark implications of surmounting nature. He might also have recognized John Roebling, about whom there was something of Melville's awful and outsized Ahab.

"Fulton Ferry House and Brooklyn Bridge"
The Illustrated Christian Weekly, December 9, 1871. From the author's collection.

The Death of John Roebling

John Roebling was a mess of contradictions. He was a staunch, lifelong abolitionist, yet, equally, a tyrannical husband and a "bloodthirsty" father who treated his family as chattel. An accomplished musician, engaged philosopher, inspired designer and inventor, he was also a severe, intolerant, and deeply rude individual. In the words of his son Washington, "there was something of the tiger in him, the sight of blood following the strokes of the raw hide, brought on fits of ungovernable fury … it was a fortunate thing that his engineering engagements kept him away for prolonged periods, otherwise his children would have all died young."[1] As a thinker and a builder, John Roebling was a visionary genius; as a man, he was odious and intractable. He was also dead by the time the first stones of the Brooklyn Bridge were laid.

On June 25, 1869, the last official hurdle to the East River Bridge was removed when the U.S. Board of Engineers approved Roebling's designs.[2] Three days later, Roebling's right foot was crushed by a ferry as he surveyed the Brooklyn waterfront. As his cries reverberated around Fulton Street, Roebling was bundled into a carriage and carted off to Brooklyn Heights. Over the next ten days his idiosyncratic views on medicinal science brought the story of the Brooklyn Bridge into the realm of surrealist nightmare.

Roebling's bailiwick was bridges not bodies, and when it came to modern medicine the world's most progressive engineer was a bit of a quack. Roebling believed solely in hydrotherapy, a view he imposed on his son. "Brought up to look upon hospitals as the abode of the devil and upon a doctor as a criminal," Washington took his wounded father, somewhat inexplicably, to a Turkish bath and then home to Hicks Street, where he was attended by Dr. Barber, a local surgeon. With Roebling still in shock, the doctor was able to amputate the toes, dress the wound, and put his patient to bed. It would be the last time a qualified physician would have his way with John Roebling.[3]

Roebling dismissed Barber as soon as he awoke, declaring that he would "take command of his own case." He ordered a tinsmith to construct a large round dish into which he placed his foot. A hose positioned above the dish supplied a constant stream of water, and the distinguished engineer sat back to await his recovery. Barber returned to warn Roebling that he was "inviting sure death," but the engineer was bull-headed. He banished Barber "in a violent manner" and returned to his bucket and hose.

Roebling soon contracted lockjaw, and within days the scene in his sickroom was horrific. As Roebling's body jerked uncontrollably, his facial muscles slowly petrified, welding his mouth shut in a demonic grin. The son tended the dying father throughout: "I was the miserable witness of the most horrible tetanic convulsions, when the body is drawn into a half circle, the back of the head meeting the heels, with a face drawn into hideous distortions." "Hardened as [he] was by … scenes of carnage"—Washington had witnessed the bloodshed at Antietam and Gettysburg—"these horrors often overcame me."

PUBLISHED BY CURRIER & IVES.   Entered according to act of Congress in the year 1872 by Currier & Ives, in the Office of the Librarian of Congress at Washington.   125 NASSAU ST. NEW YORK.

The Bridge is to cross the river by a single span of 1600 feet, to start on the New York side from the City Hall, rising by a gradual approach of 2261 feet in length, and on the Brooklyn side by an approach of 1361 feet, its elevation above the river, in the

THE GREAT EAST RIVER BRIDGE.
To Connect the Cities of New York & Brooklyn.

centre of the bridge will be 130 feet, its floor is to be 80 feet wide with tracks for steam-cars, roadway for carriages, and walks for foot-passengers; it is to have an elevated promenade commanding a view of extraordinary beauty and extent, and its cost is to be about $8,000,000.

The Great East River Bridge, To Connect the Cities of New York & Brooklyn, 1872.
Published by Currier and Ives. Courtesy of the Library of Congress.

On the morning of July 22, the spasms were so violent that the engineer sprung clear out of his bed, landing, apparently, in the arms of one of his assistants. By 6 a.m., John A. Roebling was dead. His bridge, however, was not.[4]

Roebling's death caused a crisis for the bridge's board of directors. Suddenly, they needed a new chief engineer, someone who could be trusted to transform several million dollars into the world's longest suspension bridge. They also needed the public's favorable opinion. Roebling's reputation was the key to the public's confidence, and rightly so. Yet the great engineer had just displayed a willful disregard for established science and modern medicine. Certainly, Roebling was a figure of great repute, but if he couldn't be trusted to make sensible decisions about his own health, what errors might he have already woven into the bridge's design? To question Roebling's judgment was to question the very foundations upon which the bridge would be built.

Into this breach stepped the ever-reliable *Brooklyn Daily Eagle*. The *Eagle* acted as the bridge company's attack dog throughout the construction, savaging anything that questioned or threatened the venture. And no wonder: both its owner (Henry Murphy) and its editor (Thomas Kinsella) were major stock-holders. As Roebling's illness worsened, the *Eagle* waged a bizarre war of misinformation, reporting that the engineer was "bright and cheerful"—an odd description for someone in the last stages of lockjaw—and "busily engaged on the plans." Even more bizarre was the *Eagle*'s postmortem: Roebling's "death did not ensue from irregular treatment of the wound received. On the contrary, the wound was progressing rapidly and favorably, and the surgeon remarked that it was getting better faster than he supposed, and acknowledged that he was getting well as fast under his own treatment, as he would have done under [the surgeon's]." This was pure propaganda, but the *Eagle* achieved its aim. Roebling's death went down as a tragedy, not a self-imposed fiasco.[5]

Only a few hours after Roebling's death, the *Eagle* described a conversation it had allegedly had with the chief engineer just a month earlier. "He scarce knew why, at his age, he was undertaking to build another and still greater bridge," reported the *Eagle*. His son Washington, he thought, should build this bridge: he was younger, less jaded, and just as competent. Whether this conversation took place or not, the *Eagle*'s "report" was as prescient as the bridge's beginnings were inauspicious. At a meeting of the bridge's executive committee just eight days after Roebling's funeral—attended, portentously, by a new director: one William H. Tweed—Washington Roebling was named chief engineer at the tender age of 32, and put in charge of the entire operation.[6]

Over the next seven months, the new chief engineer busied himself ordering parts, equipment, and machinery in readiness for the work proper. The bridge's construction was divided

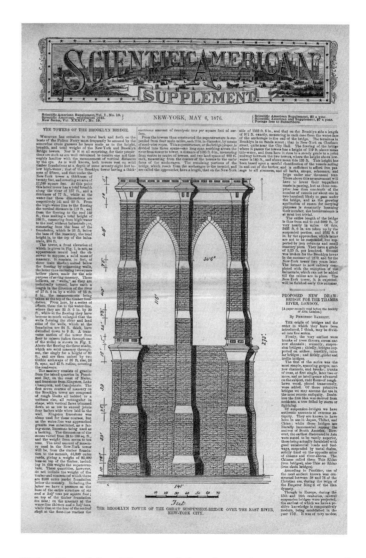

"The Brooklyn Tower of the Great Suspension Bridge"
Scientific American, May 6, 1876. From the author's collection.

into two broad phases: the visible (building the towers, fixing the cables and laying the roadway) and the invisible (the mysterious work conducted in the shadowy regions beneath the East River). The later was the project's first major task: excavating the foundations upon which the giant towers would stand, a process otherwise known as the "sinking of the caissons."

Down in the Caissons

Caissons are massive diving bells used for underwater excavations. They are sunk to the river bed, secured, and filled with compressed air. Workers descend into them and dig down, while above water the towers are constructed. The bridge's caissons were huge upended wooden boxes, approximately 168 by 102 feet and 30 feet tall. Three rotating gangs of 100 men descended through air locks into the caisson every day and spent two four-hour shifts digging, blasting, and removing earth and boulders; all the while clearing space for the colossal boxes to inch further down. And, as the caissons descended through the river bed, the towers rose up above the East River. The work was conducted around the clock, with short breaks on weekends.[7]

The mood was festive on March 19, 1870, as the first caisson was sunk on the Brooklyn side. Yet in May, when the work began in earnest, so did the rumors. Tales of hellish conditions and bizarre operations soon began to swirl around the city, reaching the ears of the press after only a few days. In June, two "Busy-Bodies" (as they termed themselves) described the journey through the air locks and into the caisson: "an unearthly and deafening screech … is the immediate result, and … as the sound diminishes we are sensible of an oppressive fullness about the head, not unaccompanied by pain, somewhat such as might be expected were our heads about to explode."[8]

Inside the caisson, compressed air made breathing difficult and voices weak and reedy, adding to the unnatural feel. The work of hauling and removing thousands of tons of debris would have been taxing on the surface; the increased atmospheric pressure made it agonizing. To make matters worse, the site of the New York foundation, in the all-too genteel words of Washington Roebling, "had for many years been the … principal dumping ground for city garbage. The mud abounded in decaying animal and vegetable matter. Although the odor of these was checked while imbedded in the salt water mud, it came forth in its original strength when brought into contact with the caisson air."[9] For several months, the sandhogs dug down through a rotting cesspool.

With an interior height of nine feet, the caisson was hell for claustrophobics. Likewise, one can only imagine the insecurity of working in a wooden box—albeit a very large wooden box buttressed by compressed air—upon which a 75,000-ton granite tower was being constructed. Gas and calcium lamps made for poor lighting and intense heat. Equally, the compressed air—at best an inexact science in the early 1870s—was

"The East River Bridge"

Harper's Weekly, December 17, 1870. Courtesy of the Library of Congress.

Anonymous, "Brooklyn Bridge, New York Tower under Construction," n.d.
Negative number 79153d. From the Collection of The New-York Historical Society.

itself the cause of myriad problems. If the caisson was not lowered uniformly, air could escape under any of the edges, shifting the caisson's balance and partially flooding the work area. Such events were common in the early stages, and they scared the living daylights out of the workmen.[10] Unfortunately, still more dangers loomed.

Early one Sunday in October, one of the caisson's two dredging shafts—which together functioned as a sort of atmospheric circuit breaker: if the shafts became unbalanced, the compressed air below would erupt out of the caisson—emptied and a huge "volume of water [came] bursting out of the shaft, carrying with it, mud, Indian-rubber

"Inside Views of the East River Bridge Caisson, Brooklyn"

Frank Leslie's Illustrated Newspaper, October 15, 1870. Courtesy of the Library of Congress.

overalls, boots and wheelbarrows, high up [over one hundred feet] in the air ... the force of the water was so great that it threw up the immense iron dipper a distance of thirty feet."[11] Luckily, no one was inside the caisson or the death toll might have been enormous.

The most fearsome aspect of working within the cramped confines of the caissons was the risk of fire or explosion. Gas lamps could leak, and with explosives used to reduce large boulders to rubble, all within the limits of a wooden box full of highly oxygenated compressed air, the caisson was an incredible fire hazard, bordering on a death trap. It is a testament to the diligence and skill of those supervising the work that a major catastrophe was avoided. Yet small fires plagued the early stages of the project, and on December 2, 1870, it shut it down entirely.

The caisson's roof caught fire during the evening of December 1 and, "once kindled," the flames were "driven by the immense force of the compressed air within the caisson with such rapidity as to defy all ordinary methods of extinguishment."[12] When the fire disappeared into the roof's interior, no one had any idea if the blaze raged on unseen. As rumors circulated—the caisson, it was said, had exploded and all the laborers had been blown to pieces—Washington hurried to the caisson and stayed down throughout the whole ordeal, working, consulting, experimenting, and, most of all, worrying. By 5 a.m. the next morning he was close to collapse and returned home for some rest.

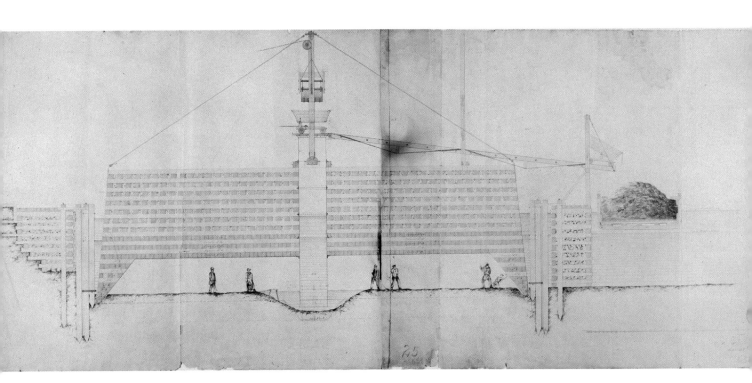

Washington Roebling, "Caisson in Position: Brooklyn Side," 1869.
Courtesy of the New York City Municipal Archives.

On the way there he experienced paralysis in his limbs, but he recovered and was back in the caisson four hours later when fire was again discovered. Washington decided to flood the caisson and leave it waterlogged for three days. This quenched the fire but not the mystery surrounding Washington's brief visit home. The warning would come back to haunt him and many of his staff: it was his first encounter with the dreaded "caisson's disease."

Now more commonly known as the bends, caisson's disease plagued the sinking of the New York foundation. The Brooklyn tower had reached bedrock at 44½ feet, but the New York tower would have to be sunk to at least twice that depth, perhaps further. All proceeded well until the depth reached 50 feet, when workers began to experience dizziness, vomiting, temporary paralysis, and acute joint pain—"like tearin' the flesh from yer bones," as one laborer described it—soon after exiting the caisson. On April 22, the first fatality occurred, quickly followed by another eight days later. On May 2, a workman by the name of Heffner began vomiting after he left the caisson. He did not stop for over 24 hours, and soon the entire workforce went on strike.[13]

The strike came to a quick end when management threatened to fire the workers, but the fear of caisson's disease persisted. Andrew Smith, a doctor brought in to study the situation, correctly divined that rapid decompression was the key to the problem, but his solutions focused on the blood vessels, not the build up of nitrogen in the blood. By mid-May solid bedrock was still a long way off, and Washington made his most significant and inspired decision: he stopped digging. With expenses mounting and men dropping like flies—Washington estimated that it would cost an extra half a million dollars and a further hundred lives to reach bedrock—the chief engineer gambled on his unparalleled knowledge of geology. He calculated that the sand at 78 feet had not moved in millions of years and was so compact "that it was next to impossible to drive in an iron rod without battering it to pieces."[14] Balancing the lives of his workers with that of the entire project itself, Roebling settled for a tower built on sand.

No one knows how many fatalities occurred in the New York caisson, or how many suffered life-long, crippling paralysis. Roebling himself noted that "scarcely any man escaped without being somewhat affected by intense pain in his limbs or bones, or by a temporary paralysis," before adding that "they all got over it."[15] A more somber judgment came a little later from one of the bridge engineers. When asked how the bends had affected the workers, he replied: "very seriously. Some are today hopeless invalids … a number died and only the most robust fully recovered. In four months there were 110 cases."[16] Among them, eventually, and perhaps inevitably, was Washington himself.

Roebling suffered another attack of the bends during the spring of 1872, and this time it nearly killed him. Washington's second attack—neither whispered nor reported—was one of the most closely guarded secrets of the entire venture, and for good reason.

Anonymous, "Workers on Brooklyn Tower (of Brooklyn Bridge)," n.d.

Negative number 79152d. From the Collection of The New-York Historical Society.

"Fulton Ferry House, Brooklyn," 1873.

Published by the American View Company.

From the author's collection.

Public opinion had yet to rally behind the bridge, and an open admission that successive chief engineers had been unable to keep themselves out of harm's way might well have ended the whole project. The management simply could not replace Washington so soon after the death of his father, nor admit that the bridge was destroying not only the workers but, one by one, the Roebling family itself.

Against the odds, Washington limped on for the rest of the year, but by December, he was unable to leave his bed. He would never again visit the construction site nor move without the aid of a nurse and a wheelchair.

William Kingsley and the Culture of Corruption

As the year turned, the bridge was four years into construction and two Roeblings down. Yet surprisingly, the bridge's stockholders had more pressing problems to deal with. On July 8, 1871, the *New York Times* ran with the headline "More Ring Villainy. Gigantic Frauds in the Rental of Armories … Over Eighty Per Cent of the Money Stolen," and the hunt for the seemingly untouchable "Boss" William M. Tweed was on.[17]

The fallout from the Tweed scandal led to a single, irrefutable conclusion: for years, Tammany Hall had used large building projects to loot the public treasury. With millions of dollars of public money already sunk into their bridge, Brooklynites were alarmed, and they mobilized. On October 24, 1871, the "Committee of Fifty" (or "Rink Committee") was formed "for the sole purpose of ascertaining the truth, detecting frauds wherever they may exist, redressing … the wrongs of the past, and obtaining by legislation … security for the future." The committee's report on the bridge's financial dealings hit the newspapers in April 1872, just as men started to fall ill in the New York caisson.[18]

The committee found fault with only a few facets of the bridge's management, and recommended only minor changes. They worried about Brooklyn's representation on the board of directors—despite providing over half of the money, the city had virtually no say in its management—but saw "no reason to conclude that the accounts of this company are not properly kept." This did not stop the *Eagle* from blowing a gasket. In an editorial that was shrill to the point of screaming, it charged that the committee had only one purpose: to bring ruin and "discredit" to the entire bridge project.[19]

The committee's most serious complaint focused on bridge superintendent and prime mover, William Kingsley. And, unfortunately, its concerns would prove justified. Under the terms of his contract, Kingsley was assigned 5 percent of the total expenditures "for his services in getting the [bridge] Company under way, and for prosecuting the work." Over the first three years, this equated to more than $200,000, a sum the committee thought "exorbitant." Under pressure, the board renegotiated Kingsley's fee down to $125,000 before the committee's report was published.[20]

BROOKLYN SIDE OF THE TOWER AT FULTON FERRY, WITH THE NEW YORK TOWER IN THE DISTANCE.
THE BROOKLYN BRIDGE.

"Brooklyn Side of the Tower at Fulton Ferry"

The Daily Graphic, July 1, 1873. Courtesy of the University of Texas Libraries,
The University of Texas at Austin.

The committee's report called for a measured tone and a reasoned defense. Alas, Kingsley opted for insults and all-out attack. He called the committee "vagabonds," "scoundrels," "perjurers," and "miserable drivellers," whose motives betrayed a "foulness and rottenness of heart." In comparison, Tweed and his cronies were angels: "their characters … infinitely better." Whether this was true or not was a moot point. There are unwritten rules to politics and public relations, and broadcasting (approvingly no less) one's own dealings with a disgraced city boss is surely not one of them.

Kingsley adamantly defended Brooklyn's representation on the board of directors: "no sane individual will contend that the interests of Brooklyn … would be better conserved by … successful candidates for election by the people, than by the eminent, wealthy and honorable men who now constitute its Board of Directors." Dangerous words to address to a city clamoring for public accountability.

Even more dangerous was Kingsley's rather ill-advised boast that, personally, he had already poured $250,000 into the project. According to the bridge company, the $125,000 owed to Kingsley was "fair compensation for services rendered and expenditures made." Where then had this extra $125,000 come from, wondered critics, and what had it been spent on? Surely, the people of Brooklyn deserved an itemized "bill of particulars." After all, with a chief and a consulting engineer, four assistant engineers, a bevy of foremen, workers, and contractors, what was Kingsley doing, exactly, to warrant such a magnificent salary?[21]

As April turned into May, little was established, other than Kingsley's petulance and the *Eagle*'s loyalty to Brooklyn's "eminent, wealthy and honorable men" on the board of directors. The rest was all aspersion and conjecture. In public life, however, truth is often less important than allegation, and anyone passing a newsstand in July 1873 would have seen that the rumors continued unabated. Emblazoned on the cover of *Frank Leslie's Illustrated Newspaper* was an illustration of Kingsley and William Fowler (of the Brooklyn Board of City Works) passing contracts and checks (signed by Tweed)

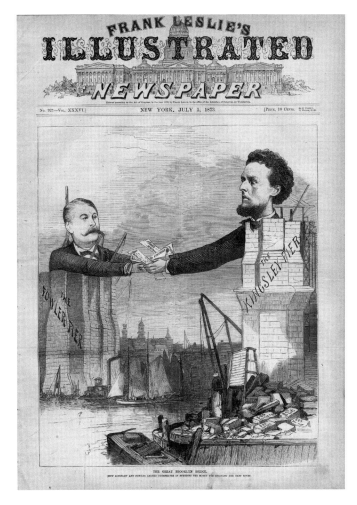

"How Kingsley and Fowler Amused Themselves in Spending the Money for Bridging the East River"
Frank Leslie's Illustrated Newspaper, July 5, 1873.
From the author's collection.

back and forth over the East River. Accompanying the image was a caption: "How Kingsley and Fowler Amused Themselves in Spending the Money for Bridging the East River."[22]

The whiff of corruption never went away, and neither did Tweed, although he tried his best, escaping New York first to Cuba and then to Spain. By 1877, he was hauled before the Board of Aldermen where he spilled the beans about his dealings with the East River Bridge. Tweed's first revelation concerned the old patriarch Henry Murphy. In 1866, when the bridge was no more than an idea in need of funding, Murphy paid Tweed a visit. He wanted to know if the Tammany chief could arrange the passage of legislation in New York authorizing a $1,500,000 appropriation. He could, as it turned out, although it would cost about $65,000 to grease a few politicians. Murphy happily agreed and several weeks later, traveled to New York with a bag full of cash.[23]

So far, so good for Kingsley, until the subject of his salary came up. Apparently, Kingsley's original fee was not 5 percent but 15 percent of the total budget. Upon "microscopical examination" it was discovered that the original documents had been altered, presumably at about the same time as the Rink Committee was nosing around.

OVERWEIGHTED

"Overweighted"
Harper's Weekly, October 19, 1901. From the author's collection.

When the aldermen asked how Kingsley had finagled such a fee, Tweed explained that it was for monies extended for the passage of all necessary legislation and appropriations. Clearly, if Murphy had carried a bag of cash to New York, then Kingsley had carried numerous other bags of currency around Brooklyn, Albany, and Washington.[24]

As the questioning continued, it became increasingly obviously that monies had been deployed not just to effect the passage of legislation, but to rig it. As a stockholder, for example, Tweed attended almost no board meetings, but he was there when Kingsley was granted his 15 percent. In fact, he proposed the resolution, although he didn't write it. When asked who had, Tweed let the cat out of the bag: "Mr. Kingsley handed it to me, and I think he prepared it."[25]

How had Kingsley earned such generosity from the infamous Tweed? The same way anyone did during the sachem's reign: cold, hard kickbacks. Tweed owned $42,000 worth of bridge stock, but paid only $8,400 for it. The balance was paid by Kingsley, as it was for three other Tammany heels.[26] Apparently, if *Frank Leslie's* had substituted Tweed for Fowler in its cover image of 1873, it couldn't have been more right.

"Cowboys of the Sky"

As rumors and accusations flew around courtrooms and newspapers, the bridge's construction continued somewhat quietly. The Brooklyn tower was finished in June 1875, and by July 1876 "the grand obelisk-like towers of the bridge … giant brothers twain," as Walt Whitman described them, stood complete amid the river traffic of the East River. Finally, the visible work of joining Brooklyn to New York could begin.[27]

The first step was to thread two large wire ropes through a series of guide wheels from one anchorage, up over both towers, to the other before splicing them into a

Great East River Suspension Bridge, 1874.
Published by Currier and Ives. Courtesy of the Library of Congress.

"The First Passenger Across the East River Bridge"
Frank Leslie's Illustrated Newspaper, September 9, 1876.
Courtesy of the Yale University Library.

massive loop. The second step was to test its fortitude, a task that fell to 59-year-old assistant engineer Edwin F. Farrington, Washington's most trusted man at the site.

"Farrington's Ride," as it became known, took place on August 25, 1876 during the height of the nation's centennial summer. The happy occasion provided a welcome relief from the scandal and doubt surrounding the construction. That morning, crowds arrived at the waterfront while journalists and local dignitaries stood atop the completed towers. The weather was stifling, the atmosphere jovial. All were eager to witness the daredevil's historic journey. A boatswain's chair—"a mere swing"—was attached to the cable and by 1:35 p.m. all was ready. Leaving the Brooklyn anchorage, Farrington swung high over the housetops and streets of Brooklyn and, somewhat inexplicably, stood up.

The crowds cheered; Farrington waved his hat and resumed his seat. Farrington reached the top of the Brooklyn tower in less than four minutes only to drag his swing over the tower and slide off again. The trip between the two towers took almost seven minutes. The throngs lining both shores cheered relentlessly while the boats in the river stopped to blow their whistles. Farrington passed over the western tower as quickly as he had Brooklyn's and was soon on his way to the New York anchorage, where he was greeted like a conquering hero.[28]

Farrington was typically understated when describing the experience: "the ride gave me a magnificent view, and such pleasing sensations as probably I shall never experience again," before going on to complain about the "troublesome and annoying notoriety" he had gained from the feat.[29] Suddenly, he was a celebrity, and it was easy to see why: for the first time, someone had traveled *over* the East River from Brooklyn to New York. Roebling's Bridge—so long haunted by death and injury, scandal, and distrust—was up and running. People could believe in the bridge as a heroic venture and envision its completion. Farrington's ride was more than a stunt, however. It proved to nervous workmen that travel between the two anchorages on a rope no thicker than a man's thumb was safe. Once convinced, they took to the job with gusto.

The next day, a second traveler rope was attached to the first, lashed every 50 feet, and dragged over the structure. Once in place, men were sent out to cut the ties. And again, the public was treated to a spectacular show. First up was swashbuckling Harry Supple, a 25-year-old riggers' foreman and a six-year veteran of the bridge works. "Lithe and active," Supple boarded his "swing" and "shot away" from the New York tower too quickly. Applying the brakes, Supple screeched to a halt, leaving him and his contraption "quivering and trembling above the wharves that lay below at a seemingly immeasurable distance." As the crowd held their breath, Supple collected himself and proceeded. Within eleven minutes all the stays had been severed and Supple stood proudly atop the New York anchorage surrounded by an adoring crowd.

Anonymous, "Brooklyn Bridge, During Construction, from Temporary Foot Bridge," 1877.
Negative number 58839.
From the Collection of The New-York Historical Society.

43

"Cable Making of the East River Bridge"
Scientific American, August 4, 1877. From the author's collection.

William Korner was no Harry Supple. Chosen to cut the ties on the Brooklyn side, Korner was clearly frightened and worked at a painfully slow rate. Shouting out from the tower, his colleagues teased him and joked that he wouldn't be done in a week. Nevertheless, he grasped onto the rope for dear life and completed the job, finally arriving at the anchorage in a "somewhat nervous condition" two hours later.

The center span was manned by Thomas Carroll—a "portly" Englishman who had fought in the Crimean War and helped to lay the Atlantic cable—and Patrick Timms, both of whom "sat in their little boatswain's chairs apparently as unconcerned as if they were seated in the family circle at the fireside."[30] When Carroll's pulley-block jammed between the first and second stays, Supple shimmied down the rope, unhitched Carroll, and climbed back up to his perch, all the while "holding an easy conversation with those on the tower."[31] Carroll soon got stuck again, and this time Timms came to his rescue,

Anonymous, "Cable Rigger," n.d.
From the author's collection.

strenuously pulling himself up the incline. After all the lashings were cut, however, neither Carroll nor Timms—both stranded over the middle of the river—could figure out a way to get back to the tower. Again, Supple came to the rescue. With a rope fastened around his waist, he slid down the wire, caught hold of his two colleagues, and was drawn up to the New York tower. An unknown foreman at lunch time, Supple was a hero by supper.

Over the next few days, more and more men went up on the wires, and soon the air was thick with workmen swinging hither and thither about the ether. Like so many trapeze artists, these were the original "Cowboys of the Sky."[32] They brought a festive atmosphere to the construction, providing a daily show of bravado. As the *Tribune* noted, "with its princes of the lofty wire the Brooklyn Bridge is now the cheapest, and most entertaining, and the best-attended circus in the world."[33] Finally, there was an end to the dark caverns and the wild rumors; progress was now visible and joyous. Over the next seven years, hundreds of workers took to the skies to weave the bridge's cables, attach the suspenders and cable stays, and piece together the roadway.

Supple's Death and Hewitt's Shame

Just after noon on June 14, 1878, Supple, Farrington, and four other workers were up on the New York anchorage when a "purchase" cable "suddenly snapped asunder with a loud, sharp noise like the report of a gun." A massive five-ton "shoe" around which the cable had been wound "shot clear of the anchorage, and flew through the air over the housetops." It landed with "terrible force" in the bridge yard on South Street, while the loose suspension strand uncoiled, shot over the New York tower, and plunged into the East River, barely missing a passing ferry.[34]

People rushed into the streets, sure that the bridge must be falling down. Miraculously, Farrington was unhurt, yet two others were seriously injured and another,

"Terrible Accident on the New York Tower of the East River Bridge"
New York Illustrated Times, June 29, 1878. Courtesy of the Library of Congress.

46

"The Great Suspension Bridge
Between New York and Brooklyn"
Scientific American, November 9, 1978.
From the author's collection.

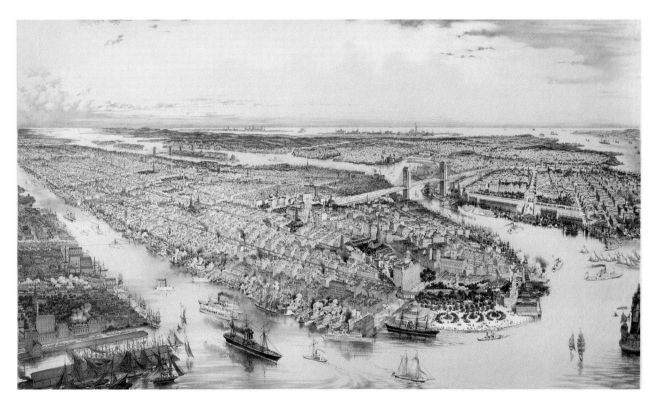

View of New-York, 1877.
Lithograph by John Bachman. Negative number 79629d.
From the Collection of The New-York Historical Society.

Thomas Blake, lay dead with his head cracked open. Supple was nowhere in sight. A cable had struck him squarely, "tearing open his chest and knocking him backwards under the wooden guard-rails, whence he fell seventy feet or more into the graveled yard, a frightfully mangled, insensible but still living man. His back, arms and legs were broken and crushed in the fall." Supple, "the best foreman in his specialty," as Farrington described him, was whisked to the Chambers Street Hospital where he died at 2:15 p.m. He left behind a wife and a young child.[35]

The purchase cable snapped because it slipped its guide wheel. When the motor was engaged, the side of the wheel scored the wire rope, causing several strands to break. Once a few strands had ruptured, a full break was inevitable when further pressure was applied. The accident, it seems, was exactly that, but privately it must have sent the engineers into fits. For, at exactly the same time, they were beginning to suspect something else about the cables wires: something much more dangerous.

On July 22, 1878, Washington Roebling announced to Henry Murphy that "a colossal fraud" had been committed. Unbeknown to the engineers, substandard wire had been woven into the cables. Washington had been furious when Joseph Lloyd Haigh was

Anonymous, "Cable Wire Spool," n.d.
Courtesy of the Institute Archives and Special Collections, Folsom Library,
Rensselaer Polytechnic Institute.

awarded the wire rope contract; he thought Haigh was a crook and a charlatan, and he was right. Washington caught Haigh's first move—bribing the inspectors—but not his second, at least not in time. Sound wire was inspected at Haigh's Red Hook factory, and hauled off. Yet, while traveling through South Brooklyn, the wagons ducked into a warehouse and the spools were switched. The good wire was taken back to Red Hook to be re-examined, while substandard wire that had failed inspection was taken up to the bridge and incorporated into the span's main cables.[36]

How had such a disreputable character managed to win such a large and important contract? Haigh had an invisible partner in the board of trustees: the honorable Abram S. Hewitt.[37] Hewitt was known as a reformer of great integrity—Henry Adams even described him as "the most useful public man" in Congress—who had been instrumental in the clean-up that followed the Rink report

"Manufacturing Wire for the Great Cables"
Frank Leslie's Illustrated Newspaper, May 19, 1877.
From the author's collection.

and the Tweed scandal.[38] But Hewitt had also led the charge to divert the wire rope contract from John A. Roebling's Sons to Haigh, on whose business he held a mortgage. In return for "brokering" the contract, Hewitt received 10 percent of Haigh's profits from the deal. Hewitt had loosened Kingsley's grip on the bridge project, it seems, only to tighten his own.

How much of this was known to the board of trustees is uncertain. But, despite Haigh's flagrant dishonesty and Hewitt's nefarious double-dealings, the crime went unpunished. Perhaps fearing yet another public scandal, the trustees "decided not to do anything at all about Haigh. The whole unfortunate affair would be very neatly and quietly swept beneath the carpet." For his part, Roebling acted quickly, weaving an extra 150 sound wires into the bridge's cables. He could not remedy Hewitt, of course, although he spent much of the next three years badmouthing him to anyone who would listen. As for Haigh, his dishonesty caught up with him shortly after the wire scandal. In 1880, he was sent to Sing Sing for defrauding a local bank. Thirteen years later, he was arrested on the Upper West Side of Manhattan for stealing an eight cent loaf of bread.[39]

John Mackie Falconer, (American, born in Scotland), 1820–1903,
The Building of Brooklyn Bridge, 1877.
Mixed manner, Roulette work. Platemark: 9.4 × 6 cm (3 ¹¹⁄₁₆ × 2 ⅜ inches), sheet: 18 × 11.8 cm
(7 ¹⁄₁₆ × 4 ⅝ inches). Museum of Fine Arts, Boston. Gift of Sylvester Rosa Koehler, K 1053.

"From Tower to Tower"
Harper's Weekly, April 14, 1877.
From the author's collection.

Management: Headless and Heedless

The bridge's trustees were the bane of the span's construction. They were neither publicly accountable, nor themselves engineers, yet they meddled and obfuscated their way through the entire construction, never surrendering the belief that this was their bridge, and that they were the principal builders. Neither, of course, did the chief engineer, despite serious illness. After quitting the bridge site at the end of 1872, Washington was rarely heard from and never seen. Some feared that the chief engineer, addled by years of pain, was a broken shut-in and that the project was proceeding ungoverned:

J.W. Pach, "Brooklyn Bridge Under Construction: Footbridge, Anchor Bars and a Finished Strand of Cable," October 15, 1878.
Courtesy of the Museum of the City of New York. Gift of Mr. Shirley Burden (57.15.16).

It has become the deepest of mysteries in the Board of Bridge Trustees, too solemn for the keenest reporters to penetrate, and far too solemn for gossip, where the chief engineer is, and what is his condition. For aught any public act or appearance of his may indicate, he may be dead or buried for six months. He is surrounded by clouds impenetrable. … We declare the great East River Bridge in peril, because it has no head, because its wires of control run into somebody's closely guarded sickroom.[40]

Washington survived the innuendo and the attacks, mainly due to his remarkable team of assistants—Farrington, William Paine, Francis Collingwood, Wilhelm Hildenbrand, all of whom deserve to be ranked as some of the finest bridge engineers of their era—and his equally remarkable wife, Emily, who shepherded the project throughout her husband's illness, more so perhaps than anyone has heretofore realized. Writing to her son in 1898, Emily confided that if not for her own efforts the bridge "would never have had the name of 'Roebling' in any way connected to it!" "Your father," she concluded, "was for years *dead* to all interest in" the bridge.[41]

Things reached a head for Washington in 1882 when Brooklyn Mayor Seth Low led a mean-spirited movement to oust the chief engineer just as the bridge was nearing completion. Low failed, but only by a single vote. Yet, as head of the board of trustees, Low was able to mold the opening ceremonies into a personal vanity project. After, that is, he failed to make it a private party. As reported by Brooklyn's Common Council: "the opening of the Bridge is to be attended by some ceremonies, apparently private in character, access to which is debarred to the public and to be granted to the few by an arbitrary selection to be exercised by the Trustees of the Bridge."[42] Such hopes were never going to fly after such a long and difficult construction, all paid for with public money, but the trustees did manage to control the guest list. They invited President Chester Arthur—who showed up, strolled over the bridge, and then refused to shake hands with anyone at the official reception—local politicians and the reliably mute New York state militia, but

Rensselaer Polytechnic Institute 53rd Annual Commencement, 1879.
Courtesy of the Institute Archives and Special Collections, Folsom Library, Rensselaer Polytechnic Institute.

Anonymous, "The Four Great Cables, Bound, Wound, and Wrapped,
Looking Towards NY Terminal Base," n.d.
Negative number 79151d. From the Collection of The New-York Historical Society.

"New York and Vicinity," n.d.
Published by the American Scenery Company.
From the author's collection.

A THRILLING ADVENTURE.

THIRTY DISTINGUISHED POLITICIANS ATTAIN LOFTY POSITIONS ON THE BROOKLYN BRIDGE AND HAVE TO CRAWL, TO THE DELIGHT OF
MANY SPECTATORS.

"A Thrilling Adventure"
National Police Gazette, August 26, 1882. Courtesy of the General
Research Division, The New York Public Library, Astor, Lenox
and Tilden Foundations.

William H. Wallace, *Fog Under Bridge Tower*, 1882.
Engraving. Negative number 79627d. From the Collection of The New-York Historical Society.

none of the engineers, laborers, or anyone who had actually worked on the bridge. The opening ceremonies would be a blank page upon which the trustees could inscribe their own message, unchallenged by even the meekest alternative.

Opening Testimony

Chock-full of social and political rhetoric, the bridge's opening was a poor testament to the bridge's construction, and poor conclusions followed. One observer, clearly unaware of the Hudson River, triumphantly declared that "with the completion of this bridge, the continent is entirely spanned, and one may visit, dry and shod and without the use of ferry boats, every city from the Atlantic to the Golden Gate."[43] Others produced remarkably uncomplicated paeans to the glories of American society and character of the American people.

S.A. Holmes, "New York and Brooklyn Bridge:
Cost, Fifteen Million Dollars," n.d.
Courtesy of the Museum of the City of New York.

For the Reverend Richard S. Storrs of Brooklyn's Church of the Pilgrims, an official speaker at the opening, the bridge was "a durable monument to Democracy itself." "After all," he continued, "the real builder of this surpassing and significant structure has been the people," which was a stretch to say the least. Even more so was Abram Hewitt's assertion that the bridge was physical proof that "notwithstanding the apparent growth of great fortunes, due to an era of unparalleled development, the distribution of the fruits of labor is approaching from age to age to more equitable conditions, and must, at last, reach the plane of absolute justice between man and man." Apparently, the United States, deep in the heart of the Gilded Age, was seeing "the steady and certain amelioration of the conditions of society," a claim that might well have surprised most of the country's labor force.[44]

The opening's key theme was the wonders of American progress, how humankind had—"in the never-ending struggle … to subdue the forces of nature to his control and use"—carved out of the "green monotony of forested hills, the piled and towering splendors of a vast metropolis." Yet New York's "restless renewal," as Henry James put it, has its victims as well as its victories. In Brooklyn, the bridge's construction ruined the "pleasant residential neighborhood" of Old Ferry, transforming it into a "slum," a "Brooklyn Bowery … haunted by vagabonds and derelicts." As the editors of *Scientific American* realized back in 1867, a bridge would devastate Brooklyn's thriving waterfront community. With the bridge's flanks stretching many blocks inland, "property on the line of these approaches would be more or less injured by the darkening of the windows and the obstruction of travel on the streets." Building the Brooklyn Bridge was tantamount to sticking a massive ten-block-long, 120-foot-tall skyscraper in the middle of a charming, low-rise community (a fact which continues to plague the borough to this day).[45]

The most serious implication concerned the shops and businesses that lined the East River. Both Manhattan and Brooklyn flourished by the river's edge, especially at the ferry terminals. The bridge ruined all this, taking traffic, trade, and business inland, away from the water, all the while casting dark shadows over the once flourishing neighborhoods. The fate of the grand old Fulton Ferry Hotel in Manhattan was typical:

The first bad blow was the bridges over the East River, beginning with the Brooklyn Bridge, that gradually drained off the heavy traffic on the Fulton Ferry that the hotel saloon got most of its trade from. … Little by little, the Fulton Ferry Hotel got to be one of those waterfront hotels that rummies hole up in, and old men on pensions, and old nuts, and sailors on the beach.[46]

Although the bridge's opening ended with a marvelous public fireworks display, few public voices broke through the speechifying, jingoistic nationalism, and general "glorification." This is not to say there were no accurate assessments of the project. To find them, however, one must look beyond the official PR to those with first-hand knowledge of the project, the sort of voices that were excluded from the opening.

"A Never Ending Job"
Puck, September 21, 1881.
Courtesy of the Cornell University Library.

"Finis Coronat Opus"
The Daily Graphic, May 24, 1883.
Courtesy of the University of Texas Libraries,
The University of Texas at Austin.

John Mackie Falconer, *Fireworks at the Opening
of the Brooklyn Bridge*, 1883.
Oil on canvas board: 7 × 9 ⅞ inches.
Courtesy of the Brooklyn Historical Society.

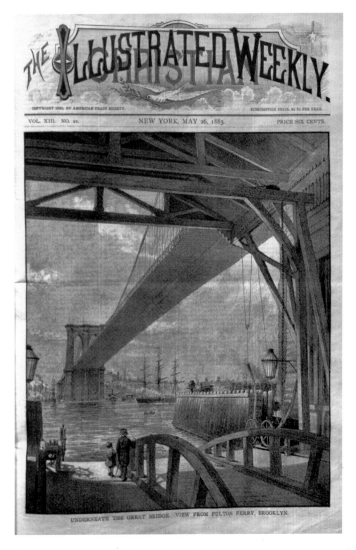

"Underneath the Great Bridge"
The Illustrated Christian Weekly, May 26, 1883.
Courtesy of the Special Collections Department and
University Archives, Stony Brook University Library.

At the conclusion of a lecture at Cooper Union's Great Hall, E.F. Farrington offered what might stand as the bridge's most poignant and somber tribute:

On a work of this description, running through so many years, many changes and casualties must occur. In the morning you greet your old friends and fellow workmen, at night his mangled remains are all that is left to you; and the impressions of familiar faces glide down the vista of time, farther and farther away, like objects seen from the rear of a railway train; and you feel, that the time may not be far away when you too must drop off and be forgotten. Meanwhile, the roar and rumble of the busy world will resound from the bridge. The sun and the stars, will shine upon it; the zephyrs will toy with its stays, and the storms will howl through its latticed sides; but through all, it will stand emotionless and firm, an enduring monument to engineering skill, and daring, patient, laborious effort.[47]

Yes, the bridge was "an enduring monument," but so was the collective effort that created it: that dug its foundations, pieced together its stonework, and strung up its cables. For Farrington, progress was worthy and commendable but complicated, and it often came at a high price. As an engineer, he accepted this, as did Roebling and many others, yet Farrington retained throughout a fervent hope: that the "laborious effort" of his departed colleagues would not be forgotten within "the roar and rumble" of the modern world.

Farrington's lament is a haunting reminder of the struggle to erect great monuments, yet no amount of words can fully or accurately describe either the bridge's construction or the experience of the span itself. For that, we must look to the visual arts, and not just any visual art. Painters initially ignored the bridge's construction; photographers, on the other hand, loved it. They scampered all over the span, producing hundreds of prints and plates. Yet photographers of that time worked at a distinct disadvantage.

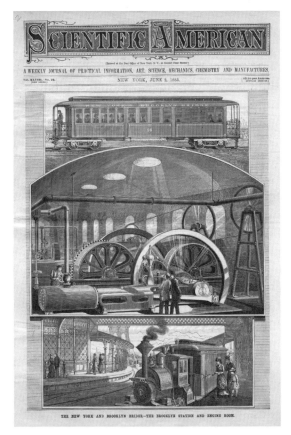

"The Grand Opening March Over the Brooklyn Bridge"
Puck, May 30, 1883.
From the author's collection.

"The New York and Brooklyn Bridge—Brooklyn Station and Engine Room"
Scientific American, June 2, 1883.
From the author's collection.

Anonymous, "Construction of the Anchorage," n.d.
Courtesy of the Institute Archives and Special Collections, Folsom Library,
Rensselaer Polytechnic Institute.

With shutter speeds still painfully slow, they were unable to convey movement or action. As a result, the construction's photographic archive is limited to posed group portraits and still, silent images of the looming structure. Viewed as a narrative, these static images read like the separate frames of time-lapse cinematography. The bridge miraculously grows with each new image, although how it grows is left unsaid.

The most enduring record of the bridge's construction is found in the great illustrated weeklies that proliferated in the second half of the nineteenth century. From 1867 to 1883, *Harper's Weekly*, *Scientific American*, and *Frank Leslie's Illustrated Newspaper*, among numerous others, documented the bridge in countless illustrations and articles. What readers were able to see and understand was the strenuous activity and profound human drama of the bridge's construction. The illustrated weeklies helped fuel the nation's fascination with the span—illustrations were quickly reprinted throughout Europe, stoking interest there—providing an intimate glimpse into the work: the look of the structure, the feel of the undertaking, and the sense of achievement and momentum. In their pages we find laborers deep in the caissons, and riggers high up above spinning, wrapping, and painting the cables; aristocratic New Yorkers brought low by vertigo and anonymous bridge-hands shifting dirt and blasting boulders; Farrington's roller-coaster ride over the towers, Supple's tragic accident, and Washington Roebling gazing out at the monument that made his fame and broke his health. The illustrated weeklies supplied a glorious visual chronicle of the construction and conveyed it to a waiting world.

"Demolition of Buildings for the New York Approach"
Harper's Weekly, November 24, 1877.
From the author's collection.

"Pedestrians on the Footpath of the Brooklyn Bridge"
The New York Illustrated News, August 18, 1877.
Courtesy of the Institute Archives and Special Collections, Folsom Library, Rensselaer Polytechnic Institute.

"Held in a Vise"

Frank Leslie's Boys' and Girls' Weekly, January 27, 1883.

Courtesy of Department of Special Collections, Stanford University Library.

"The Young Girl Plunged Headlong from the Bridge"

Street and Smith's New York Weekly, May 16, 1881.

Courtesy of Department of Special Collections, Stanford University Library.

"Baptized in Blood"

The illustrated weeklies allowed the nation to share in New York's triumph, and they didn't shy away from the horror that visited the span a week after its opening. Officially, the bridge's opening was called "The People's Day," yet the people played no part. As local dignitaries strolled over the bridge, the public were corralled into holding pens to await their turn. This arrived at midnight, and chaos followed quickly. One man complained of the "helter-skelter" amid those "willing to … pound one another to mincemeat"; others sustained broken ribs. The crowds and the mayhem only increased when the morning arrived. Crushes were a constant, as was lawlessness: horse races drew sporting types, while others dropped rocks on passing ships.[48]

"Completing a Great Work"
Frank Leslie's Illustrated Newspaper, April 28, 1883.
Courtesy of the Library of Congress.

"Thrilling Adventure of Four
Brooklyn Bridge Workmen"
National Police Gazette, October 18, 1879.
Courtesy General Research Division, The New York Public
Library, Astor, Lenox and Tilden Foundations.

Summing up the bridge's first days, *The Daily Graphic* offered the following: "when you see a man with his coat torn off of him and a lady with her hat jammed over her eyes it is pretty safe to say that they have crossed the bridge. That noble structure has thus far been ruled by the mob." Never slow to note the irony in any situation, *Puck* proffered its own advice: "To keep cool while people are being crushed to death on the Bridge—why, don't go *over* but *under* it [in a ferry]." Clearly, a catastrophe was in the making. And it didn't take long to arrive.[49]

Memorial Day fell just six days after the opening, and thousands used the holiday to take their first stroll across the cities' new attraction. By 3:30 p.m., about 20,000 people were on the bridge, an hour later twelve people were dead and hundreds more were injured or missing. What had begun as a pleasant day to mark the nation's war dead had turned into a nightmare, generating its own list of casualties.

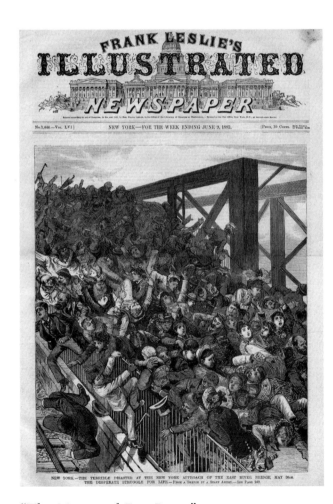

"The Memorial Day Panic"

Frank Leslie's Illustrated Newspaper, June 9, 1883.

From the author's collection.

"The Tragedy on the Brooklyn Bridge"

Harper's Weekly, June 9, 1883.

From the author's collection.

The tragedy began with the bridge's design, and developed through confusion. Today, the bridge's walkway inclines gradually down from the western tower into Manhattan, but in 1883 there were two set of stairs, ten feet wide and seven feet apart, just past the great granite arches. Crowds moving towards Manhattan were forced into a bottleneck where the walkway narrowed and the stairs began. A Brooklyn-bound crowd coming in the opposite direction helped form a vice around those in the middle. As the two crowds pushed inward, the pressure mounted and a woman tumbled down the steps. Immediately, someone screamed, everyone surged forwards, and the front of the descending crowd toppled. When a shout rang out—"the bridge has broken"—the frenzied mob made for the quickest route off the bridge: towards the mass of fallen bodies.[50]

"The writhing, struggling mass of those on the fatal steps formed a picture that made the strongest heart turn pale," reported one eyewitness, "men and women, with their limbs contorted and their faces purpling in their agonized efforts to breathe were held … by the struggling mass on top of them."[51] No one, of course, knew exactly what was happening, outside of the fact that *Puck*'s little joke had turned deadly serious.

Help arrived shortly after 4:30 p.m., too late for many. According to fireman Francis Mahedy, "an inextricable mass of women and children, dead and dying, were lying heaped together and uttering the most heartrending shrieks and groans." One boy's "face had been trampled out of all semblance to humanity," and hundreds were staggering around bloodstained and tattered. By 5 p.m., "two grocery wagons, hurriedly brought in, drove away full of bodies, dead or living."[52]

Finger-pointing abounded amid the shock and horror. One eyewitness testified that local "toughs … hooting like so many demons" had staged a diversionary fight on the stairs for the benefit of pickpockets. Others blamed incompetent management and lazy policing. Apparently, only a single police officer was on the span when the tragedy struck, and the bridge employees themselves seemed more than a little indifferent: "I don't take orders, go see the superintendent," one toll clerk reportedly replied when notified of the unfolding disaster.[53]

The official report censured the bridge's narrow stairway. The trustees, however, deferred all responsibility, claiming, despite all evidence to the contrary, that "there was no reason for anticipating such a tragedy." Unsurprisingly, the *Eagle* went further: "the unreasoning and erratic tendencies of the crowd" and their "exaggerated visions of danger" were "beyond calculation." Being so far above "terra firma emancipates the mind," they editorialized, making people "liable to discomposure by the most trivial circumstance." Frederick Richards, the only policeman to make it to the scene, concurred: "the woman who screamed did more to create the trouble than anything else."[54]

The Brooklyn Bridge was a glorious leap forward in the culture of American achievement. New Yorkers and Brooklynites, however, needed time to process and adjust to their new monument. The essential daring of the undertaking and the sheer size

"Removing the Bodies"
Frank Leslie's Illustrated Newspaper, June 9, 1883.
From the author's collection.

of the result—its towers loomed above both cities as the tallest structures in North America—prompted great awe and excitement, alongside equal measures of trepidation and dread. Although the bridge took fourteen difficult years to build, the public remained leery. Yet awe fades and terror abates. While the bridge was "baptized in blood" during the Memorial Day Panic (as the *National Police Gazette* described it), it would go on to take its place as one of the most remarkable treasures in the restless and frenetic metropolis.

Spectacle and Show (1883–1911)

The most imaginative of all the illustrated weeklies—equally the most scurrilous, sensationalistic
and disreputable—was the wonderful, the incomparable
National Police Gazette. The *Gazette* eschewed respectability in favor of the lurid and the strange, and, in so doing,
brought as much human drama to the bridge as *Frank
Leslie's* or *Harper's* had brought to the construction. With
purple prose and graphic pictures, the *Gazette* treated
life on the span as a bizarre soap opera filled with odd
characters, dark deeds, and the occasional moment of
pure human wonder.

Reading the *Gazette* was the antidote to the over-
blown opening day. From the "agile beauty" who scaled
the bridge to write "her name and address" on a suspension cable, through a gaggle of young girls who
traded kisses for admittance and a young couple who
used their "pistols as passports" to gain entrée to the as-
yet-unopened bridge, to a local prizefighter who was
"garroted and robbed at the entrance to the bridge," the
Gazette shunned the famous and embraced the anonymous. Underdogs were a special favorite, especially
women. In December 1883, they led with "Popping
a Cop," the story of Anna Garvey's attempt to shoot a
bridge officer, who, she claimed, "had trifled with her
affections." In May 1895, the magazine's cover featured

MAKING HER MARK.

AN AGILE BELLE LEAVING HER NAME AND ADDRESS ON THE CABLE OF THE BROOKLYN
BRIDGE.

"Making Her Mark"

National Police Gazette, June 23, 1883. Courtesy of the
General Research Division, The New York Public Library,
Astor, Lenox and Tilden Foundations.

FACING PAGE
"Welcoming Admiral Dewey" (detail)

PISTOLS AS PASSPORTS.

"Pistols as Passports"
National Police Gazette, May 26, 1883. Courtesy of the General Research Division,
The New York Public Library, Astor, Lenox and Tilden Foundations.

Miss Vera Irving, a "nervy and athletic young actress" (the tabloid *loved* nervy and athletic young actresses) punching the lights out of a young man on the bridge. Inside, the *Gazette* lifted its "editorial hat" to Miss Irving, for drawing "the claret from a masher's nasal organ before an applauding crowd on the Brooklyn Bridge."[1]

Gleefully flaunting the standards of Victorian morality, the *Gazette* focused on the bizarre subculture that thrived on and around the bridge. And, in doing so, it supplied an alternative narrative to that found in more genteel publications, one that would blossom into an enduring legacy. Fueled by the *Gazette*, the bridge underwent a cultural change in the late nineteenth century. From a sublime urban thoroughfare, the span was transformed into a public stage, a site of human activity, and a place of stunts. By the dawn of the twentieth century, the Brooklyn Bridge was defined by spectacle and show.

P.T. Barnum and the Culture of Spectacle

If P.T. Barnum had chosen publishing over showmanship, he would have founded a magazine like the *National Police Gazette*. Born to the thrill of the spectacle, Barnum understood the bridge's unique appeal and singular geography. Unsurprisingly, it didn't take him long to find his way to the span. And, when he arrived, he brought a few friends.

Just after nine o'clock on the evening of Saturday May 17, 1884, dozens of ferries arrived at Manhattan's Cortlandt Street dock and began discharging their strange cargo. As thousands of onlookers stood in awe, twenty-one elephants, ten dromedaries, seven camels, untold giraffes, and any number of zebras gradually spilled out onto the wharf and began to amble east. With his usual aplomb, Barnum had arrived in New York.

The spell was broken when the last of the passengers made his appearance, a massive white pachyderm named Jumbo. Purchased from London's Royal Zoological Gardens—much to the consternation of Queen Victoria—Jumbo was Barnum's latest superstar. As he emerged, the crowds roared and the procession moved off. The animals lumbered up Broadway, galumphed their way over to the Brooklyn Bridge, and drew to a halt at the tollgate. "What do you charge for 'helephants?" asked Barnum's lead zoo keeper, "how much for zebras, crocodiles and red ants?"[2] The gatekeeper was flummoxed: there

EVACUATION-DAY—THE GREAT MARINE PARADE, AS VIEWED FROM THE BROOKLYN TOWER OF THE BRIDGE.—Drawn by Charles Graham.

"Evacuation Day—The Great Marine Parade, As Viewed from the Brooklyn Tower of the Bridge"
Harper's Weekly, December 8, 1883. From the author's collection.

were rates for cattle and horses, but none for circus animals. The superintendent of tolls soon arrived, however, and allowed the horde to pass without charge.

Barnum's parade was one of the strangest spectacles to ever visit New York. As the *Times* noted: "to the people who looked up … at the big arch of electric lights it seemed as if Noah's ark were emptying itself over Long Island."[3] Over the next hour, Barnum's menagerie clumped over the bridge while officers stood sentry on the off chance that Jumbo might take a dislike to the city's new ornament. Instead, the elephants took a shine to the railroad cars that slid back-and-forth across the span. With each passing car, they raised their trunks and let forth a huge trumpet. Jumbo and his cohorts spooked a few passengers and disturbed the occasional eardrum, but otherwise the animals were well-behaved.

Barnum could have landed at Fulton Street in Brooklyn, or at the Navy Yards, but he drove his animals over the bridge for a single reason: publicity.[4] Barnum understood what millions of protestors would also realize over the next century or more: that the bridge was an unrivalled location, a magical backdrop, and a great place to get attention. Like Barnum himself, the bridge guaranteed publicity. And the relationship was reciprocal: "Barnum added a new lustre [sic] to the bridge," as one scribe put it, yet the bridge also added a new luster to the showman. Much as it would for another group of publicity seekers, those who established that most enduring of all bridge stunts: the one that involved getting onto the span only to get off it again. Very, very quickly.

"The Rights of Suicides"

On what must have been a *very* slow news day during the bridge's construction, the *Eagle* printed an odd little item entitled "The Bridge as a Spur to Artistic Suicide." The article described the recent death of a man in Indiana who'd set up a guillotine, placed a candle near the release rope, and filled the "catch basket" with chloroform-saturated cotton. With all his props in place, he lay down, breathed deeply of the anesthetic, and was beheaded while he slept. The *Eagle* thought this was marvelous: "artistically considered, this was beautiful. It was novel, graceful and ingenious." Sadly, mused the *Eagle*, neither New York nor Brooklyn could boast of a comparable "artist." Yet, with the opening of the Brooklyn Bridge, it predicted, this would change. Troubled residents would have a fantastic new stage upon which to act out their final moments, be it jumping—"it is hardly necessary to point out to thoughtful men the splendor of a suicide committed from this virgin height"—or otherwise: "let us imagine a man addicted to hanging, and think of the unique picture which the early passengers would behold should they turn up their eyes in the ghostly dawn and see a man hanging by his neck fifty feet from the water's edge!" In more ways than one, apparently, the bridge promised a new era of artistry and invention.[5]

Donaldson Brothers, Five Points, NY, "Try Our Cable Screw
Wire Boots and Shoes," 1875.
From the author's collection.

Brandishing its trademark sarcasm, *Puck* soon joined the fun. In "The Rights of Suicides,"
it told of a New Yorker who'd "patiently waited for several years" to "throw himself from the
Brooklyn Bridge." "Finding it as far from completion as ever," the man had resorted—"under
protest"—to suicide by other means. Always the civic watchdog, *Puck* took up the man's
cause: "Are suicides to be compelled to wait till the bridge is completed?" it demanded, and
if so, "what assurances have they that it will ever be done?" If the delays continue, "some
foolhardy man will be saying some day that the bridge never was intended for suicide."[6]

Puck's tale was laced with bitter irony. By contrast, the *Gazette* was licking its lips:
"What a beautiful chance the Brooklyn Bridge will offer for sensational suicides! All
our artists are sharpening their pencils in anticipation."[7] Unfortunately, they weren't
looking on July 19, 1883, when a "crazy Philadelphian" by the name of John Bower
made the first recorded suicide attempt. Bower failed—he was dragged back from
the edge by a police officer—and, despite such advance promotion, so did the suicide
craze.[8] The press had been right about jumping and wrong about the angle. From the
moment the roadway was in place, people took to the bridge to throw themselves off.
Their intention was not death, however, but fame and fortune.

The Jumping Craze: Fame and Fortune

The bridge was a challenge not only to science and engineering, but to daredevils as well. And on April 20, 1882, the great era of the bridge jumper was born. Naturally, it all began in the *Gazette* with an "articles of agreement":

> The said Daniel Foster [a local champion dog fancier] hereby agrees to wager the sum of two hundred and fifty dollars ($250) that on May 14, 1882, or the nearest date after possible, Robert Donaldson of Tain, Scotland, cannot jump from the Brooklyn bridge … into the East River, the said Richard K. Fox [owner and editor of the *Gazette*] wagering the sum of two hundred and fifty ($250) that the said Robert Donaldson will accomplish the feat.
>
> It is further agreed that neither the party of the first or second part shall claim any part of the stakes should there be any magisterial interference.[9]

Unsurprisingly, the local constabulary also read the *National Police Gazette*, so an earlier date was fixed: May 11, although this was hardly much more of a secret. By 11 a.m., crowds began to gather and at noon a small barge complete with "300 sporting men, reporters and curiosity seekers" drifted out into the river. Meanwhile, Donaldson had made his way to the bridge's outer roadway. In plain sight, Donaldson, all five feet ten inches of him, jumped up on the rail, discarded his outer garments, and stood there bold as brass decked out in pink tights, red trunks, and a maroon shirt emblazoned with the words: "POLICE GAZETTE, R.K. Fox, proprietor." Despite his heroic pose, Donaldson struggled to gain his balance. He stood up, wobbled, grabbed hold of the bridge, and tried again, but it was all for naught. Out of nowhere, five bridge officers materialized and hauled Donaldson away.

Assorted Trade Cards, 1880–90s.
From the author's collection.

Donaldson's failure left the publisher and the dog fancier without a wager, and hundreds of onlookers without their sport. Within minutes a new wager was agreed to, that a friend of Fox's, the mysteriously named Professor Bibbero, could swim the East River with his feet bound and his hands tied behind his back. The curious

74

"man-fish" cast off from Brooklyn and began to "propel himself like a porpoise." Bibbero made good headway but was caught in a strong tide halfway across and carried south. Chilled to the bone and nearly drowned, he fetched up on Governor's Island over an hour later.[10]

Donaldson was back in the news three years later when he announced he would jump again. At the same time, an obscure, large-nosed Washington swimming teacher called Robert Emmet Odlum also signaled his intentions. Odlum got there first and Donaldson was never heard from again.[11]

At 5:15 p.m. on May 19, 1885, a suspicious black cab, carrying a masked and visibly nervous passenger, set out across the bridge. Forewarned, dozens of watchmen surrounded the vehicle. Meanwhile, with all eyes trained on the ensuing commotion, a swarthy young man in a red shirt and gray tights jumped out of another cab and made for the edge. Odlum hopped on the railing, raised his right arm straight above his head, pressed his other arm against his side, and bounded off the bridge.[12]

"Brooklyn Bridge (Roadway, Cable Road and Promenade)," n.d.
Published by the Keystone View Company.
From the author's collection.

Some witnesses swore that Odlum was chuckling as he left the bridge, no doubt at the success of the distraction, but his amusement didn't last long. About two seconds probably. Odlum took three and a half seconds to reach the river, and for two-thirds of the journey, about 100 feet, his flight was as straight as an arrow. With 50 feet to go, he began to drift. Before anyone could register the fact, he was out of control, spinning and thrashing wildly. He was almost horizontal when he hit the water with a sickening sound, like a "pistol-shot."[13]

A tugboat, the *Chancellor Runyon*, crowded to capacity with reporters, local sports, businessmen, and politicians took almost ten minutes to find Odlum's unconscious body, but he was still alive when they dragged him on board. So were the local police, who chased the *Chancellor* around Governor's Island before the tug docked in lower Manhattan. With firm ground reached, the passengers bolted for fear of arrest, leaving poor Odlum in the care of a handful of friends. He regained consciousness long enough to ask about the jump, but his fate was sealed. At 6:18 p.m., he hoisted himself up to utter his last, immortal words: "Oh God! My back's killing me!" apparently. Cause of death was

ROBERT EMMET ODLUM.

CLIMBING THE RAIL.

CAPTAIN BOYTON BRINGING THE BODY TO THE BOAT.

THE LEAP TO DEATH—ODLUM'S FATAL LEAP FROM THE BROOKLYN BRIDGE ON TUESDAY AFTERNOON.

"The Leap to Death"

The Daily Graphic, May 21, 1885.

From the author's collection.

hemorrhaging of the lungs, along with rupturing of the liver, spleen, and kidneys.

The press treated Odlum as a tragic fool, reserving its vitriol for his friend, the marginally famous crackpot Captain Paul Boyton.[14] Boyton was credited with devising the scheme and convincing Odlum to jump. He was excoriated in the press, although one suspects he wasn't very popular to begin with:

> ODLUM is dead, but BOYTON and many other well known persons are still painfully alive. There was every reason why BOYTON should have jumped from the bridge. For the last ten years the public has endured his advertising voyages in his rubber suit, and he has never failed to outrage public decency by arriving safely at his destination. Had he decided to jump from the bridge there is not a man in this city who would have been so heartless as to interfere with him … Indeed, it would have been easy to raise by popular subscription a large sum of money to induce BOYTON to jump.[15]

Boyton swore that he had tried to talk his friend out of the feat, which failed to convince Odlum's mother, who openly charged the Captain with murder in a book she wrote about her son. As it turned out, Boyton had been to see our old friend Richard K. Fox of the *Gazette* about a wager. Burned by Donaldson's boast, not to mention his own "man-fish," Fox wouldn't be fooled twice: "there's no money in it," he replied.[16]

Over the next decade, various people "in various degrees of sobriety" jumped or fell from the bridge.[17] Yet history has remembered only one, and certainly only one profited from the feat. Ironically, of course, he probably didn't jump at all.

"The Late Tragedy at the Brooklyn Bridge"
Frank Leslie's Illustrated Newspaper, May 30, 1885.
From the author's collection.

Steve Brodie and the Culture of Celebrity

Steve Brodie was born in 1858 into the "poverty, wretchedness and vice," as Charles Dickens termed it, of New York's Five Points.[18] His father was killed in a street fight between the Bowery Boys and the infamous Dead Rabbits three weeks before Brodie was born. Out of necessity, Brodie soon learned how to survive on the streets and, by the late 1870s, he was locally famous—described by the *Times* as "the Napoleon of newsboys, the George Washington of bootblacks"—and living in the Newsboys' Lodging House made famous by Horatio Alger.[19] Brodie, however, was no Algeresque Ragged Dick. He aspired to notoriety, not respectability.

Brodie gained a little money and some fame as a long-distance walker and, after the privations of his youth, must have thirsted for more. Rumor has it that Isaac Myers, a curio dealer from the Bowery, told Brodie that if he wanted "to make a name for himself," he should "jump off the Brooklyn Bridge."[20] Whether this conversation took place or not, Brodie decided to jump off the bridge, or at least pretend to, as a career move.

Before Odlum, bridge jumping was common and vulgar, the province of the *Gazette* and its readers. Afterwards, it went mainstream. The nation's reputable broadsheets embraced it, and the *Boston Medical and Surgical Journal* even ran an article on the "physiology of falling bodies" prompted by Odlum's "experiment."[21] As daredevils had been proving since the 1820s, jumps of around 150 feet were relatively easy for those who knew what they were doing. After Odlum's fateful leap, for example, Sheriff McKee of Paterson, New Jersey, where young men had been jumping the Passaic Falls for generations, claimed to know at least 20 men who could have jumped the bridge.[22] Brodie was a master of the main chance and must have sensed this cultural turn. Clearly, he needed to get busy and jump.

The details of Brodie's "leap" were mundane, but the reaction was spectacular. On July 23, 1886, what appeared to be a body dropped from the bridge into the East River. Shortly afterwards, a boatload of Fourth Warders with a sodden Brodie in tow, reached the shore and declared that their friend had just successfully jumped from the bridge. No one questioned the claim, and Brodie was hauled off to the Tombs. As the city awoke the next morning, the leap was front and center on every newspaper in the city. The illustrated press sustained the momentum in the following weeks by faithfully printing images of Brodie mid-jump. Leap or no leap, the story clearly had legs, and within days, Brodie's legacy was secure: he had gone over the bridge and all subsequent jumpers would live in his shadow.

Suspiciously, no journalists were forewarned or present for Brodie's leap, as was the custom of the day. Instead, Brodie and his minions put themselves about with remarkable efficiency in the hours after the event, granting interviews and feeding the media

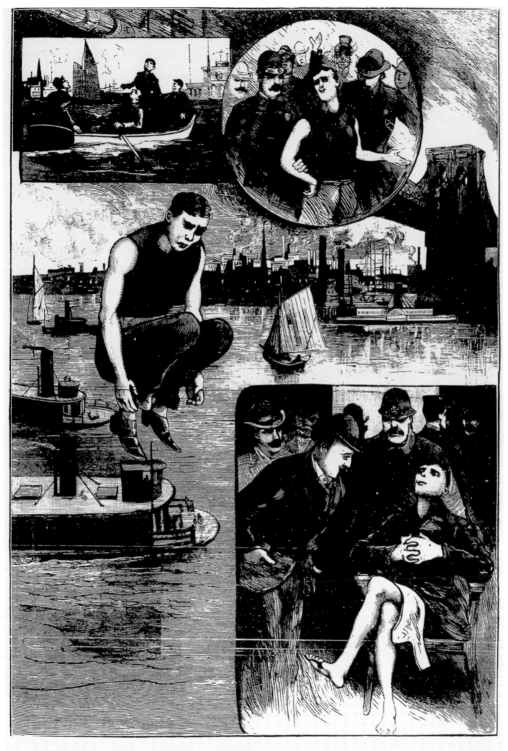

HE DID IT.

STEVE BRODIE, THE WELL-KNOWN NEW YORK NEWSBOY, MAKES A FLYING LEAP FROM THE BIG BROOKLYN BRIDGE.

"He Did It"

National Police Gazette, August 7, 1886. From the author's collection.

frenzy. Everyone wanted the story and they got it, straight from the horse's mouth. No one wanted to upset the apple cart, and for years no one did. Until, that is, journalist Ernest Jarrold decided to write an account of the leap and went searching for witnesses. He didn't find any, despite interviewing everyone associated with the event.[23]

The most convincing evidence against Brodie is Brodie himself. He was not a professional jumper, yet he survived his purported leap without sustaining a single bodily injury. At the Tombs, he complained, quite theatrically by all accounts, of "a terrible pain" in his side, although his wife let it slip that it "was an old complaint." The examining physician thought Brodie was "shamming a little" but declared that he was "in excellent condition." Given the injuries suffered by Odlum, it is doubtful that Brodie could have accomplished the same feat without sustaining a single bruise. But it is possible. Brodie was a very good liar, but that didn't mean he wasn't also very lucky.

The most effective evidence against the leap came two years later when Brodie jumped from the Poughkeepsie Bridge. Eventually. His first "attempt" in September was hailed as a triumph before it was revealed that "an effigy with the trousers filled with stones" had been tossed from the bridge.[24] To clear his name, he went through with the jump two months later, and it very nearly killed him. The following year he apparently went over Niagara Falls wearing, in an odd twist of fate, Paul Boyton's rubber swimming suit. Again, the feat was lauded in the press, although two days later a couple of local men testified that Brodie came down from the Falls in a coach and horses.[25]

None of this really mattered, of course. As Luc Sante points out, the most salient fact about Brodie's leap was not the truth of the claim but the life of the myth. At his arraignment, Brodie overheard a private conversation between two men—"he's fixed now," said one, "he's got a big fortune within his reach"—and immediately butted in: "Indeed I have and I mean to reach it."[26] Brodie had created the myth and persuaded the people, now he just needed to cash the check. And he did, with remarkable *élan*.

Within weeks Brodie was appearing at the Bowery's Alexander Museum and at Coney Island, pulling down over $250 a week for the privilege. At Huber's Palace in New York a waxwork model of Brodie was put on display alongside a dancing monkey and, for some reason, "a den of performing alligators." After a few more doubtful and dubious stunts, he began a successful stage career. His first performance was in *Money Mad* (1892), a remodeled version of an earlier play with a leap from the Chicago's Clark Street Bridge shoehorned into the finale.[27] Thereafter, Brodie mainly played himself, and the dramatic center of these plays was always his leap. *On the Bowery*, written by Robert Stevens, opened in 1894 and was wildly successful: it "was like inauguration day in Washington," reported the Bowery's unofficial biographer, Alvin Harlow, who attended the opening, "to say that the play was a success is an absurd understatement."[28]

The apotheosis of Brodie's stage career arrived in 1898 with *One Night in Brodie's Barroom*, a play designed for a single reason: to publicize Brodie's leap and his bar. Brodie

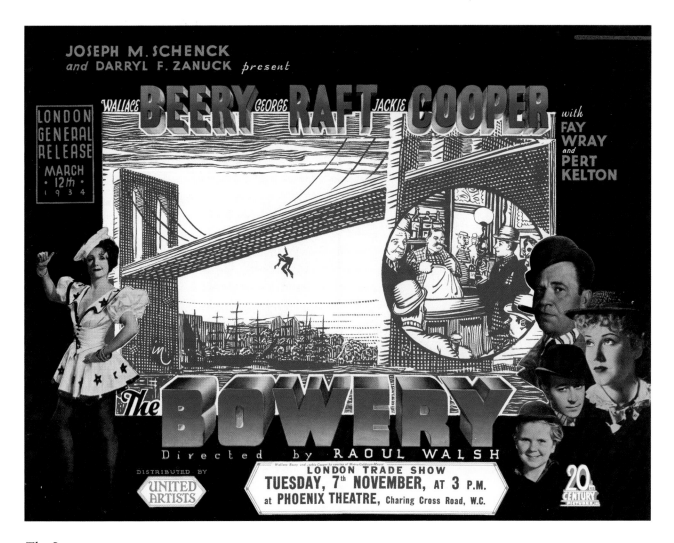

The Bowery, 1933.
Film poster. From the author's collection.

opened his famous saloon in 1888 at 114 Bowery, and it quickly became a tourist hotspot and a popular hangout. In 1895, Brodie hit the jackpot when he was raided by Anthony Comstock's obscenity police—the New York Society for the Suppression of Vice—for displaying reproductions of old French paintings. As any self-respecting businessman knew, the Bowery crowds followed in Comstock's wake.

Brodie lived for publicity. As he once remarked, "say something about me … say I'm a crook and a faker, that I never jumped off a curbstone; anything, so you print my name."[29] After all, publicity meant customers, both on the stage and in his bar. Sure, it came with a few embellishments—by the late 1890s, he had invented his own accreditation: Steve Brodie, B.J. (Bridge Jumper)—and a few lies, but wasn't that the point? Brodie didn't know anything about high-wire jumping, but he knew, implicitly, about

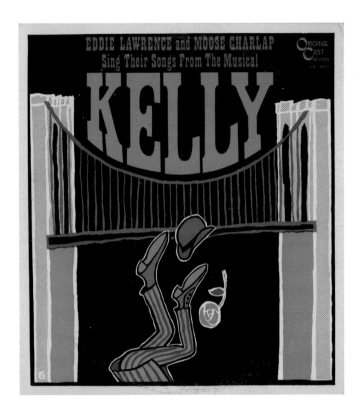

Kelly, 1965.
Original cast recording.
From the author's collection.

the mechanisms of fame. He was Bowery Barnum serving up humbug to an insatiable audience, a low-rent Gatsby who re-created himself with remarkable ease. From his supposed leap to his death, Brodie milked his fame for all it was worth. When he died in 1901, his estate was valued at $100,000. Subsequently, of course, Brodie was enshrined in the language and folklore of New York City. He was played by George Raft in *The Bowery* (1933), turned into a basket case by Bugs Bunny in *Bowery Bugs* (1949), and in 1965 had a musical written about him, the fantastically expensive flop *Kelly*.[30]

In Brodie's Wake

If Brodie wasn't the first man to jump off the Brooklyn Bridge, then who was? The answer is probably Larry Donovan, or "Crank No. 3" as the *New York Times* preferred to call him. Donovan, a 24-year-old printer at (surprise, surprise) the *Gazette*, jumped from the bridge at 5:15 a.m. on the morning of August 28, 1886, just over a month after Brodie. His secret was blue baseball shoes each filled with five pounds of zinc. The extra weight kept him straight and stopped him spinning in mid-air.

"Cable Road, Brooklyn Bridge," n.d.
Published by the Keystone View Company.
Courtesy of the Library of Congress.

After his leap, Donovan told reporters that "I aint no star freak and I won't go on exhibition. I'm going to work on at my trade."[31] Although a member of the Pressmans' Union and the Knights of Labor, he didn't mean printing. In October, Donovan applied for permission to jump the Genesee Falls at Rochester and was turned down. From there, he high-tailed it to Niagara Falls—the nation's jumping Mecca—where he leapt from one of Roebling's other great bridges, sustaining a concussion and several broken ribs. The next year he jumped from the Chestnut Street Bridge in Philadelphia, and by 1888 he was invited to jump the Clifton Suspension Bridge in England. Donovan never saw Brunel's first great triumph, although he did make it across the Atlantic. Early in May he wrote home that he'd given up jumping and was working for a London printer. Sadly, his change of heart didn't last too long. The following August, he jumped from the Hungerford Bridge and was drowned in the Thames.[32]

After Donovan came a deluge of imitators and accidents. In 1887, bridge worker James Martin tumbled from the span after slipping on a freshly painted beam. Two years later, Patrick Carroll spent all day drinking in Brodie's bar before announcing he was off to jump the bridge. He was so drunk no one believed him, but he ended up in the East River all the same. By all accounts his leap was less a jump than a trip, stumble, and fall, but he survived. In 1893, Bostonian John Mulrennin jumped after dark and missed the river altogether, landing on the roof of the Clyde Steamship Company "like a big lump of iron."[33]

In 1895, the bridge finally achieved equal-opportunity status when Clara McArthur leapt from the span. Her first attempt, to which she brought her husband and five-year-

"Our Champion"
National Police Gazette, September 11, 1886.
From the author's collection.

"Fell from the Bridge"
National Police Gazette, August 20, 1887. Courtesy of the
General Research Division, The New York Public Library,
Astor, Lenox and Tilden Foundations.

old son, was foiled after word got out of her intentions. No fan of bridge-jumpers, social equality or the "New Woman," the *Eagle* flatly declared that Mrs. McArthur "deserves the palm."[34] Yet, ten days later, at 3:30 a.m. on September 7, 1895, McArthur calmly stepped off the bridge, wearing a yellow cat suit and an American flag tied around her waist. To maintain balance, McArthur filled her stockings with twenty pounds of sand; to keep afloat, she held two inflatable "bladders" under her arms. This may sound like a good idea in principle, but it was nearly suicidal in practice. McArthur, it turned out, couldn't swim. Her water wings burst as she hit the water, and the impact knocked her unconsciousness. From there she sank under the weight of her loaded stockings. Luckily, her husband had arranged for a couple of friends to

"Selfish Objections to a Good Match"

Puck, January 18, 1893.

From the author's collection.

patrol the river and one of them finally found her. She was bruised and senseless, but otherwise unharmed.[35]

A Tremendous Place to Take a Stroll

The bridge made Brodie famous, but Brodie also helped to make the bridge famous. And to this we can add myriad new cultural forms that flowered in the late nineteenth century. Postcards, guidebooks, and advertisements all profited from the bridge, and in turn helped build its reputation. During the bridge's first 25 years it was established as a prime Victorian icon, a sublime American monument, and a hot topic of conversation.

Tourists from all over the world flocked to it as images of the span spread infectiously around the globe. The verdict, however, was not unanimous. The legendary critic Montgomery Schuyler famously described the bridge as "architectural barbarism"; for some its aesthetic failed to fit the age: the gothic too old, the steel too new. For others, it was too functional, too removed from the Beaux-Arts mainstream. Yet far more people saw the bridge as a miracle in stone and steel, a perfect expression of the coming age. Needless to say, it was also a tremendous place to take a stroll.[36]

In 1867, John Roebling envisioned the finished structure as a new "Broadway," a "great avenue between the two cities." And to achieve this he designed the bridge's *elevated promenade*, its most captivating feature. "In a crowded commercial city, such a promenade will be of incalculable value," he wrote, "because its principal use will be to allow people ... to promenade over the Bridge on fine days, in order to enjoy the beautiful views and pure air."[37] Roebling was right, of course; although not everyone agreed. Three days before the span's opening, C.C. Martin—a Kingsley man, the only bridge engineer not appointed by Washington Roebling—put out a circular:

"Types of Life on the Promenade" 1904.
Published by the American Stereoscopic Company.
Courtesy of the Library of Congress.

The bridge was constructed for the purpose of providing sure and rapid communication between the two cities and not as a place where leisure hours are to be spent ... it is earnestly urged upon all citizens and visitors to remember that the bridge is a great business thoroughfare, and when necessary everything must be sacrificed to the demands of business.[38]

Thankfully, Martin was roundly ignored. Visitors and residents took to the bridge like ducks to water.

Photographers swarmed all over the span. They climbed the cables and towers, prowled the riverbanks, and sauntered along the walkway. George P. Hall, A.S. Johnson, and the Detroit Publishing Company all produced photographic series of life on and around the bridge, as did most of the stereoscope companies that flourished in New York. In the American Stereoscopic Company's "Types of Life on the Promenade" (1904), a prosperous-looking dad with his two young kids strolls side-by-

"Stroll in the Rain"
Harper's Weekly, November 5, 1887.
From the author's collection.

side with a couple of laborers, one of whom sports a rather goofy but charming grin. Behind, workers and city-gents chat among themselves while a top-hatted chap walks the bridge with his smiling wife. In a city increasingly divided by money, class, ethnicity, and geography, such images showed the bridge as a popular, democratic space where the well-heeled shared space with the downtrodden.

As the Memorial Day panic showed, however, the bridge's crowning triumph could also be a liability. Over 9,000,000 people used the bridge in its first year. By May 25, 1889, a remarkable 21,396,935 people had walked over the bridge and 125,138,594 had ridden over.[39] These numbers were a testament to the bridge's popularity, but also proof that overcrowding was already a very real problem. Day by day, the scene on the bridge was increasingly chaotic as thousands battled through a massive human traffic jam to get to work or home. And it was equally bad for straphangers. Trains were

Anonymous, "Photographers on the Brooklyn Bridge," n.d.
Courtesy of the Institute Archives and Special Collections, Folsom Library, Rensselaer Polytechnic Institute.

so unreliable, and lines so long, that many gave up after an hour's wait and joined the throngs on the walkway. In 1907, William F. Slater immortalized the feeling in his musical parody "Bridge Crush March": "Say au revoir but not good bye / We won't get home till morning."

Overcrowding was exacerbated by other problems. On June 26, 1883, an alert went out to bridge officer Dooley that three "runaways" were headed over the bridge. Dooley opened the toll gate, cleared the roadway, and braced himself. Before long he spied a wagon careening towards him—the driver shouting "like a madman"—followed by three charging camels.[40] Even though the bridge was only a month old, Dooley was familiar with runaways, just not those of the humpbacked variety. From the off, runaway horses were a fact of life on the bridge and just as serious a problem as crushes. Horses often got spooked on the span and bolted.

Spooked horses spooked other horses, and before anyone knew what was happening the outer roadway was a crazy equine mess. On June 8, 1889, 26-year-old Mary Ellison was killed by a runaway horse as her four-year-old son looked on.

Life on the interior trains was no less fraught with danger and delay. Cables and axles broke, brakes and grips failed, and collisions occurred at regular intervals. During rush hour, cars were forced to run almost constantly, and if it rained, all hell broke loose. Fewer people walked the bridge during a rainstorm, so demand increased. Yet, with slippery tracks, so did braking time. It was a delicate balance: the margin of error was tiny, and it was often breached. Fog was also a liability. On December 20, 1889, a trolley dropped a coupling as it entered the Brooklyn station. Warning lights went out, and the following two cars ground to a halt. The fourth car failed to pick up the alarm in the dense fog, however, and it slammed into the stationary logjam at full speed. Luckily, none of the passengers was killed, but 2,500 people—packed into the cars "like sardines"—were left battered and bruised.[41]

By 1889, the span itself began to misbehave. In February 1889, the alarm was raised when a cable girder broke. Worse news was to come nine years later on the evening of July 26, 1898. In the middle of rush hour, a huge jolt rocked the bridge, and the

"The Poor of New York City—A Hot Night on the East River Front: An Officer on Watch"
Frank Leslie's Illustrated Newspaper, July 13, 1889.
Courtesy of the Yale University Library.

"The Recent Blizzard in New York— Pedestrians Struggling with the Storm on the Footpath of Brooklyn Bridge"
Leslie's Illustrated Weekly, February 21, 1895.
Courtesy of the Yale University Library.

Anonymous, "Casino Advertising Coach," 1896.
Courtesy of the Museum of the City of New York.
The Byron Collection (93.1.1.3216).

Anonymous, "Photographer on the Brooklyn Bridge," n.d.
Courtesy of the Institute Archives and Special Collections, Folsom Library, Rensselaer Polytechnic Institute.

roadway suddenly dropped several feet. City engineers brushed off the incident, but they could not dismiss what happened on July 24, 1901, when twelve suspension rods snapped near the middle of the span. As a section of the walkway began to visibly sag, some yelled that that the bridge was falling, while other frightened pedestrians scattered.[42] An investigation concluded that the bridge was safe, but the official word failed to quiet the local chatter: perhaps, whispered some, it was time to start altering the bridge.

Proposals, Upgrades, and Alterations

Proposals to upgrade, remodel, or otherwise alter the bridge were a constant fixture of the span's first half century. Most of the plans came in response to increased traffic pressure, but others were more fun and fanciful. Despite the acclaim that greeted the bridge, it took all of two and a half years before someone called for a change. And that someone was Linda Gilbert, welfare worker and founder of the Prisoners' Aid Society.

Gilbert's vision was more extension than alteration. Iron and glass columns would be affixed to either side of the bridge's towers. Inside, steam-powered elevators would carry visitors up to an observatory where they could gaze out over the developing city. Gilbert proposed a modest fee for visitors, three-quarters of which would serve as direct revenue for the bridge, while the rest would fund Gilbert's "charitable and reformatory work." Gilbert wished to purchase a tract of land outside the city to which she could "convey the class of persons who are now burdens upon the community, and set them at work and prevent their becoming either criminals or paupers." The bridge's trustees considered the proposal, but it went no further.[43]

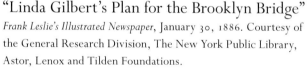

"Linda Gilbert's Plan for the Brooklyn Bridge"

Frank Leslie's Illustrated Newspaper, January 30, 1886. Courtesy of the General Research Division, The New York Public Library, Astor, Lenox and Tilden Foundations.

"New Cable Driving Plant of the New York and Brooklyn Bridge"

Scientific American, July 21, 1888.
From the author's collection.

Observation decks at the summit of the bridge's towers would have surely proved popular, and their entry points at the base of the towers would not have impeded traffic. But the bridge was already a mix of styles, the venerable gothic bulk of the towers playing against the modernist steel filigree of the bridge's cables. To add the enclosed glass would have confused the bridge's raw aesthetic power, as would the faint whiff of Moorish architecture in the observation towers. The bridge was a prime example of architectural eclecticism, a style rooted in balance. Gilbert's plan would have destroyed this equilibrium, plunging the bridge into visual and architectural mayhem.

Although Gilbert's plan was intriguing, it might have diminished the bridge. The next proposed alteration, however, would have ruined it entirely. In September 1889, the bridge's trustees met to consider the urgent problem of rapid transit. The span had

Anonymous, "Reconstruction of the Brooklyn Bridge, Modification of Towers," December 1903.
Courtesy of the New York City Municipal Archives.

"Proposed Endless Train Loop and Rotating Station for Brooklyn Bridge"
Scientific American, March 18, 1905.
From the author's collection.

already exceeded its planned capacity and change was needed. The approaches needed widening, the terminals needed replacing, and, most controversially, the transit system's carrying capacity needed doubling. To address this last issue, the trustees wanted to add a second set of train tracks immediately above the existing deck. The only problem was that the central walkway was immediately above the existing deck.

The proposal roused Washington Roebling from his self-imposed exile in upstate New York. Washington had made no public comments since leaving Brooklyn the day after the bridge was opened. With these new developments, however, he could no longer hold his tongue. Removing the central walkway would be a disaster, he noted, and unfeasible to boot. The extra weight of an added deck might well loosen the main cables from their anchorages. Whether this was true or not is debatable, but the point

NEW PLANS TO PREVENT OVER-CROWDING AT BROOKLYN BRIDGE DURING RUSH HOURS

When the plans already prepared and approved for the reconstruction and extension of the Manhattan terminal of the Brooklyn Bridge are put into effect, New York will have one of the handsomest and most spacious structures of the sort in the world. The plans, which are intended to do away with the present congested and dangerous conditions at the bridge terminal, provide for radical changes. The new terminal station will extend from the southerly line of the bridge property at its intersection with Park Row, across and over Park Row, and thence along a line almost parallel with the easterly line of Centre Street to the southerly line of Pearl Street. The trolley and railroad tracks will be extended across Park Row and into the Station Building on different grades, and are to be so arranged that passengers will reach them by unobstructed approaches to separate platforms. As shown in the drawing, the Subway tracks, as well as the Elevated, will be easily accessible from the new terminal.

"Plans to Prevent Overcrowding"

Harper's Weekly, September 23, 1905.
From the author's collection.

was somewhat moot. Clearly, Washington didn't want anyone messing with his bridge's most beloved and endearing feature.[44]

If the city wanted to enlarge East River travel, Washington counseled, they should build more bridges, which is exactly what they did. Three new East River bridges opened during the first decade of the twentieth century, but that didn't staunch the tide of new plans. In 1893, a new Brooklyn terminal was proposed with wider platforms, better turnaround times, and a direct link to the elevated system. Twelve years later, a proposal to make the Manhattan terminal "the handsomest and most spacious structures of its sort in the world" was discussed. That same year, Edward Whitehead Curtiss proposed an endless train loop that did away with "dead space" between cars, not to mention the problems of collision.[45]

"Design for a Plaza in Brooklyn"
Harper's Weekly, March 2, 1907. From the author's collection.

Designs for the Proposed Washington
Memorial Portal, 1928.
Courtesy of the Brooklyn Collection,
Brooklyn Public Library.

Often, proposed alterations came in the form of improved surroundings. In 1907, the New York City Improvement Commission proposed a gigantic new plaza in downtown Brooklyn. The roundabout would be enclosed by public buildings and radiate out to the East River bridges, the Navy Yard and Borough Hall. A similar set of plans appeared in April 1912 in the *Eagle*. More extravagant, this proposal sought to convert downtown Brooklyn into a series of monumental intersections and grand, tree-lined boulevards.[46]

At their meeting in 1889, the bridge trustees worried that "the stations now in use are ... inappropriate portals to the grand engineering work."[47] And others did also. In 1923, the American Institute of Architects recommended a rather uninspiring neo-classical portal. Five years later the newly formed Brooklyn Bridge Plaza Association began drafting plans for the Washington Memorial Portal, an ostentatious approach that displayed all the brash self-confidence and showy excesses of the 1920s. By the time the Plaza Association's plans were ready for presentation in 1929, however, the U.S. economy had collapsed and America had stopped building superfluous new monuments to its own glory.

Brooklyn Planning Section

Brooklyn Daily Eagle, April 12, 1912. Courtesy of the
Institute Archives and Special Collections, Folsom Library,
Rensselaer Polytechnic Institute.

"The Columbian Celebration in New York City"

Frank Leslie's Illustrated Weekly, October 20, 1892.
From the author's collection.

City of Spectacular Night

If Barnum and Brodie made the bridge a place of spectacle and show, so did the city.
A massive fireworks display greeted the bridge's opening in 1883, and its popularity
guaranteed future displays. The bridge hosted two different fireworks shows to mark
the Columbian celebrations of 1892. The first was the largest in the city's history. For
almost an hour and a half, "rockets, bombs and all other forms of pyrotechnic brilliancy"
were fired from the walkway in "bewildering profusion," while "prismatic lights"—
changing from red to green to blue—burned atop the towers. The second display featured C.T. Brock's famous "Niagara Falls," a 500-foot-long cataract in fire. In 1899, the

"Welcoming Admiral Dewey"
The Sketch, October 18, 1899. From the author's collection.

The Electric Light, 1880.
Published by Currier and Ives. Courtesy of the Library of Congress.

"The Brooklyn Bridge Standing Against the Sky
like a Huge Piece of Jewelry"
Harper's Weekly, October 2, 1909. From the author's collection.

Anonymous, "Reflection," 1910.
Courtesy of the Library of Congress.

bridge was the centerpiece of the city's celebrations to welcome home Admiral George Dewey, hero of the Battle of Manila Bay. On the evening of September 29, arc lights shone from the bridge's towers as fireworks exploded all over the city. Across the center of the bridge, thousands of little electric lamps spelled out, in 36-foot-high letters, "WELCOME DEWEY."

Displays of "grand illumination" confirmed that the bridge was the city's most spectacular stage. Yet pyrotechnic displays were temporal, fleeting moments of dramatic illumination. Electricity was permanent and it arrived, conveniently enough, at the same time and place as the bridge. Thomas Edison opened his Pearl Street Station on September 4, 1882, eight and a half months before the bridge was opened and only a few short blocks away, and suddenly the battle for the electrification of New York was on.

The Brooklyn Bridge was New York's first electrified icon, lighting up the sky well before the Great White Way in the 1890s and 1900s. And the span helped spread the word about electrification, not only through direct experience, but also in the press. While shipping interests complained that "the electric lights on the Brooklyn Bridge continue to blind our pilots," illustrated magazines printed images of the new phenomenon throughout the 1880s, a trend buoyed by the refinement of the half-tone process in the 1890s.[48] Before long, no publication was complete without a special photographic spread devoted to the new-look city.

Anonymous, "Sperry Lights on the Brooklyn Bridge," 1919.
Courtesy of the Library of Congress.

The bridge was a major icon in the development of a new urban aesthetic: the electrified cityscape. And again, the span's unique geography played a role. Harsh arc lights were softened by halation and distance, and the river lent the scene a romantic aura, as if a thousand moons were reflecting on the bay. "In all the glare of" illumination, noted the *Times*, the bridge "stood out more massive than ever, its graceful lines gained new beauty."[49] At the Hudson–Fulton celebrations in 1909 the bridge was described as "an aerial pathway of fire" and a "huge piece of jewelry … standing against the sky."[50] Following on from the exploits of Barnum and Brodie, electrification ushered in a new era of what *Harper's* described as "Spectacular Night."

Artists Approach the Bridge

While shutterbugs flocked to the bridge, painters kept their distance. Lacking the documentary imperative that drove early photography, fine artists shuffled towards the bridge slowly, seemingly unsure how to incorporate the gargantuan new structure into their vision of the city. Setting up their easels on Governor's Island or the shores of South Brooklyn, painters depicted the bridge, but only as a small part of the larger harbor scene. Thomas Moran's *New York from the Bay* (1883), William Bliss Baker's *View of New York Harbor* (1883), Charles Bierstadt's *New York Harbor* (1890), and August Fricke's *New York Harbor* (1890) all feature the bridge, but did not confront it directly. These paintings are about life on the harbor, about sailboats, ferries, and skiffs, while the bridge is an incidental aspect of the unexamined, unimportant urban backdrop.

Painters began to tackle the bridge as its own subject in the 1890s, and the results follow two, somewhat divergent, trends. Emile Renouf's *Le Pont du Brooklyn* (1891) and William Louis Sonntag's *Brooklyn Bridge* (1895) form the beginning of what might be called the heroic mode. Here, the bridge is all thrusting energy and visual greatness.

Thomas Moran (American, 1837–1926), *New York from the Bay*, ca. 1883.
Transparent and opaque watercolor, brown ink, and graphite on wave paper. Sheet 25.8 × 43.3 cm.
Fine Arts Museums of San Francisco, Gift of Mr. and Mrs. John D. Rockefeller 3rd, 1979.7.74.

Emile Renouf, *Le Pont du Brooklyn*, 1891.
From the author's collection.

For both Renouf and Sonntag—standing transfixed beneath the bridge—the structure is less a part of the evolving cityscape than an aspect of national movement, of transport and linkage. Appearing suddenly out of the left-hand side, the bridge vaults over the ill-defined city and extends, infinitely it seems, into the horizon. Closely allied to the visual iconography of the Hudson Valley School and the ideology of Manifest Destiny, the heroic mode imagined the bridge as a symbol of physical expansion and national glory.

Charles Graham, *The Sky Line of New York*, 1896.
Courtesy of the Eno Collection, Miriam and Ira D. Wallace Division of Arts,
Prints and Photographs, The New York Public Library, Astor, Lenox and Tilden Foundations.

Impressionist painters also embraced the bridge, albeit slowly and with a certain apprehension. Yet, together, they helped to supply a visual counterpoint to the heroic mode. After several rather pedestrian efforts, most notably John Twachtman's *Below the Brooklyn Bridge* (1888), the Impressionist vision really came alive through the work of Childe Hassam. Hassam painted the bridge at least four times, and each time it was nighttime and snowing. Like any good impressionist, Hassam loved the play of light around the bridge: the snow in contrast with the night sky, the bridge's towers against the river and sky. His *Brooklyn Bridge in Winter* (1904) is an impressionist benchmark. Painted from a similar vantage point to Henry Ward Ranger's *Brooklyn Bridge* (1899), Hassam's image is significantly more Tonalist. The white foreground contrasts with the blue upper section to subdue its subject. The thin veil of falling snow that suffuses the painting masks the bridge, diminishing its impact and de-emphasizing its heroic outline. The bridge is patently there, but understated; its form a softened figure in a romantic landscape. While there is much beauty in Hassam's scene, there is no power in the structure.

Hassam's approach influenced Edward Redfield's *Brooklyn Bridge at Night* (1909), Edmund William Greacen's *Brooklyn Bridge, East River* (1916), Ernest Lawson's *Brooklyn Bridge* (1917–1920), and Guy Wiggins's *Brooklyn Bridge in Winter* (1920), all of which shunned the span's bold outlines and soft-pedaled its place in the urban landscape. Redfield's view

Charles Frederick William Mielatz,
Catherine Market with Brooklyn Bridge, 1903.
Engraving. Negative number 79626d.
From the Collection of The New-York Historical Society.

John Francis Strauss, "The Bridge," 1903.
Courtesy of the Library of Congress.

Childe Hassam (American, 1859–1935), *Brooklyn Bridge in Winter*, 1904.
Oil on canvas, 30 × 34 ⅛ inches. Courtesy of the Telfair Museum of Art, Savannah, Georgia.
Museum purchase 1907.2.

Franz Šedivý, "Afton på Brooklyn-bron"

Allers Familj-Journal, September 17, 1905. From the author's collection.

George P. Hall, "Brooklyn Bridge, View Towards Lower Manhattan," ca. 1905.

Negative number 77380d. From the Collection of The New-York Historical Society.

is particularly skillful, managing to combine all the elements of the modern city—the electrified cityscape, the evolving skyline and bridge's massive form—into an image of profound romantic nostalgia.

Between 1892 and 1894, Hassam painted three similar images of the bridge, all from the perspective of the promenade, all set during rush hour. As with his later image, the combination of winter light and raging snowstorm undermines the bridge's essential strength. In the first and second paintings, the bridge is a shaded, ghostly presence looming above the commuters; in the third, the towers are entirely absent.

In his earlier paintings, Hassam was clearly less interested in the bridge than in the human traffic that choked the span during rush hour, which is exactly why his paintings should have influenced the artists of the Ash Can School. Ash Can artists were interested in social realism, not monumental architecture. Their city was defined by people and the places they gathered: by street corners, tenement fire escapes, el tracks, and boxing rings. For them, the Brooklyn Bridge must have seemed too removed from the hustle and bustle of the daily grind, not a part *of* the city but apart *from* it.

Unsurprisingly then, Ash Can artists virtually ignored the bridge, including it in only in a handful of canvases, as if the bridge just happened to exist in the background of the scene they were really interested in. In William Glackens's *East River from Brooklyn* (1902) and George Bellows's *Snow Dumpers* (1911) and *Splinter Beach* (1916), the bridge is in the distance, a backdrop to life on the river front. In 1949, at the end of his life, John Sloan finally got around to sketching the bridge he loved. Tossed off in an afternoon, *Wake on the Ferry* is Sloan's least serious work, a comic play on an earlier etching. George Luks was the only Ash Can artist to paint the bridge directly. His *Brooklyn Bridge* (1916), although a fitting and evocative rendering of New York's harsh urban milieu, is at heart a grubbier, darker version of Hassam's *Brooklyn Bridge in Winter*.

Childe Hassam, *Bridge in Snow (Brooklyn Bridge in Winter)*, 1894.

Oil on canvas: 32 × 25 inches. Purchased with funds from the Coffin Collection of the Des Moines Art Center, 1961.47. Photo credit: Michael Tropea, Chicago.

Jonas Lie, *Morning on the River*, ca. 1911–12.
Oil on canvas: 50 × 60 inches. Memorial Art Gallery of the University
of Rochester: Gift of Ruth Sibley Gade in memory of James G. Averell.
Photo credit: James Via.

The Ash Can artists were wrong, of course. The bridge's walkway was as much an
urban thoroughfare as Hester, Allen, or Monroe streets. Granted, it wasn't surrounded
by tenements, fire escapes, or street vendors, but it was alive to the sights and sounds of
daily human life. As with "Types of Life on the Promenade," Hassam's bridge is a place
of urban commingling where high and low walk side by side. This is no genteel urban
boulevard, but a scene of strenuous effort as hundreds of New Yorkers battle through a
driving snowstorm. Hassam's pedestrians are not escaping the city but confronting its
daily challenges.

Like Hassam, Everett Longley Warner painted the bridge numerous times, including once in 1919 from a seaplane. His favorite vantage point, however, was Peck Slip
between Water and Front streets, an angle he used at least three times: once in a snowstorm and twice during the bright sunshine of spring. Artistically, Warner's paintings

George Wesley Bellows, *Splinter Beach*, 1916.
Lithograph, 15 × 19 ¾ inches.
Courtesy the San Diego Museum of Art. Museum purchase 1998.85.

John Sloan, *Wake on the Ferry*, 1949.
Etching on paper: 5 × 7 inches. Printer: Ernest D. Roth. Bequest of Frank McClure.
Courtesy of the Smithsonian American Art Museum, Washington, DC/Art Resource, NY.

Everett Longley Warner, *Peck Slip, NYC,* n.d.
Oil on canvas: 40 × 50 inches (accession number 1945.343).
From the Collection of The New-York Historical Society.

connect the Impressionists' nineteenth-century aesthetic with the emerging dynamism of twentieth-century Modernism; formally, they are divided by contrasting architectural styles: the eighteenth-century row houses of Peck Slip and the massive modern bridge. These two urban places are linked by the commercial traffic that moves around one and over the other. Yet, despite their formal similarities, Warner's paintings show a distinct evolution. From *Falling Snow*, through *Along the East River Front, New York* to *Peck Slip*, Warner drags himself into the twentieth century. With each image the bridge grows starker and stronger, as does the sense of modern commercial activity. The effect is like a flip-book: as we scan the images we witness the morphing of a city dominated by Peck Slip to one dominated by the bridge. *Peck Slip* falls short of true Modernism, yet the painting is more akin to Stieglitz's photograph "City of Ambition" (1911) than it is to Hassam. In *Falling Snow*, the bridge is quaint; in *Peck Slip* it is dynamic.

Make It New!

Hassam was way ahead of the Ash Can school, and Warner was way behind the Modernists; neither was any match for popular culture. From the off, illustrated magazines, daredevils, and showmen embraced the bridge, as did ordinary New Yorkers. Together they helped to establish the span as an energetic, fascinating new arena, a new Broadway and a forerunner to Times Square. Brodie, Barnum, and Richard Fox of the *Gazette* helped nurture the proto-modernist cult of celebrity and self-promotion; J.S. Eldridge, Fahy's Coin, Max Stadler, Willimantic, among many others, used the bridge to advertise everything from "electromagnetic products" and medical cure-alls to watches, boots, and baking powder.

Slowly at first, and then with gathering momentum, artists experimented with the bridge—as if testing it out—incorporating the structure into their vision of the city. Less impulsive than the showmen, artists followed quietly, keeping their distance. In time, of course, they would gain confidence and join the parade. Likewise, poets would learn to appreciate the bridge's industrial aesthetic and dispatch reams of verse into the publishing ether. Disquisitions on beauty were also found in travelogues—both native and foreign—and novelists gradually began to explore the span's unique setting. As the twentieth century arrived, the bridge was poised to lead a new movement. Popular culture had reached the halls of high culture and found itself a seat.

The disparate streams of high and low culture that swirled around the bridge combined and rolled on into the new century. As technological Modernism began to reshape the downtown landscape, the bridge seemed like all things to all people: an advertising icon and a fit subject for art, a staple of the mass-market and of earnest poets, a place of escape and engagement, the home of philosophers and philanderers, of the showy and the stuffy, of critics and comedians. This groundwork would reap rich rewards in

Everett Longley Warner, *Falling Snow, New York*, n.d.
Oil on canvas: 32 × 40 ⅛ inches. Courtesy of the Smithsonian American
Art Museum, Washington, DC/Art Resource, NY.

the years to come. While city planners, engineers, and architects discussed altering the bridge, a new group of cultural performers took hold of the span and modernized it. Over in Europe in the 1920s, Ezra Pound exhorted his fellow modernists to "make it new!" Back in New York they were already on the case.

CHAPTER THREE

Modernism Takes Command (1912–1929)

Modernism was a revolution. And in many respects a distinctly American one. Few artistic movements have blended sensibility, style, and place quite as perfectly as modernist America. Yet why? One answer may lie in Gertrude Stein's somewhat off-hand comment that the U.S. was the oldest country in the world because it had been in the twentieth century the longest. While Edgar Degas was painting ballerinas, the Vatican initiating papal infallibility, John Ruskin venerating "The Stones of Venice," and Queen Victoria celebrating her golden jubilee, Elisha Otis was perfecting the elevator, William Le Baron Jenney was building the first steel-framed skyscraper, and New Yorkers were watching the construction and completion of the Brooklyn Bridge.

If the United States was the home of Modernism in action, then New York was its Mecca. And as the twentieth century roared around Gotham, the city had no more beloved shrine than Roebling's grand old bridge. Combining a new spatial phenomenon (height) and a new structural material (steel), the Brooklyn Bridge single-handedly dragged Victorian America into the new century. Where the Eiffel Tower—Europe's great modernist icon—stuck up out of Paris like a sore thumb, the bridge helped synthesize and balance the emerging downtown landscape, combining reverence for both the traditions of the gothic and the innovations of skyscraper steel. Subsequently, of course, it assumed a central role in New York's most famous downtown triad: the bridge is the cross brace that anchors the Woolworth Building to Trinity Church.

Understandably, modernist pilgrims flooded into New York from all over the world and made straight for the span. Once there, they stood transfixed. Through their imagination, the Brooklyn Bridge became exalted as the nineteenth century's most twentieth-century structure. They fused the vitality and energy of Futurism, Cubism, Expressionism, and Constructivism (amongst other artistic creeds) with the cityscape of lower Manhattan to produce some of the most striking images the bridge has ever

FACING PAGE
Ernest Fiene, *Brooklyn Bridge*, 1929 (detail)

inspired. Equally, of course, modernity had its detractors, many of whom came from within Modernism's own literary ranks. Where some saw a technological utopia, others saw a spiritual wasteland.

The Proto-Modernists, 1905–1911

The origins of the modernist contradiction can be examined through two friends who visited New York within a year of each other early in the twentieth century. Neither the staid Henry James nor the adventurous H.G. Wells were modernists in any strict sense of the word, yet both saw the city as a distinctly technological, fundamentally modernist place. There were no soft snow filters or evening twilight for these two. Instead, they saw the city with the same harsh glare that electrified its streets, skyscrapers, and bridges.

James departed the U.S. within months of the bridge's opening and returned 21 years later to find the city of his birth utterly transformed. In his absence, New York's population had more than doubled to over 4,000,000 people, many of whom were crowded into tiny tenements where they spoke little or no English. This new polyglot

Alvin Langdon Coburn, "Brooklyn Bridge from the River"
New York, 1910, plate 7. Courtesy of the Rare Books Division, Department of Rare Books and Special Collections, Princeton University Library.

city was physical as well as demographic. Gone was the discrete charm of low-lying brick row houses and the open spaces of James's youth. In their well-planned stead, tall new buildings had sprung up everywhere "like extravagant pins in a cushion already overplanted, and stuck in as in the dark, anywhere and anyhow."[1] While James was forging a new life in Europe, the skyscraper—and all that it represented—had come and claimed New York.

Raised on the virtues of genteel society—on form, manners, and propriety—James placed great stock in the past. For him, age and tradition were the ultimate source of value and worth. Accordingly, James returned to his native soil in excited anticipation, glad to be back and eager to visit the haunts of his youth. Yet James soon discovered that, during his absence, New York's past—his own past—had been obliterated by the onrush of technological Modernism. Unable to locate the city of his youth—either socially or physically—James was scandalized and bewildered, cast adrift in a suddenly foreign city. Map-less and lost, James was forced to confront the present (and future) reality, in the process becoming a momentary, reluctant modernist. "Crowned not only with no history, but with no credible possibility of time for history," New York was "like a train covering ground at maximum speed, and pushing on, at present, into regions unmeasurable."[2] To his credit, James took off after it.

What he found was a city reduced to the logic of a commercial machine. To him, New York had abandoned art, culture, and refinement in favor of "the commercial at any cost." Viewing the city from the bay, James saw a massive, single-minded dynamo driven by the "dauntless power" of the "mere market," not a home and haven for humanity. Searching for the root of this transformation, James focused on the Brooklyn Bridge:

> This appearance of the bold lacing together, across the water, of the scattered members of the monstrous organism … does perhaps more than anything else to give the pitch of the vision of energy. One has the sense that the monster grows and grows, flinging abroad its loose limbs even as some unmannered young giant at his "larks," and that the binding stitches must for ever fly further and faster and draw harder; the future complexity of the web, all under the sky and over the sea, becoming thus that of some colossal set of clockworks, some steel-souled machine-room of brandished arms and hammering fists and opening and closing jaws. The immeasurable bridges are but as the horizontal sheaths of pistons working at high pressure, day and night, and subject, one apprehends with perhaps inconsistent gloom, to certain, to fantastic, to merciless multiplication.[3]

The bridge was the perfect symbol for everything James loathed. It was a forerunner to the skyscraper, the heart of the new reality, and, stretching between Manhattan and Brooklyn, the sinew and muscle that bound the new urban body together. Equally, it

Photograph by Alvin Langdon Coburn.

BROOKLYN BRIDGE AT DAWN

BY RICHARD LE GALLIENNE

Out of the cleansing night of stars and tides,
Building itself anew in the slow dawn,
The long sea-city rises; night is gone,
Day is not yet—still merciful, she hides
Her summoning brow; and still the night-car glides

Empty of faces; the night watchmen yawn
One to the other, and shiver and pass on;
Nor yet a soul over the great bridge rides.

Frail as a gossamer, a thing of air,
A bow of shadow o'er the river flung—
Its sleepy masts and lonely lapping flood;
Who, seeing thus the Bridge a-slumber there,
Would dream such softness, like a picture hung,
Is wrought of human thunder, iron and blood?

Richard Le Galliene and Alvin Langdon Coburn, "Brooklyn Bridge at Dawn"
Metropolitan Magazine, February 1905.
From the author's collection.

was an engine room fueling the city's growth. Revolted by the city, James was nevertheless comfortable on the "breezy brightness of the Bay," a reminder, perhaps, of his youthful city. But, as he glanced up the East River from the harbor, he saw three further bridges in various stages of completion. This "merciless multiplication" threatened to do away with the last vestiges of James's New York, "in the light of" which the bay seemed like a "vast white page that awaits … the black overscoring of science." Having taken New York, the dynamo now threatened the bay with industrial vandalism and eventual elimination.

James never recovered from New York. Realizing, perhaps, that he was a man out of time and place, James retreated into comfortable nostalgia. He spent the last ten years of his life holed up in his little house outside London composing his memoirs (of life in pre-modern New York and Boston) and laboring over previously written books (the famous New York edition of his collected works). He took British citizenship, never returned to his native land, and wrote no more contemporary novels.

For his part, H.G. Wells arrived in New York a year after James, clutching some of the Master's travel essays as his guide. There, however, the similarities between the two men ended. Where James recoiled from the physical presence of Modernism, Wells loved it. Despite writing two large histories of the world, Wells cared little for the past. The future was his specialty, and he came to the U.S. to see it. And see it he did.

Wells disliked Americans, especially those he met on the trans-Atlantic voyage, but he adored new technologies, particularly those on display in New York. Arriving from the bay, Wells lets out what can only be described as a proto-modernist "yawp." He is dazzled by the skyline, in thrall to the city's "furious energy," and enraptured by its "immensity," what he elsewhere terms "Growth Invincible." Bombarded by a wealth of new stimuli, Wells seems afflicted by A.D.D., yet, amid the whirl of hyperactivity, his eyes, like James's, finally settled on the East River:

> Much more impressive than the skyscrapers, to my mind, is the large Brooklyn suspension bridge. I have never troubled to ask who built that, its greatness is not in its design, but in the quality of necessity one perceives in its inanimate immensity. It *tells*, as one goes under it up the East River, but it is far more impressive to come

Eugene de Salignac, "Brooklyn Bridge, Showing Painters and Foremen, October 7, 1914," 1914.
Courtesy of the New York City Municipal Archives.

Eugene de Salignac, "Brooklyn Bridge, Showing Painters on Suspenders,
October 7, 1914," 1914.
Courtesy of the New York City Municipal Archives.

upon it by glimpses. ... One sees parts of the Cyclopean stone arches, one gets
suggestive glimpses through the jungle growth of business, now of the back, now of
the flanks of the monster, then as one comes out on the river one discovers, far up
in one's sky, the long sweep of the bridge itself, foreshortened and with a maximum
of perspective effort.[4]

Where James despaired that New York's "Growth Invincible" would destroy its accumulated culture and human scale, Wells didn't care. "The great thing is the mechanical thing," Wells wrote, and the Brooklyn Bridge was New York's "very great[est] thing." By comparison, the "unmeaning faces" of the commuters that poured over the bridge were of little consequence. "The individuals count for nothing," he affirmed: the bridge was everything.[5] With such a declaration, Wells helped set the tone and tenor of the coming modernist revolution. For Wells, the bridge was not a *place* of spectacle—of stunts and showmen—but a spectacle *in and of itself*.

James and Wells were friends in 1905—although they would not remain so for long—and discussed their impressions of the U.S. James thought Wells too simplistic and altogether "too loud"; Wells thought James not simple enough.[6] Both were also friends with the photographer Alvin Langdon Coburn, who illustrated James's collected works, Wells's short novel *The Door in the Wall*, and corresponded with (and photographed) both authors. Coburn was also in New York from 1904 to 1905, scanning the new urban landscape.[7]

Like Wells, Coburn was a proto-modernist in thrall to New York's bustling energy and monumental size; like James he saw great value in the past. His major artistic influences were Japanese wood-blocks and, after a ten-year love affair with photography, he retired with his wife to a remote Welsh village and devoted the rest of his life to religious mysticism, freemasonry, and the study of ancient texts.[8] Yet from 1904 to 1912, Coburn produced some of the most memorable and seminal images of New York. And, in the process, he helped drag the Brooklyn Bridge into the modernist limelight.

Coburn didn't soften the facts of modern urban life as so many painters did: he exposed them. He depicted the new electric lights on Broadway, the construction of the Manhattan Bridge, the commercial bustle of the harbor, the rise of the new skyscrapers, and the gargantuan scale of the Brooklyn Bridge. Stressing length and height, Coburn's bridge towered over the ferries that chugged beneath it and the city that lay beyond it. Visually, it combined the giddy exhilaration of Futurism with the modernist urban aesthetics championed by Alfred Stieglitz in his magazine *Camera Work*.

Implicitly, it seems, Coburn understood one of the central assumptions of photographic Modernism, that the camera was kin to the city, and especially to its massive bridges:

> As I steamed up New York harbor the other day ... I felt the kinship of the mind that
> could produce those magnificent Martian-like monsters, the suspension bridges,
> with that of the photographer of the new school. The one uses his brain to fashion
> a thing of steel girders, a spider's web of beauty to glisten in the sun, the other
> blends chemistry and optics with personality in such a way as to produce a lasting

impression of a beautiful fragment of nature. The work of both, the bridge-builder and the photographer, owes its existence to man's conquest over nature.[9]

Coburn believed, as Stieglitz did, that photography, like structural engineering, was a combination of science and art. And that this affinity made the camera the pre-eminent medium through which to capture and explore such technological icons as the Brooklyn Bridge. This sense of exploration was compounded by advances in photographic science, especially increased portability. In the hands of modernist photographers, the hand-held camera became "an instrument of knowledge capable of expressing the multiplicity of a monumental technological form."[10] Unlike painters, photographers enjoyed unprecedented mobility, allowing them to move about and around the bridge for days and weeks on end, capturing each and every nuance and angle. Walker Evans is often credited with exemplifying this new sensibility—depicting new technological forms in new technological terms—but the honor really belongs to Coburn's friend, Karl Struss.

The Rise of Modernism, 1912

In 1912, Struss began to photograph the Brooklyn Bridge as part of his massive ongoing portrait of modern New York. He produced images of the bridge from the ferry, from the ferry slip, from the docks, from the neighborhood now known as DUMBO, from the walkway, and, most radically, through the bridge's intricate cable-work. In his strenuous attempts to make sense of the bridge—and its relationship to the city—Struss began a tradition that would grow to include Walker Evans, Andreas Feininger, Erich Hartmann, and William Gedney, among many others. The photographic bridge series is best described as a restless attempt to somehow cover or even uncover the bridge in all its multifaceted glory. Equally, it is an investigation into the mechanics of the camera itself, in effect welding the mechanical tool with the technological object. Experimenting with light and form, Struss returned repeatedly to the same vantage point: from the ferry slip looking up at the bridge, for example, during the noon-day sun and in the dead of night. His image from the walkway is titled "Vanishing Point" (1912), hinting at a convergence of form and perception. "Cables" (1910–1912)—Struss's most enduring image

Karl Struss (American, 1886–1981),
"Cables—New York Skyline through Brooklyn Bridge," 1912.
Printed 1979 by Phil Davis (American). Photograph, platinum print. Image/sheet: 11.4 × 9.4 cm (4 ½ × 3 ¹¹⁄₁₆ inches), mount: 30.5 × 22.8 cm (12 × 9 inches). Museum of Fine Arts, Boston. Gift of Richard Germann, 2001.375.

Christopher Richard Wynne
Nevinson (British, 1889–1946),
Looking Through Brooklyn Bridge,
1921.
Drypoint: 39.05 × 23.65 cm.
The Cleveland Museum of Art, Gift of
Mrs. Malcolm L. McBride 1966.73.

Arnold H. Rönnebeck, *Brooklyn Bridge*, 1925.
Lithograph: 12 ⅝ × 6 ¹¹⁄₁₆ inches.
Courtesy of the San Diego Museum of Art (Museum purchase 1926.141).

of the bridge—replicates the act of photography itself where one is always looking through something at something. Bonnie Yochelson has described Struss's photographs as "transitional … neither purely pictoralist nor purely modernist," and in his bridge images we see this play itself out.[11] "Brooklyn Bridge, Nocturne" (1912–1913) is an image of profound romanticism, whereas "Cables" is purely modernist. Anticipating such visual works as Christopher Nevinson's *Looking Through Brooklyn Bridge* (1921) and Arnold Ronnebeck's *Brooklyn Bridge* (1925), not to mention Vladimir Mayakovsky's modernist poem "Brooklyn Bridge" (1925), "Cables" prefigures the "lines of force" that would obsess Futurists and the strict linear geometry of Cubism. Equally, the photograph speaks to the two salient aspects of physical, modernist New York: the grid system and the steel-framed skyscraper. A study in form, context, and optics, "Cables" is literally the imprinting of Modernism on the already modernist skyline of New York.

Jonathan Lethem recently captured the essence of the bridge in a wonderfully succinct manner: "the bridge," he noted, is "an argument … with space."[12] This sensibility drove Struss and numerous other photographers and artists, including John Marin, who from 1910 to 1932 produced image after image of the bridge. Encompassing countless watercolors, drawings, etchings, and oils, Marin's bridge series is the most complete effort to capture and understand the span in the fine arts. By the time he finished, he'd exhausted almost every possible angle, not to mention himself.

Marin's favorite angle became the dominant modernist perspective: from the walkway looking up at the bridge's towers. Yet, where later artists would most often depict a deserted, monumental bridge, Marin, like Hassam before him, always included pedestrians on the bridge. And the reason was simple. Other artists saw the city and the bridge in Precisionist terms, as a showcase for America's evolving industrial landscape, a place where power flowed from sheer physical presence. Marin, on the other

Karl Struss (American, 1886–1981), "Brooklyn Bridge from Ferry Slip, Evening," 1912. Printed 1979 by Phil Davis (American). Photograph, platinum print. Image/sheet: 11.6 × 9.7 cm (4 9/16 × 3 13/16 inches), mount: 30.5 × 22.8 cm (12 × 9 inches). Museum of Fine Arts, Boston. Gift of Richard Germann, 2001.374.

John Marin (American, 1870–1953), *Brooklyn Bridge*, ca. 1912.
Watercolor and charcoal on paper: 18 ⅝ × 15 ⅝ inches (47.3 × 39.7 cm): The Metropolitan Museum of
Art, Alfred Stieglitz Collection, 1949 (49.70.105) Photograph © 1989 The Metropolitan Museum of Art
© 2007 Estate of John Marin/Artists Rights Society (ARS), New York.

John Marin, *Brooklyn Bridge No. 2
(Song of the Bridge)*, 1913.
Etching, printed in grayish black: plate 10 ¾ × 8 ⅞ inches.
Purchase (83.1955). Courtesy of The Museum of Modern Art/
Licensed by SCALA/Art Resource, NY © 2007 Estate of John
Marin/Artists Rights Society (ARS), New York.

John Marin, *Brooklyn Bridge No. 6*, 1913.
Etching on off-white wove paper. Plate: 10 ¾ × 8 ¹³⁄₁₆ inches.
Courtesy of the Terra Foundation for American Art, Chicago/
Art Resource, NY © 2007 Estate of John Marin/Artists Rights
Society (ARS), New York.

hand, saw the whole thing lumped together. Yes, New York was the seat and symbol of
U.S. Modernism, but modernity could not be reduced to mere scale. It was a climate
predicated on cultural, physical, economic, and social acceleration. As James noticed,
New York was speeding into the twentieth century like a bullet from a gun.

Movement is the key to Marin's bridge images and to his understanding of modernity. "I see great forces at work," he declared in 1913, "great movements."[13] In Marin's
vocabulary, force, movement, and modernity were interchangeable terms. His city
was alive, bustling with the kinetic energy of modern life, of the crowds that poured
around the labyrinth, the motion of the rising skyline, the charged current of cultural
anticipation, and the crackling dynamism of artistic change. This sense of movement
not only surrounds his bridge but seems to propel the viewer over the span and towards
the towers. Marin's visual lexicon embraced other burgeoning cultural forms. One

Max Weber, *Brooklyn Bridge*, 1912.
Courtesy of the University of Reading, UK.

of Marin's etchings depicts the bridge carrying a tune; another has it swaying to the rhythms of the modern metropolis. For Marin, the bridge was an active participant in the process of modernity, speeding into the new century with a song and a dance.

The Polish–American artist Max Weber also painted the bridge from its walkway in 1912. Although deserted and less frantic, Weber's bridge is conceptually similar to Marin's. A sense of motion and vibrancy grips the canvas, which is dominated by a bright, fluid depiction of a tower and the long, elegant sweep of the cables. Weber made lithographs from the image and gave the original to Coburn—the painter and the photographer were good friends—along with a "cubist poem" entitled "On the Brooklyn Bridge":

> This morning early I was on the old Bridge of this New York. Midst din, crash, out-wearing, outliving of its iron and steel muscles and sinews, I stood and gazed at the millions of cubes upon billions of cubes pile upon pile, higher and higher, still piled and still higher with countless window eyes, befogged chimney throats clogged by steam and smoke—all this framed and hurled together in mighty mass against rolling

clouds—tied to space above and about by the infinitely numbered iron wire lines of the bridge, spreading interlacedly in every angle. Lulled into calm and meditation (I gazed) by the rhythmic music of vision (sight) I gazed and thought of this pile throbbing, boiling, seething, as a pile after destruction, and this noise and dynamic force created in me a peace the opposite of itself. Two worlds I had before me the inner and the outer. I never felt such. I live in both![14]

Weber's poem fuses James's and Wells's reactions to the bridge with Coburn's thoughts on "man's conquest over nature." Here modernity is a tightrope, a balancing act, wherein one must temper enthusiasm and embrace fear. More cautionary tale than poetic reaching, Weber's perspective would prove prescient once the wild mood swings of the 1920s began to kick in.

The Modernist Explosion, 1913–1924

During the first decade of the twentieth century, James, Wells, and Coburn set the parameters of the modernist conception of the Brooklyn Bridge; in 1912 Struss, Marin, and Weber filled them in. While fiddling around in his studio a year later, James Daugherty expanded them. Daugherty painted *Greater New York* (1913), his Cubo-Futurist masterpiece, as a screen to separate his kitchen from the living room of his studio at 61 Poplar Street in Brooklyn Heights. Separated into three panels, *Greater New York* is an attempt to distill the modern city into its constituent parts. On the left, skyscrapers cluster high over the city, and on the right he presents a visual evocation of electrification and kinetic motion. In the middle, the bridge links these two subjects so that they seem to bleed together into the center panel. Daugherty's canvas was part of a wider trend to broaden the significance of individual paintings, from specific things and places to "synoptic" representations of the city. George Bellows's *New York* (1911), for example, is not an accurate depiction of Union Square, but a compendium of "the economic, commercial, and political activities that made the city function": crowds, commerce, mass transit, electrification, and modern office buildings.[15]

No doubt influenced by the Italian Futurist Athos Casarini, his neighbor on Poplar Street, Daugherty was among the first to bring a distinctly modernist aesthetic to this "synoptic" approach and the first to include the bridge at the heart of his "totalizing" vision. The full extent of Daugherty's influence is difficult to pin down, but his originality is not. Stylistically, *Greater New York* predates Albert Gleizes's major bridge paintings by two years. Often regarded as some of the most original images of the bridge, Gleizes's explosive, energetic, heavily abstracted, and deeply cryptic canvases appear as direct descendants of *Greater New York*. As for content, Daugherty's approach was simplified by Weber, who also worked in the synoptic vein. In Weber's *The City* (1918), New York is

James Daugherty,
Greater New York, 1913.
Oil on burlap. Courtesy of The Charles M.
Daugherty Testamentary Trust.

James Daugherty (American,
1887–1974), *Glend Island*, n.d.
Etching: 29.5 × 30.1 cm (image).
Fine Arts Museums of San Francisco,
Achenbach Foundation for Graphic Arts,
1963.30.24427.

FACING PAGE
Albert Gleizes, *Brooklyn
Bridge*, 1915.
Black ink, gouache and watercolor
on paper, 25 × 19 cm. Photo: Banque
d'Images, ADAGP/Art Resource, NY
© 2007 Artists Rights Society (ARS),
New York/ADAGP, Paris.

Samuel Halpert, *Brooklyn Bridge*, 1913.
Oil on canvas: 34 × 42 inches. Gift of Mr. and Mrs. Benjamin Halpert (54.2).
From the Collection of the Whitney Museum of American Art, New York.

reduced to a jumble of skyscrapers over which the bridges presides. Daugherty's triumvirate was further replicated in Louis Lozowick's lithograph *New York* (1925), which reduced the city to the same three formal elements: skyscrapers, speeding el trains, and the Brooklyn Bridge.

Daugherty's main influence, hereto unnoticed by art historians, was probably on Joseph Stella. Stella met Daugherty in 1918—a year before he began to paint the bridge and just two years before he began *Voice of the City of New York, Interpreted* (1920–1922)— and may well have studied *Greater New York*. Certainly, there are numerous similarities: the "synoptic" approach to New York: the stress on skyscrapers, the harbor, the bridge,

Joseph Stella, *Study for "New York Interpreted: Brooklyn Bridge"*, (1920–22).
Watercolor and brush and ink on paper:
17 ⅛ × 11 ¾ inches. 66.4779. Hirshhorn
Museum and Sculpture Garden, Smithsonian
Institution, Gift of Joseph H. Hirshhorn, 1966.
Photo credit: Lee Stalsworth.

Joseph Stella, *Study for "New York Interpreted: Brooklyn Bridge"*, (1920–22).
Watercolor and brush and ink on paper: 13 ¹⁵⁄₁₆ × 9 ¹⁵⁄₁₆ inches. 66.4775.
Hirshhorn Museum and Sculpture Garden, Smithsonian Institution,
Gift of Joseph H. Hirshhorn, 1966. Photo credit: Lee Stalsworth.

electricity, and movement and the isolation of each individual feature within separate
panels. *Greater New York* may be closer to early Cubism than the electrified Futurism
of Stella's *Voice of the City*, but both paintings share a sense of joyous excitement at the
prospect before them.

Stella's feelings about New York fluctuated from love to loathing, and his bridge
paintings reflect this. Where *The Bridge (Brooklyn Bridge)* from *Voice of the City of New
York* is generally positive, *Brooklyn Bridge* (1919–1920) is deeply ambiguous, and

American Landscape (1929)—totalizing not just the city but the entire country down to an image of the span—is downright hostile. Yet such contradictions are less puzzling than revealing. Stella's work is central to the modernist conception of the bridge *specifically because* it replicates the roller-coaster ride of the American 1920s. Stella was certainly captivated by the bridge—"I felt deeply moved," he wrote, "as if on the threshold of a new religion or in the presence of a new DIVINITY"—but also (as often as not) repulsed by New York's "gigantic jaw of irregular teeth": "the skyscrapers like bandages covering the sky, stifling our breath, life shabby and mean, provincial, sometimes shadowy and hostile like an immense prison where the ambitions of Europe sicken and languish."[16]

The key to Stella's ambivalence was perspective. Proto-modernists like James, Wells, and Coburn gazed out at the bridge from afar and contemplated its cultural meanings. Modernists like Marin, Struss, Webber, Gleizes, and Stella took themselves to the bridge and reveled in the personal experience. The shift—from looking *at* to being *on*, from *contemplating* to *experiencing*—was central to the modernist approach to the bridge. This is what Alan Trachtenberg calls "the classic moment," the instant when the bridge—in front of our very eyes—transforms itself from a public icon to "a private event." Familiar to bridge-walkers and tourists the world over, "the classic moment" is not studied or pondered but wholly immediate and radically personal. It is a visceral, instinctual response to the bridge's unique modernity. It is the attempt "to know the bridge from the inside."[17]

Given its deeply personal nature, there are many tropes but no standards for the classic moment. Lewis Mumford, Hart Crane, and Alfred Kazin, for example, experienced profound epiphanies while walking the bridge. They found purpose and energy while enclosed within the network of granite and steel, a profound affirmation of themselves and their culture. Likewise, Paul Strand and Charles Sheeler chose to open *New York the Magnificent* (1921)—their cinematic hymn

John Paul Edwards, "The Web," 1921.
Courtesy of the Amon Carter Museum, Fort Worth, Texas.

Albert Gleizes, *Brooklyn Bridge*, 1915.
Oil and gouache on canvas: 40 ⅛ × 40 ⅛ inches. Solomon R. Guggenheim
Museum, New York (44.942) © 2007 Artists Rights Society (ARS),
New York/ADAGP, Paris.

to New York, later renamed *Manahatta*—on the bridge's central walkway. Others,
however, felt crushed, not freed, by the mighty span. As the modernist poet Lola
Ridge wrote:

> Pythoness body —arching
> Over the night like an ecstasy—
> I feel your coils tightening ...
> And the world's lessening breath.[18]

The innate sense of power that haunted Ridge and energized Mumford was also captured by Charles Reznikoff. For Reznikoff, the bridge underscored man's insignificance when placed against the mighty backdrop of New York:

On Brooklyn Bridge I saw a man drop dead.
It meant no more than if he were a sparrow;
For tower on tower behind the bridge arose
The buildings on Manhattan, tall white towers
Agleam with lights; below, the wide blue bay
Stretched out to meet the high blue sky
and the first white star.[19]

To stand before the bridge's great towers, enclosed within the grip of its cables, is to stand in a visual, aural, and cultural vortex. And the experience leads as often to confusion as to clarity. In Waldo Frank's novel *The Unwelcome Man* (1917), Quincy Burt visits the bridge in an effort to better understand New York:

Before him swept the bridge ... It seemed to Quincy that he was being caught upon a monstrous swing and swept with its pulsed lilt above the groveling life of the metropolis. Suddenly, the fancy flashed upon him that from his perch of shivering steel the power should indeed come to poise and judge the swarm above which he rocked. The bridge that reeled beyond him seemed an arbiter. It bound the city. It must know the city's soul since it was close to the city's breath. In its throbbing cables there must be a message. In its lacings and filigrees of steel there must be subtle words![20]

Unfortunately, the bridge is no "steeled cognizance" (as Hart Crane believed), and Burt finds no answers. For Frank the bridge is more sphinx than oracle, a mute witness to the search for order amid the hysteria of Modernism.

Herbert J. Seligmann (American, 1891–1984), "Brooklyn Bridge," ca. 1920s.
Gelatin silver print: 10.8 × 8.2 cm. The Cleveland Museum of Art, John L. Severance Fund 1989.397.

Tavik Frantisek Simon,
*New York—Brooklyn
Bridge*, 1927.
From the author's collection.

Samuel Halpert, *View of
Brooklyn Bridge*, n.d.
Oil on canvas: 34 × 42 inches
(86.4 × 106.7 cm). Brooklyn
Museum, Gift of Benjamin
Halpert, 54.15.

Martin Lewis, *Dock Workers Under the Brooklyn Bridge*, ca. 1915.
Oil on board, 23 ⅜ × 19 ⅝ inches. From the collection of Joseph S. Allerhand.

Stella dramatized the shifting, visceral, and often unstable nature of the classic moment in his short article "The Brooklyn Bridge (a page of my life)," published privately in 1928. Set during the First World War but written from the perspective of the late 1920s, Stella's essay tracks his attempts to make sense of the bridge, amid the wild cacophony of the city:

> Many nights I stood on the bridge—and in the middle alone—lost—a defenceless [sic] prey to the surrounding swarming darkness—crushed by the mountainous black impenetrability of the skyscrapers—here and there lights resembling the suspended falls of astral bodies or fantastic splendors of remote rites—at times, ringing as alarm in a tempest, the shrill sulphurous voice of the trolley wires—now and then strange moanings of appeal from tug boats, guessed more than seen, through the infernal recesses below.

Stella's article packs ten years of turmoil and struggle into two short pages: it fuses his youthful wonder at the bridge with his mature enervation of New York. Throughout,

Eugene de Salignac, "Brooklyn Bridge, Brooklyn, Looking from Stable's Roof East, May 6, 1918," 1918.
Courtesy of the New York City Municipal Archives.

Stella wrestles with the contradictions of industrial New York and resolution arrives not through engagement but through flight: "At the end, brusquely, a new light broke over me … from the sudden unfolding of the blue distances of my youth in Italy, a great clarity announced PEACE—proclaimed the luminous dawn of a NEW ERA." This new era would see Stella turn his back on the bridge and return to his own artistic heritage: the rural and religious folk art of Italy.[21]

The Decline of Modernism, 1925

Stella's early bridge paintings crystallized the aims, origins, and efforts of modernist New York, and his later work fixed its waning years. The bridge emerged from the cultural frenzy of 1912 as a somewhat unlikely modernist icon, yet, by 1925, the spiritual potential of new technologies and new social relations had begun to evaporate. After living through the era of industrialized death known as the Great War, modernists came face to face with the spiritual vacuity, harsh racism, failed promise, and careless brutality of F. Scott Fitzgerald's *The Great Gatsby* (1925). Just as Fitzgerald ultimately rejected the flapper aristocracy he longed to join, so modernist authors and artists began to question and abandon the landscape of industrial New York. All it required was one last hurrah

Ernest Lawson,
Brooklyn Bridge, 1917–20.
Oil on canvas, 20 ⅜ × 24 inches.
Courtesy of the Terra Foundation
for American Art, Chicago/Art
Resource, NY.

before the rot set in. Unsurprisingly, it came from a man for whom New York was entirely alien ground.

Shortly after the release of Fitzgerald's great novel, Vladimir Mayakovsky—"the plenipotentiary of Soviet poetry"—arrived in New York and discovered the Brooklyn Bridge.[22] His poetic tribute, the architectonic masterpiece "Brooklyn Bridge" (1925), is the literary kin of Struss's "Cables"—"I … look / upon New York / through Brooklyn Bridge"—and a direct descendent of Montgomery Schuyler's traveling New Zealander: "If ever / the end of the world / should arrive," and the bridge "towering over debris" was "the only / lonely / thing to survive," how might "future's geologist … remodel / these days / of ours"? As a contradiction, of course, just as Mayakovsky did. Standing on "this steel-wrought mile" where "my visions come real / in the striving / for structure / instead of style," Mayakovsky saw the bridge as means to understand the conjunction of Capitalism and technology. The bridge's towers stood for bourgeois conservatism and the cables for the revolutionary potential of new technology. It was, in fact, nothing less than the meeting ground of Capitalism and Communism, two ideologies for whom technology was central. Needless to say, it is the steel of socialism that carries the day, "unfurling" through both space and time into a new future.[23]

Sears Gallagher, *Brooklyn Bridge*, 1919.
Courtesy of the Institute Archives and Special Collections, Folsom Library, Rensselaer Polytechnic Institute.

Mayakovsky's "shout of joy," as Colum McCann so wonderfully describes it, was unencumbered by the realities of New York, or even any real sense of the city's geography (he describes "the victims of unemployment," for example, jumping "headlong" off the Brooklyn Bridge into the Hudson River).[24] The same cannot be said for John Dos Passos's *Manhattan Transfer*, which hit New York bookstores just a couple of weeks after Mayakovsky left town. Dos Passos understood the roaring twenties better than most, especially the dichotomy between aspiration and attainment: the wrecked lives and failed dreams that lay just beneath the decade's triumphant headlines. His New York is a

Guy Carleton Wiggins
(1883–1962), *Brooklyn
Bridge in Winter*, ca. 1920.
Oil on canvas, 20 ¼ × 24 ¼ inches
© University of Cincinnati Fine
Arts Collection; Gift of W.T.S.
Johnson.

frantic, Sisyphean merry-go-round where money and success are seemingly everywhere (yet always nowhere) and the worship of them so prominent and so ingrained as to make all other considerations irrelevant. Dos Passos's novel is best described as a vast treasure hunt where ordinary individuals, drunk on cheap dreams of instant wealth, roam the city like packs of toothless dogs in search of nourishment. There is no sustenance in *Manhattan Transfer*—the prize is securely locked up, high in the city's great fortresses, its unattainable, unenterable skyscrapers—only hunger and longing. The effect is itself a classic moment, perhaps best exemplified by Thomas Wolfe's bluntly titled short story "No Door" (1931), and one particular to New York. While gazing out over "great vision of the city" and "the wing-like swoop" of the Brooklyn Bridge, Wolfe's protagonist experienced the same epiphany as that experienced by the cast of characters in *Manhattan Transfer*: "that it is all here, somehow, waiting for you and only an inch away if you will touch it, only a word away if you will speak it, only a wall, a door, a stride from you if you only knew the place where you may enter."[25] Wolfe might well have called his short story "No Money," for, as *Manhattan Transfer* so clearly shows, the currency of success in the capital of Capitalism is always currency.

Dos Passos's novel opens with Bud Korpenning, a Dick Whittingtonesque upstate rube arriving in New York. Bud is drawn to the city by the bright lights of fame and

Christopher Nevinson,
Under the Brooklyn Bridge, n.d.
Courtesy of the Institute Archives and Special Collections,
Folsom Library, Rensselaer Polytechnic Institute.

Paul Berdanier, *Lower East Side—New York*, n.d.
From the author's collection.

fortune. Stepping off the ferry, he announces his intentions, "I want to get to the center of things," a catchphrase he repeats first with gusto and then with increasing fatigue throughout the rest of his short life. Korpenning doesn't last long, but in many ways he is the novel's central character, the moral soul of the tale: his story is, in one form or another, the story of all the characters. Like many before him, Korpenning's search for "the center of things" takes him to the bridge:

> Picking his teeth he walked through the grimydark entrance to Brooklyn Bridge. … The arching footwalk was empty except for a single policeman who stood yawning, looking up at the sky. It was like walking among the stars. Below in either direction streets

Joseph Pennell,
The Bridges, From Beneath, ca. 1921.
Etching. Image: 6 ⅞ × 10 ³/₁₆ inches (17.5 × 25.8 cm).
Brooklyn Museum, Gift of the artist, 24.44.

Peter Marcus,
The East Tower, 1921.
Courtesy of the Institute Archives and
Special Collections, Folsom Library,
Rensselaer Polytechnic Institute.

Conseulo Kanaga, "[Untitled]
(Horse Drawn Wagon)," 1922–24.
From the series: "Downtown New York"
1922–1924. Gelatin silver print.
Image: 2 ⅝ × 3 ⅞ inches (6.7 × 9.8 cm).
Mat: 14 ½ × 19 ¼ inches (36.8 × 48.9 cm).
Brooklyn Museum, Gift of Wallace B. Putnam
from the estate of Consuelo Kanaga, 82.65.401.

Conseulo Kanaga, "[Untitled]
(Brooklyn Bridge)," 1922–24
(printed 1946–1949).
Gelatin silver print, 4 × 3 inches (10.2 × 7.6 cm).
Brooklyn Museum, Gift of Wallace B. Putnam
from the estate of Consuelo Kanaga, 82.65.152.

tapered into dotted lines of lights between square blackwindowed buildings. The river glimmered underneath like the Milky Way above. Silently smoothly the bunch of lights of a tug slipped through the moist darkness. A car whirred across the bridge making the girders rattle and the spiderwork of cables thrum like a shaken banjo.

When he got to the tangle of girders of the elevated railroads of the Brooklyn side, he turned back along the southern driveway. Dont matter where I go, cant go nowhere now.[26]

Bud's second-to-last act is a flight of imagination—he imagines himself as a city alderman (yet more shades of Dick Whittington) in a "swallowtail suit and a gold watchchain … riding in a carriage full of diamonds with his milliondollar bride" surrounded by adoring onlookers—and his last act is a return to reality:

Ralph Briggs Fuller, *Scrambled History: Horatius at Brooklyn Bridge*, 1924.
Courtesy of the Graphic Arts Collection, Department of Rare Books and Special Collections, Princeton University Library.

Bud is sitting on the rail of the bridge. The sun has risen behind Brooklyn. The windows of Manhattan have caught fire. He jerks himself forward, slips, dangles by a hand with the sun in his eyes. The yell strangles in his throat as he drops."[27]

Korpenning's visceral, instinctual response to the bridge, unfortunately, is to throw himself off.

Dos Passos refashioned the classic moment to include a dark undertone of warning. Clearly Korpenning doesn't take himself to the bridge to celebrate the vibrancy of the modern urban environment. Instead, Dos Passos puts him there to condemn it. Bud's suicide is both pathetically ignominious and socially significant. It marked a cultural moment, where national dreams collide with personal reality, signaling the beginning of the end of Modernism's infatuation with the bridge.

New York's joyful embrace of its own modern urban landscape was as precarious as the 1920s economy. By focusing on the products of civilization, artists and writers

Arnold Rönnebeck (American, 1885–1947). *Skyline*, 1928.
Lithograph: 28.8 × 40.3 cm. The Cleveland Museum of Art, John L. Severance Fund 2000.26.

William Walcott, *Brooklyn Bridge, New York*, ca. 1925.
Aquatint and drypoint on wove paper, 1980.1.
Courtesy of the Sterling and Francine Clark Art Institute, Williamstown, Massachusetts.

Joseph Pennell, *The Bridge*, ca. 1920s.
Courtesy of the Library of Congress.

often forgot that civilization is a human endeavor: that cities are built for people not postcards. In his bizarre little book, *Mirrors of New York*, also published in 1925, Benjamin De Casseres imagined the "the resignation of New York." Standing on Riverside Drive, De Casseres spies a motley collection of New York icons—all grown sick and weary and "struck clean" from their mooring—marching out of the city in protest. "My soul is a series of pigeon-holes called rooms. I am Business. I am Profit and Loss. I am Beauty come into the hell of the Practical," declares the Woolworth Building's tower; "Justice is a dice-box. The rich always win, while the poor get the box," adds the Golden Lady from the summit of the Municipal Building. "The Brooklyn Bridge, crawling along like a tired snake, its cables making a most unearthly racket" brings up the rear, "making such an uproar that I could not hear what it said."[28]

De Casseres might well have been discussing the era's great modernists, many of whom, after the enthusiasm of the 1910s, turned their back on modern America: John Marin retreated to rural New Hampshire, Max Weber turned to social realism and urban poverty, and Joseph Stella abandoned New York as a subject and took up the mantel of folk classicist. While thousands of Americans were happily leaping

Ernest Fiene, *Brooklyn Bridge*, 1929.
Courtesy of the Graphic Arts Collection, Department of Rare
Books and Special Collections, Princeton University Library.

Adriaan Lubbers, *Brooklyn Bridge*, 1929.
Courtesy of the Graphic Arts Collection, Department of Rare
Books and Special Collections, Princeton University Library.

into the get-rich landscape, most American modernists were packing their bags and
heading out.

1929 and the Fall of Modernism

Stella remains the best lens through which to view the modernist era. After his triumphant canvases of the late 1910s and early 1920s, Stella returned to the bridge only
once more with any meaningful intent. His *American Landscape* of 1929 is the year writ
large. It portrays a caustic New York seen through the bridge's cables. The city appears

Walker Evans (American, 1903–1975),
"[Brooklyn Bridge, New York]," 1929.
Film negative: 1 ⅝ × 2 ½ inches.
The Metropolitan Museum of Art, Gift of Arnold
Crane, 2003 (2003.564.1) © Walker Evans Archive,
The Metropolitan Museum of Art.

wracked with decay, and the bridge itself is askew: the lines of its cables flow unnaturally outward, as if forcibly pulled in opposite directions. Here the bridge is no longer a gateway, but a barrier and a prison.

Needless to say, numerous artists of all descriptions—notably Louis Lozowick and Walker Evans—continued to celebrate the bridge's triumphant iconography and revolutionary form. But, by the early 1930s, they could no longer deny that America had changed. The Jazz Age had passed, the Depression was here and American art would have to respond to a new social reality. As Evans bid farewell to the bridge and took to the rural farmlands of the American South under the auspices of the Farm Security Administration, the first great moment of modernist enthusiasm came to a close.

FACING PAGE

Joseph Stella, *American Landscape*, 1929.
Oil on canvas, 79 ⅛ × 39 ⁵⁄₁₆ inches. Courtesy of the Walker Art Center,
Minneapolis. Gift of the T.B. Walker Foundation, 1957.

CHAPTER FOUR

Depression and Recovery (1929–1945)

The 1930s exposed the tensions evident in the 1920s, between image and reality, icons and individuals, high Modernism and Social Realism. As the exuberance of the Jazz Age collided with the certainty of overwhelming economic collapse, the nation's collective mindset hung a u-turn; surely, quickly, and absolutely. The collapse of the modernist revolution, albeit temporarily, and the rise of socially conscious art defined the American 1930s. The conflict can be summarized by comparing two of the period's most renowned poets, both of whom made their way to New York in the 1920s.

Drunk in a Bar in Brooklyn: Lorca, Crane, and the Stock Market Crash

Federico García Lorca arrived in New York during the summer of 1929 and stayed just long enough to witness the stock market crash and the beginnings of national panic. By April 1930, he was sick to death of America and on his way back to his native Spain. While in New York, he was shown around Harlem (which he adored) by Nella Larsen and went sightseeing on Wall Street (which he abhorred). He was also taken to Brooklyn by Angel Flores—the noted Puerto Rican translator, literary critic, and editor—to meet Hart Crane, who was then finishing up *The Bridge* (1930), his poetic tribute to the Brooklyn Bridge and the nation it symbolized.

As dedicated young poets, Lorca and Crane had both enjoyed a good measure of critical acclaim. Equally, both were driven by their love of Whitman's infectious idealism, not to mention their love of other men. Yet, their shared passions and achievements did not translate into the stuff of legend. Their meeting was an absolute non-event. According to Flores, Crane was drunk and flirting with a band of sailors by the time he and Lorca arrived in Brooklyn. With Flores's help, the two poets exchanged brief pleasantries before the conversation petered out and Crane returned to his flirting. What happened next is

Ernest Fiene, *New York Skyline (Under the Brooklyn Bridge)*, 1932.
Courtesy of American Printmakers On-Line Catalogue Raisonné Project (www.catrais.org).

anyone's guess. Some say Lorca left immediately, shocked by Crane's behavior. Others say Crane invited Lorca to stay and that the Spaniard agreed, out of curiosity, if nothing else.[1] Either way, neither Lorca nor Crane ever mentioned their exchange, nor each other for that matter, in any of their letters, essays or diaries. It was as if the encounter simply never happened, or, more likely, that neither poet was especially impressed by the other.

Nevertheless, the meeting is intriguing. Lorca was radicalized by his American experience, and must have been stunned by Crane's hedonism and willful abandon. "Never as then, amid suicides, hysteria, and groups of fainting people," wrote Lorca of post-crash New York, "have I felt the sensation of real death, death without hope, death that is nothing but rottenness, for the spectacle was terrifying."[2] While America was being brought to its knees, and suicides were raining down on the sidewalks of New York, Crane was living in oblivion in Brooklyn, obsessing over his masterpiece and cavorting with drunken sailors.

These two personal reactions to the stock market crash are revealing. Hart Crane's *The Bridge* is the most celebrated and famous attempt to capture the span in words. Unfortunately, as a poem it is often considered a failure, albeit a somewhat noble one. Based in "history and fact," Crane wanted his poem to

16250

Eugene de Salignac, "Brooklyn Bridge, Showing Painters' Scaffold, April 9, 1934," 1934.
Courtesy of the New York City Municipal Archives.

"concern a mystical synthesis of 'America'. ... The initial impulses of 'our people'
will have to be gathered up toward the climax of the bridge, symbol of our construc-
tive future, our unique identity, in which is to be included also our scientific hopes
and achievements of the future."[3]

Unfortunately, Crane wasn't too interested in either "history" or "fact"; spiritual transcendence was more his game. And this was fine during the high symbolism of the
1920s, but Crane dallied too long and failed to get his poem finished in time.

When Crane finally emerged from Brooklyn in 1930, his manuscript in hand, he must have wondered where the hell everyone had gone. As he put the finishing touches to his modernist masterpiece, Modernism crashed into the Great Depression and fractured, sending its advocates scurrying. The Depression was a cultural juggernaut that decimated the mores, standards, and tastes of the 1920s, leaving artists scrambling to make sense of the dizzy new reality. Aesthetic contemplation and stylistic experimentation slipped quickly out of vogue, for the world was no longer listening. Most modernists morphed, changed, and survived. Poor old Hart Crane could not.

The Bridge failed to formulate any meaningful connection between the Brooklyn Bridge and the realities of American life, a complaint the critics of the day made loudly, clearly, and often. Crane admitted as much in 1926: "intellectually judged the whole theme and project seems more and more absurd. ... The bridge as a symbol today has no significance."[4] Yet he did as all good poets do: after finding no "mystical synthesis" to celebrate, he conjured one up.

Earl Horter, *Brooklyn Bridge*, 1931.
Courtesy of the Institute Archives and Special Collections, Folsom Library,
Rensselaer Polytechnic Institute.

Crane gave up on the bridge *as a bridge*, and retreated into the welcoming arms of a mythic past, a past found not in American history, but in the early poems of Walt Whitman. Under Whitman's influence, Crane transformed the structure into a symbol of pure affirmation, an "inviolate curve," a "harp" and an "altar." It became an icon of deep spiritual significance—so much so that it could "lend a myth to God," as if God needed the bridge's charity—and an instrument upon which Crane could tease out his own personal rhythms. No longer the key to America's soul, it became the key to Crane's utopian longing, his dreams of poetic transcendence. Ultimately, as Alan Trachtenberg notes, the bridge of *The Bridge* exists nowhere in the world, only in the mind and imagination of the poet. After all, few symbols can honestly sustain and hold the level of significance that Crane demanded.[5]

Crane hoped *The Bridge* would refute the negativity of T.S. Eliot's *The Wasteland* (1922), but, by 1930, Eliot was as popular as ever, and for good reason. Eliot used the Great War to smash the myth of Western progress; Crane tried the opposite and failed.

Earl Klein, *Brooklyn Bridge*, n.d.
From the author's collection.

The utopian promise of American progress couldn't dent the Great Crash. Eliot's living dead, who flowed over London Bridge and around the "Unreal City," had, as Lorca perceived, found their way to America. Crane, unfortunately, was too busy binge drinking and dreaming of Whitman to notice.

Crane saw the bridge as the gateway to a modern utopia, a new Atlantis. Lorca saw it as hell's lobby. The Spaniard saw New York as poisonous and aberrant, and he articulated this through several key metaphors. Writhing serpents populate and patrol the New York streets, haunting and shadowing the frenzied crowd. This hysteria is compounded by the city itself, which allows no rest or slumber. The "genuine pain" of insomnia "keeps everything awake": "crowds stagger sleeplessly through the boroughs / as if they just escaped a shipwreck of blood." Lorca understood morning as Ronald Reagan did, as a time of optimism, revitalization, and renewal, yet there is no morning in America for this poet—"morning and hope are impossible," he laments—only a "counterfeit dawn" where "life is neither noble, nor good, nor sacred." Whispering back down the years to Whitman, Lorca passed judgment on the now-rotten, long-lost world of Whitman's youth: "This is the world, my friend, agony, agony."[6]

Lorca's impressions of the city coalesce in "Sleepless City (Brooklyn Bridge Nocturne)," his great ode to spiritual exhaustion. On the bridge, Lorca confronts the city before him, and can make no sense of the mess. "Out in the sky, no one sleeps. No one, no one. / No one sleeps," he mumbles over and over again. Even the dead can't rest here—"a boy who was buried this morning cried so much / they had to call the dogs to quiet him"—and on the off chance "someone closes his eyes," the answer is swift: "whip him, my children, whip him!"

A boy weeps because he can't understand the bridge, but the structure—the span's history and symbolism: its *meaning*—is as irrelevant as Crane's proved to be. It is merely a place to stand and gaze at Manhattan—an "incredible crocodile resting beneath the tender protest of the stars"—while "lunar creatures sniff and circle the dwellings" and "iguanas and serpents wait" for the "brokenhearted fugitives" that roam the streets. Staring out from the bridge at the "panorama of open eyes" Lorca sees only "bitter inflamed wounds." The energy, awe and sublimity of the electrified cityscape collapse into a series of open sores, an unhealing blight on the sky. There is no triumph or exhilaration on Lorca's Brooklyn Bridge, only alienation, isolation, and despair. As the poet and critic Conrad Aiken observed, "he hated us, and rightly, for the right reasons."[7]

FACING PAGE

Yun Gee, *Wheels: Industrial New York*, 1932.
Oil on canvas: 84 × 48 inches. Private collection, USA © Estate of Yun Gee.
Photo credit: Kevin Ryan.

Lorca and Crane: Legacies and Influence

Crane's poem has often been debated, but its utopian premise has found few adherents. Lorca, however, seemed to capture the moment. Writing later in the decade, Henry Miller also understood the bridge as a platform upon which to gaze at and try to comprehend America. And his answers were no less bleak than Lorca's. Miller wrote about the bridge throughout the 1930s—in *Black Spring* (1936), *Tropic of Capricorn* (1939), the unpublished novel *Moloch*, and finally, at the end of the decade in an essay devoted to the span—and his frantic, hate-fueled words spoke directly to a world gone wrong. On the bridge, Miller was possessed by thoughts of suicide, violence, and murder. The bridge was "destructive of hope and longing," wrote Miller, a "harp of death."[8]

In the visual arts, Yung Gee imagined the bridge as a site of death. In *Wheels: Industrial New York* (1932), the bridge—its towers human bones and its cables sinew—exists in a garish, almost post-apocalyptic, landscape beneath which menacing figures circle the scene armed with mallets. At the center of the painting, a young Asian male enacts a depression ritual: jumping to his death. Through the 1930s, artists and writers placed the bridge in relation to the national crisis, not the national dream. O. Louis Guglielmi painted numerous dour images of sorrow and hopelessness—*South Street Stoop* (1935), *Wedding in South Street* (1936) (which may be the most funereal wedding in art history), and *The Widow* (1938)—all of which feature the bridge as a backdrop. In *Mental Geography* (1938) he depicted the span in ruins, the result of a coming world war. The bridge was Maxwell Anderson's great symbol in the verse drama *Winterset* (1935), his tragic retelling of the Sacco and Vanzetti case. While the play's action takes place in a rundown tenement on the East River shore, the bridge flies high overhead, above both the stage and the audience. Like Crane, Anderson saw the bridge as a promise and an escape; unlike Crane, Anderson's bridge is out of reach and inaccessible, a cruel tease in a hard-luck society of ingrained prejudice and rampant inequality.

We should not dismiss Crane so quickly, however. Not for nothing did the young poet embrace Whitman so fully. Like many writers, he was attracted to Whitman's vision of a more open, democratic, and accepting society, a vision that was as at odds with the realities of the 1850s as Crane's was with the 1930s. That Crane held faith with Whitman was perhaps naïve, but also devoutly optimistic and, in many respects, admirable. And he was not alone. Crane was part of a larger movement that helped establish Whitman as a great American icon. Coincidentally, the resurrection of Whitman and the canonization of the Brooklyn Bridge took place at much the same time. Odd perhaps—although Whitman and the bridge were contemporaries, the poet had almost nothing to say about the span—but revealing. Amid the seeming vacuity of commercial America, intellectuals and artists of the early twentieth century were on a mission to discover what Van Wyck Brooks called "a usable past." "I suspect," Brooks wrote, "that

Yun Gee, *Oil Study for "Wheels: Industrial New York"*, ca. 1932.

Oil on canvas: 29 × 24 inches.

Private collection, USA © Estate of Yun Gee.

Photo credit: Kevin Ryan.

O. Louis Guglielmi, *Mental Geography*, 1938.
From the collection of Barney A. Ebsworth.

the past experience of our people is not so much without elements that might be made to contribute to some common understanding in the present."⁹ Whitman was often at the heart of this cultural longing, as was the bridge; as if the spirit of the poet might fuse with the physical presence of the bridge to point the way forward. Put simply: if we can think like this, and build like that, then we might finally achieve a "more perfect union." Alfred Kazin certainly felt that way, as did Lewis Mumford, two of the bridge's (not to mention Whitman's) biggest fans.

Crane, Kazin and Mumford all stood on the side of Whitmanesque optimism, but Crane couldn't keep his vision rooted in the context of city life, the same context that had fueled Whitman. He couldn't see the wonder and majesty of people, only the sublimity and visual awe of the bridge's outline. Crane wasn't too happy that the bridge only led from one slightly dingy neighborhood to another; he wanted it to lead elsewhere, someplace radiant and extraordinary. Mumford wasn't especially happy either, but he lived with it. Kazin, on the other hand, embraced it and in the process made himself the real heir to Whitman's expansive soul. Kazin saw the bridge as a massive metaphor for life, as a visual marvel and as an incredible place to spend some time and see the city.

Kazin wrote about the bridge whenever he got the chance, but his greatest description concerned his "efforts to understand one single half-hour at dusk, on a dark winter day, the year I was fourteen." Coincidentally, and remarkably, this was the same winter in which Crane and Lorca met:

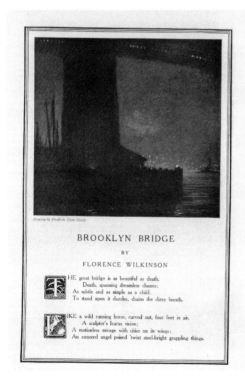

Florence Wilkinson, "Brooklyn Bridge" illustrated by Frederick Dorr Steele.
From the author's collection.

Evening was coming on fast, great crowds in thick black overcoats were pounding up the staircases to the El; the whole bridge seemed to shake under the furious blows of that crowd starting for home ... trolley cars bounding up into the air on each side of me, their bells clanging, clanging; cars sweeping off the bridge and onto the bridge in the narrow last roadways before me. ... Suddenly I felt lost and happy as I went up another flight of steps, passed under the arches of the tower, and waited, next to a black barrel, at the railing of the observation platform. ... I saw the cables leap up to the tower, saw those great meshed triangles leap up and up, higher and still higher—Lord my Lord, when will they cease to drive me up with them in their flight? ... Somewhere below they were roasting coffee, handling spices—the odor was in the pillars, in the battered wooden planks of the promenade under my feet, in the blackness upwelling from the river.[10]

All the sights, sounds, and smells of the great city converge here to form an image of profound vitality and connectedness. Baudelaire, the great poet of Paris and one of the world's finest urban observers, called this experience "enjoying a crowd-bath."[11] Crane spent too long looking for a higher purpose in the bridge when he really should have just dived into the mêlée, like Kazin and Baudelaire before him.

The Bridge is part of a long tradition of poetic contemplation that has focused its attention on the products of the industrial age, a tradition that has lent energy, passion, and soul to Brooklyn's grand old span since its very beginnings. (Poetry and bridges are natural companions, of course, as well suited as Keats and his urn.) Crane's noble failure is also a key text in another long tradition that has come to define our understanding of the bridge: the illustrated text. Artists and writers have long juxtaposed words and images in an effort to better understand the

Henri De Ville, "The Gothic Arch"
Architectural Record, June 1915. From the author's collection.

Walker Evans (American, 1903–1975)
"[Brooklyn Bridge, New York]," 1929,
printed ca. 1970.
Gelatin silver print: 17.0 × 21.0 cm (6 ¹¹/₁₆ × 8 ¼ inches).
The Metropolitan Museum of Art. Gift of Arnold H. Crane,
1972 (1972.742.4) © Walker Evans Archive,
The Metropolitan Museum of Art.

Walker Evans (American, 1903–1975)
"[Brooklyn Bridge, New York]," 1929,
printed ca. 1970.
Gelatin silver print, 24.6 × 16.2 cm (9 ¹¹/₁₆ × 6 ⅜ inches).
The Metropolitan Museum of Art, Gift of Arnold H. Crane,
1972 (1972.742.1) © Walker Evans Archive,
The Metropolitan Museum of Art.

span, from the illustrated weeklies of the nineteenth century to the modern photo-text. In 1905, *Metropolitan Magazine* used two of Coburns photographs to illustrate Richard Le Galliene's "Brooklyn Bridge at Dawn." Previously, Florence Wilkinson employed one of Frederick Dorr Steele's drawings of the bridge to lend mood and atmosphere to her dark poetic tribute, and in 1915 Henri DeVille's etchings were used to highlight the shifting perspective of Mildred Stapley's literary exploration of life around the bridge. Yet *The Bridge* remains at the apex of this tradition combining, as it does, the words of a renowned poet with images by one of America's foremost photographers.

Walker Evans (American, 1903–1975), "[Brooklyn Bridge Tower and Cables, New York City]," 1928–1930.
Film negative: 1 ⅝ × 2 ½ inches. The Metropolitan Museum of Art, Walker Evans Archive, 1994 (1994.251.39) © Walker Evans Archive, The Metropolitan Museum of Art.

Crane's poem helped introduce the world to the photographic genius of Walker Evans. Three of Evans's bridge images accompanied the first edition of *The Bridge* (published in Paris by Black Sun Press), and two others helped decorate the first and second American editions (both published by Horace Liveright). Evans's photographs are credited with anchoring Crane's bridge to Roebling's. If not for Evans drawing us back to the span's sheer physical presence, Crane's poem would take flight into the heavens leaving us all in its wake. In short, Evans's photographs remind us that Crane is actually writing about a real bridge moored to a real location.[12] While this is certainly true on a number of levels, the interpretation fails to account for two divergent trends in Evans's work: the documentary and the aesthetic.

Evans struggled to reconcile the impetus to record with the impetus to make art throughout his life, and the breach expressed itself in two distinct photographic modes:

Walker Evans (American, 1903–1975), "[Horse-Drawn Cart Through Trussing on Brooklyn Bridge, New York City]," 1928–1930.
Film negative: 1 ⅝ × 2 ½ inches. The Metropolitan Museum of Art, Walker Evans Archive, 1994 (1994.251.40) © Walker Evans Archive, The Metropolitan Museum of Art.

studies of animate objects (people) and studies of inanimate objects (buildings, signs, etc.). Evans spent much of the late 1920s and early 1930s producing vivid depictions of New York street life. Yet Evans's photographs of the bridge, taken at the same time, seem removed from the life of the city, more still life than life study. As a group, they are kin to Evans's studies of African artifacts, Civil War monuments, and American architecture, not to his work on the streets of Havana or with the tenant farmers of Hale County, Alabama. Outside of a man asleep on a bench and a horse-drawn cart, Evans's bridge photographs are devoid of human life. While they are marvelous studies in form and substance—as sleek and efficient as the bridge itself—they are poor evocations of New York. Evans himself seems to have realized this. Interviewed later in life he described his early forays in photography as "romantic in a way that I would repudiate now," a charge that seems to serve as a fitting epilogue to *The Bridge* project itself.[13]

Social Realism: The New Deal Effect

In 1935, Evans did what many artists did to survive the Great Depression: he signed up to work for the government, specifically for the photographic arm of the Farm Security Administration (FSA). The FSA was part of a much larger body of government-sponsored art produced during the Roosevelt administration. Beginning with the Public Works of Art Project (PWAP), created in 1933, to the FSA, the Treasury Section of Painting and Sculpture (SECTION), and the Federal Art Project (FAP), a subdivision of the Work's Progress Administration (WPA), all of which ran through to 1943, New Deal art differed wildly in quality; it was chaotic, amorphous, and it quite possibly saved American art.

The economic insecurity of the Depression chased many traditional buyers from the art market. And with dealers, patrons, and collectors all running for cover, most artists had little but soup kitchens and labor lines to look forward to. The Roosevelt administration responded to the enduring depression by putting Americans to work.

Harry Taskey, *Frozen Assets*, 1934.
Print: 23 × 31 cm. Courtesy of the New York Public Library/Art Resource, NY.

Charles Ernest Pont, *Peck's Slip*, 1936.
Wood engraving on paper: 8 ¾ × 11 ⅞ inches. From the Collection of the Queens Borough
Public Library on long-term loan from the United States General Services Administration.

New Deal work projects employed thousands of Americans in jobs as diverse as construction and conservation. They also provided relief to a whole host of artists, writers,
musicians, and theatrical workers. The government employed artists to teach classes,
design posters, create public murals, help decorate federal buildings, photograph and
document the country, put together exhibitions, and most of all, to keep producing art.
New Deal programs allowed countless artists to continue practicing their profession,
and the upshot was remarkable. American art didn't die during the Depression, as many
might have imagined: it flourished.[14]

New Deal art reversed all the rules in the modernist playbook and ran with them.
Above all, Modernism celebrated the self and the city, and not just any old city, but
the new sleek skyscraper city, the city directed and determined by technology. But
with millions in breadlines and even more clamoring for relief, personal introspection
fell quickly out of fashion. Likewise, the magical promise of technology—backed by
commerce and Capitalism—was punctured by the harsh new social climate. Something terrible had happened to America and it needed to be understood. Artists could
no longer revel in "aesthetic obscurity ... high falutin symbolisms and devious and

Howard Simon, *Pecks Slip*, 1936.
From the author's collection.

indistinct meanings," as Thomas Hart Benton put it; engagement was the name of the game, and the result was a sudden left turn, towards Social Realism, documentary expression, and radical politics.[15] Wall Street was out and the working-class were in.

The prevailing impression of the 1930s is rural—the Joads of *The Grapes of Wrath* (1939), Woody Guthrie's *Dust Bowl Ballads* (1940), stark images of Southern poverty, the Midwest Regionalism of Benton and Grant Wood—but with 44.5 percent of FAP artists residing in and around Manhattan, New Deal art was very New York-centric.[16] Images of Gotham proliferated under the auspices of federal art programs, although the city was less the subject than the backdrop: the stage on which artists could explore the dignity of labor, the stoicism of hardship, and the social reality of unemployment. Situated by the working of docks of South Street, the McCauley Water Street Mission, and the homeless shelters on the East River, life around the Brooklyn Bridge was a natural subject.

In 1934, Harry Taskey produced *Frozen Assets* for the PWAP, a playful comment on unemployment. Beneath the bridge, in what is now Empire–Fulton Ferry State Park, a homeless man warms his "frozen assets"—his hands and his backside—on a pile of smoking trash. (Taskey produced a more traditional view of the bridge the same year while working for the PWAP.) In 1935, FSA photographers captured the

Milford Zornes, *Master Bridge*, 1936.
Linoleum block print. Courtesy of the artist. Photo courtesy of Jeffrey Coven.

breadlines that ran the length of the bridge's approach on Dover Street, and Charles Wheeler Locke produced the lithograph *Furman Street, Looking North to Brooklyn Bridge*. At the height of FAP activity in 1936, Howard Simon, Charles Ernest Pont, and Milford Zornes, who also did murals in Texas and California for SECTION and the Treasury Relief Art Project (TRAP), all produced bridge images. Zornes's linoleum cut, *Master Bridge*, contrasts the bold outlines of the bridge with life on the street below. Unemployed men loiter, warming themselves by an ash-barrel, while others search the classifieds for jobs. A few lucky ones haul produce, but they are a distinct minority. Simon and Pont both drew from the scene that fascinated Everett Warner 20 years before: the corner of Water Street looking towards Peck Slip and the bridge. Like Warner, both Simon and Pont foregrounded the work carried on beneath the bridge, but from a different perspective. Warner looked down on the scene from several floors up, whereas Simon and Pont drew from the street, on the same level as, and eye to eye with, the laborers. The workmen here are nearer and more tangible than the tiny abstractions painted by Warner. A year later Greek–American Theo Hios painted *Brooklyn Bridge Workers* (1937), a canvas he subsequently produced as an etching. Again labor is the topic as red-faced, bundled-up workers strain to fix a problem with the bridge's cables. Always, it seems, the weather is cold and the work, where it can be had, is arduous.

Leon Bibel, *Brooklyn Bridge*, 1938.
Courtesy of the Estate of Leon Bibel/Park Slope Gallery (www.parkslopegallery.com).

FACING PAGE

Louis Lozowick, *Bridge Repairs (Repairing Brooklyn Bridge)*, 1938.
Lithograph on paper, 12 ⅝ × 7 ½ inches. Printer: George C. Miller. Museum purchase.
Courtesy of the Smithsonian American Art Museum, Washington, DC/Art Resource, NY.

Ukrainian immigrant Louis Lozowick produced three different lithographs of workers toiling up in the bridge's cables in the late 1930s while working for the FAP, having previously depicted the bridge in *New York* (1925) and *Brooklyn Bridge* (1930). Lozowick, one of the few artists whose vision and style barely changed between the 1920s and the 1930s, was one of the most famous and revered New Deal artists, but in many respects an anomaly of the time. Lozowick was no less radical than any of his colleagues—he was a member of the left-wing American Artists' Congress and sat on the editorial board of *The New Masses*—but he focused less on the plight of the people than on the idea of the modern city. Lozowick celebrated the city's Cubo-Futurist form as "an icon of a socialist future."[17] Like Mayakovsky, Lozowick saw the bridge as the physical expression of a coming revolution.

Most federal artists abandoned the walkway view favored by modernists during the previous decade, preferring to feature the bridge as a background to labor, unemployment, or, in the case of Guglielmi, whose grim bridge images were created on a government salary, despair. Leon Bibel didn't and neither did Joseph Stella, who worked briefly for the FAP, producing *Bridge* (1936), a sleek, stripped-down version of an earlier work. Bibel was a radical Polish immigrant who thrived under the New Deal. He was an active member of the Harlem Art Center who taught printmaking at various schools in the Bronx. He was one of the rare artists to depict the bridge from its walkway during the 1930s. Most of Bibel's FAP work was politically-conscious protest art: pro-labor, anti-war, always driven by social justice. His *Brooklyn Bridge* (1938) was less overt. The serigraph shows a sun-filled, oddly distorted bridge sweeping gently toward Manhattan. On the bridge a peddler pushes his cart, a couple takes a stroll, and an elderly man sits slumped on a bench. The scene is similar to John Marin's great bridge images minus the kinetic energy. Bibel's pedestrians seem to belie the bright scene before them, they seem tired and old: static where Marin's figures were all movement. The comparison is an apt summation of the contexts in which the images were created. Marin's figures rush towards the bridge in a frenzy of excitement, Bibel's plod on.

The 1930s was *the* era of reproducible art. Etchings, screen-prints, woodcuts, lithographs, and photographs were the great triumphs of the New Deal art programs. Cheaper to produce, easier to distribute, and orientated towards a mass audience, they seem to fit the tone of the times. In equal measure, they prospered inside and

FACING PAGE

Joseph Stella, *Bridge*, 1936.
Oil on canvas: 50 ⅛ × 30 ⅛ inches. The United States General Services Administration, formerly Federal Works Agency, Works Projects Administration, allocated to the San Francisco Museum of Modern Art (3760.43).

Thomas Hart Benton, *The Brooklyn Bridge*

outside government programs. Many older, more established artists produced etchings and lithographs of the bridge independent of federal patronage: James Daugherty, Kerr Eby, Ernest Fiene, Earl Horter, Bror Nordfeldt, amongst others. Viennese artist Luigi Kasimir visited the U.S. in 1936 and produced two etchings of the bridge. Even Benton, whose vision rarely extended past rural America, produced an etching of the bridge for Leo Huberman's *We, the People* (1932), a Pulitzer Prize-nominated Marxist history of the United States. The lateral view of the bridge prevailed outside as well as inside federal art, although the social element was often lacking. Few workmen, or even people, found their way into non-federal images of the bridge. As a result, the bridge was less a backdrop for a subject—city life—than the subject itself.

New Deal programs contributed to the bridge in other ways. In 1936, the WPA built the wonderful art deco Purchase Building—sadly, recently slated for demolition to make way for the Brooklyn Bridge Park—on Water and New Dock streets

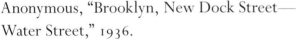

Anonymous, "Brooklyn, New Dock Street—
Water Street," 1936.
Courtesy of the New York Public Library/Art Resource, NY.

Berenice Abbott, "Brooklyn Bridge, Water
and Dock Streets, Brooklyn," 1936.
Gelatin print mounted on paperboard. Courtesy of the Smithsonian American Art Museum, Washington, DC/Art Resource, NY.

in the shadow of the bridge's Brooklyn overpass. WPA photographers documented
the construction, as did Berenice Abbott, who was roaming the waterfront at the
same time. Abbott spent four years (1935—1939) on the government payroll, and the
result—*Changing New York* (1939)—was the great triumph of the FAP's photographic
division. Oddly, Abbott's massive photographic archive contained little in the way of
change: her focus was on older, soon-to-change New York. This fact made her "Brooklyn Bridge, Water and New Dock Streets" (1936) somewhat unique, depicting as it
does, the new rising amid the old.[18]

Just as the city built, it also demolished. In 1934, the city announced it would tear
down the bridge's Manhattan railroad terminal—long deemed an "eyesore"—with
the help of a WPA loan. In August of the following year New York's "Little Flower,"
Mayor Fiorello LaGuardia, took a jack hammer to the structure during a public ceremony, and in just a few short months relief workers razed the terminal completely.

James Suydam, "Front Street, Manhattan," 1937.
From the WPA/Federal Writers Project.
Courtesy of the New York City Municipal Archives.

The demolition was the first step in a plan to improve the area around City Hall, but it was also the first blow to public transportation on and around the bridge.[19]

One June 4, 1944, Brooklyn Borough President John Cashmore announced plans to bulldoze many of the old buildings that surrounded the bridge to make way for a new "Brooklyn–Queens Connecting Highway." The creation of the BQE signaled the rise of the automobile at the expense of public transit, but the process, by that time, was already well under way. Three months earlier, at 12:02 p.m. on March 5, 1944, Harry Page piloted his Lexington Avenue el train over the bridge for the final time. After 46 years of continual service, the era of the Brooklyn Bridge el trains was over. And few were there to mourn its passing: a handful of city officials, some journalists, and about 150 ordinary citizens took the trip. One old man spent the entire journey gazing out at the harbor in a daze. "It is very sad," he whispered as the train left the bridge. Hearing the comment, a conductor nodded.[20]

New Deal Art: Murals

Much New Deal art was ephemeral: thousands of art pieces were lost, destroyed or, in one notorious case, sold at 4 cents a pound when the federal art agencies were closed down.[21] The great federal mural projects were not. The 1930s was an age of murals, and the New Deal was its great facilitator. Almost 4,000 murals were produced during Roosevelt's presidency, helping to enliven myriad public buildings, from schools and post offices to military buildings and bases. Thousands more were commissioned to decorate private buildings, perhaps most famously by Diego Rivera, who produced murals for such diverse clients as the San Francisco Stock Exchange, the Detroit Institute of Art, and ultimately (and ill-fatedly) Nelson Rockefeller's new midtown office complex.

The bridge featured in numerous public murals and in two distinct ways: as a symbolic version of exactly what it was—a passageway from one place to another—and as a vital part of the region's history. One of the first planned murals to feature the span

Anonymous, "Renovating the Roadway," n.d.
Courtesy of the New York City Municipal Archives.

was drawn up by long-time bridge fan James Dougherty. In January 1934, the New York Regional Committee of the PWAP began to cast around for an experienced muralist to decorate the central rotunda of the U.S. Custom House. Dougherty was a front runner for the much-coveted commission and a committed New Dealer (he called the PWAP a "momentous step in the cultural life of the nation"). He also completed a set of preliminary sketches for the project, only one of which survives. In his study for *The Immigrants*, Dougherty revived his interest in cubism and the modern metropolis, this time with the addition of people. In the foreground, a family of immigrants—husband, wife, and babe in arms—disembark from the steerage surrounded by other new arrivals. A triumvirate of skyscraper, ship's prow, and Brooklyn Bridge loom over the newcomers.

Dougherty never received the Custom House commission. Problems emerged with the rotunda's ceiling before the PWAP could make a final decision, and the project was postponed. In 1937, it passed into the hands of TRAP, which finally awarded the commission to Reginald Marsh.[22]

Anonymous, "Painting the Brooklyn Bridge," n.d.
Courtesy of the Brooklyn Collection, Brooklyn Public Library.

Alexander Alland, *Approach to Manhattan*, 1938.
Courtesy of the Art Commission of the City of New York.

Another abandoned mural project was Alexander Alland's *Approach to Manhattan* designed for the Riker's Island Penitentiary Library. Like Dougherty, Alland's design was site-specific, as he explained in his submission statement:

> The subject of this photomural utilizes the familiar aspects of the normal and happy family in the City. The main purpose of this decoration, besides that of relieving the monotony and changing the aspects of a huge prison hall, into a livable library, where those prisoners who have gained the privilege through their behavior, can enjoy the uses of this library, is to reestablish in the inmates (by suggestion) the desires and the values of a wholesome life.[23]

Alland's mural combined two of the bridge's most symbolic attributes: the enclosure of the cables and the freedom of the footpath. Just as the towers function as gateways, and the walkway as an open road, so the cables, as Stella understood, often function as the bars of a prison. Most artists utilized one or the other of these motifs, Alland combined them. Designed specifically for prison inmates, *Approach to Manhattan* portrays ("by suggestion") the journey towards social reentry, the passage from incarceration to liberation and the "wholesome life" of the ideal social unit: the "happy family."[24]

Understandably, prison murals were often controversial, but so were many others. In 1936, Vertis Hayes was commissioned to decorate the central corridor of the nurses' residence at the Harlem Hospital. A transplanted black Atlantan, Hayes was only 25 years old at the time but already a master muralist and something of an FAP veteran. Befitting the hospital's location and the community it served, Hayes designed an eight-panel mural depicting the sweep of African-American history, from life in an African village, through the cotton-picking years in the South, to settlement and establishment in the North. He titled the work *The Pursuit of Happiness*.

The mural's key central image depicted black migration from the South to the North. In the lower right-hand corner, a rural black

Alexander Alland, "The Old Bridge," 1939.
Courtesy of the New York Public Library/Art Resource, NY.

Andreas Feininger, "Walking on Brooklyn Bridge, going towards Manhattan," 1940.

Courtesy of the Artist's Estate and Bonni Benrubi Gallery, NYC. Photo courtesy of the Center for Creative Photography, University of Arizona.

family surrounded by broken farm tools gazes up towards the bright image of a modern, industrial city. The two halves of the picture are linked by a massive cog, representing progress, and an image of the Brooklyn Bridge. Here, the span symbolizes the passage from rural poverty to urban achievement and sophistication. The mural's remaining panels depict successful black Americans in a variety of occupations: architect, professor, doctor, musician, and artist.

Hayes's mural was a fitting tribute to the hospital's location, and its predominantly black nursing staff, but it caused a fuss anyway. The hospital's superintendent, Lawrence Dermody, along with the city's commissioner of hospitals, Sigmund Goldwater, both objected to the subject matter. "Harlem Hospital is a city institution," they argued, "and should not be singled out because of its location in the city for the special treatment indicated in the mural designs; i.e., that the subject matter deals with the various phases of Negro endeavor and community life."

The white administrators' disapproval created a *cause célèbre* that galvanized the local community. The Harlem Artists' Guild and the Artists' Union issued a joint statement of rebuke, and Louis T. Wright—the first black American doctor appointed to the hospital and a future director of the medical board—helped finance a national publicity campaign. Dermony and Goldwater withdrew their objections in response to the outcry, and Hayes's mural was unveiled less than a year later to far more fanfare than it might have otherwise enjoyed.[25]

As a major New York icon, the Brooklyn Bridge was a key component of many state and city murals. Bertram Hartman, for example, included a large image of the span in the foreground of his *Imaginary Projections of the State of New York* at the Homer Folks Tuberculosis Hospital in Oneonta. The most notorious mural to feature the bridge was Alois Fabry Jr.'s massive two-part *Brooklyn Past and Present* commissioned by the FAP in 1937 to adorn the central rotunda of Brooklyn Borough Hall. Fabry's two murals—*Historic Brooklyn* and *Brooklyn Today*, each an impressive 900 square feet—took over two years to complete and were unveiled to a less than enthusiastic reception. Despite Brooklyn Borough President Raymond Ingersoll's claim that "these murals will be of

Andreas Feininger, "Oliver Street with Bridge in Background," 1940.
Courtesy of the Artist's Estate and Bonni Benrubi Gallery, NYC.
Photo courtesy of the Center for Creative Photography, University of Arizona.

great interest and value to the people of Brooklyn," the people of Brooklyn were unimpressed. One woman derided the murals as "amateurish, garish monstrosities," others hated their modern style, yet the most serious charge was the same one that terminated Rivera's employment at Rockefeller Center.

Fabry's *Historic Brooklyn* celebrated the borough's myriad achievements from European settlement in 1609 to consolidation in 1898. It featured Henry Hudson communing with the Lenape Indians, Revolutionary War heroes at the Battle of Brooklyn, Walt Whitman at the offices of the *Brooklyn Freeman*, Henry Ward Beecher addressing Civil War soldiers from the pulpit of Plymouth Church, and John and Washington Roebling perusing plans in front of the Brooklyn Bridge, all interspersed with craftsmen, farmers, shopkeepers, newsboys, and other ordinary Brooklynites. This was all very wholesome and historic, until rumors began to swirl around Brooklyn that one of the figures surrounding Beecher bore a striking resemblance to Lenin. Unlike August Henkel, whose WPA murals at Floyd Bennett Field in Brooklyn were summarily torn down for including an image of Stalin, Fabry was no communist radical, in fact, no sort of a radical at all, and the offending face bore almost no resemblance to the Soviet icon. Yet the talk continued, and in 1946 the murals were removed by Borough President, John Cashmore, who had long harbored a grave dislike for the work. As with Rivera's *Man at the Crossroads*, Fabry's Brooklyn murals are now sadly lost.[26]

As the Decade Turns

The Great Depression was a moment of profound trauma, but as the decade turned, so did the economy. By the early 1940s, the free-fall had reversed, jobs were available, and two of America's most famous photographers took to the streets of New York City. Arthur Fellig (a.k.a. Weegee) and Andreas Feininger were as different as two photographers could be: the former raised on the Lower East Side, the son of a peddler; the latter, the son of a painter who taught at the Bauhaus art school. What they found on the streets of New York were, predictably, two very different cities. Yet in their own way, Weegee and Feininger helped shape and form the image of New York in the post-war world. They extended the documentary aesthetic of New Deal art and helped set the stage for the post-war boom in documentary photography.

Feininger's New York photographs are some of the most renowned ever taken of the city. Feininger saw a city bathed in the bright rays of the noon-day sun, an island community of suits, ties, and hats, and of trade, transport, and linkage. In Feininger's "clean, uncluttered photographs,"[27] the city emerges as a peacock: a great strutting display, its magnificence self-evident. Emerging from the abject depression of the 1930s, Feininger helped the city reclaim its monumental greatness and thrusting vitality. The photographer took more images of the Brooklyn Bridge than of any other object in New York,

Andreas Feininger, "View of the Brooklyn Bridge," 1946
© Time & Life Pictures. Courtesy of Getty Images.

Weegee, "Striking Beauty," 1940
© International Center of Photography.
Courtesy of Getty Images.

assigning it a central role in his portfolio. Under his influence, the bridge again took its place as the central icon of a great city. Feininger's bridge is an epic sculpture, the city's most vibrant symbol, an overpowering work of civic art.

When Feininger arrived in New York from Europe in 1939, Weegee was already totting his bulky Speed Graphic camera around the city. Like Feininger, Weegee was a tour guide to a city of great vitality. Unlike Feininger's photographic project, however, Weegee's New York is a "city of sensational night" illuminated by the harsh glare of the flash-bulb. His New Yorkers are not well-dressed shoppers, day-trippers or workers enjoying a break but drunks, cross-dressers, murder victims, and petty criminals. Weegee's subject was the bizarre spectacle of urban disorder and the audience it attracted.[28]

From the late 1930s to the mid-1940s, Weegee prowled the New York night with a police radio and a beat-up Chevy, and in 1945, he published *Naked City*, the fruits of his night-time wanderings.

Naked City is Weegee's most enduring statement on the people of the city he loved, yet its opening image—"Striking Beauty" (1940)—features no people. Instead, the first thing one sees in the book is the New York skyline and the Brooklyn Bridge, illuminated during the dead of night by a massive lightning bolt. The effect is similar to the beginning of a film, the other visual medium closely associated with Weegee. The title page is an establishing shot: the Naked City is New York City and we, as readers, are poised at its gates. "Striking Beauty" is significant, however, beyond merely establishing location, it also seeks to encapsulate. No one image can do justice to the contents of *Naked City*, but it can capture the mood and flavor of what follows. "Striking Beauty" defines New York as a place of night-time activity, noirish mood, and sudden spectacle. In a violent flash, the thrill of an intensely powerful event is played out along the rugged outline of the Naked City to form a prologue and an outline to the book that follows. In the briefest of moments, the real New York is transformed into the mythic Naked City: blink and you'll miss it.

Weegee was a direct descendent of the culture that produced the *National Police Gazette*; if he had lived during the nineteenth century, he might well have worked for Richard Fox and hung out in Brodie's Famous Saloon. Fox himself would have loved the 1930s, much as Weegee did. Both understood that the weird and bizarre, existing just beneath the collective consciousness, have always played a major role in New York's history. Dig deep enough in news files of the 1930s, even those of the respectable *New York Times*, and one finds the sort of screwball antics that so captivated Weegee and, many years earlier, the *Gazette*.

Edwin Kaufman (American, Cleveland School, 1906–1939), *Brooklyn Bridge, New York*, ca. 1930s. Drypoint. The Cleveland Museum of Art. Gift of Robert Hays Gries (1942.910.1942) © 2007 Artists Rights Society (ARS), New York/ProLitteris, Zurich.

William Thon, *Under the Brooklyn Bridge*, 1944.
Oil on canvas. Image: 22 ¼ × 36 ¼ inches (56.5 × 92.1 cm); frame: 32 × 46 inches (81.3 × 116.8 cm).
Brooklyn Museum, Gift of Midtown Galleries, 68.211.

This Just In: Breaking News from the 1930s

A hundred and seventeen police officers and sixty detectives were sent out to patrol the East River bridges on July 18, 1931, after the Police Commissioner received a bomb threat. "Every car passing over the Brooklyn Bridge tomorrow morning at the Brooklyn end is going to be bombed, and there is no maybe about it," warned the saboteur.

On June 23, 1932, 21-year-old Joseph Pellerito was spotted "cavorting" atop the bridge's Brooklyn tower "skipping from cable to cable and swinging from the guy ropes." Pellerito's antics caused a traffic jam and soon aroused the interest of the police. When questioned, Pellerito shouted down that he had no intention of jumping. He'd been unemployed for two and a half years and had scaled the tower merely to "think things over." Pellerito was finally coaxed down when challenged to a race. As a police car navigated the traffic jam, the youth sped down the cables. He was finally apprehended at the center of the span. Unfortunately, the press failed to mention who won the race.

In October 1934, the Narcotics Squad uncovered a massive crop of "loco weed"—the largest thus far cultivated in the Northeast—growing in an empty lot right by the Brooklyn entrance to the bridge. The weed, "which produces a pleasant, relaxed sensation when smoked and eventually drives the habitual user insane," was discovered after "an ever increasing number of soldiers" stationed at Governor's Island began to "show signs of lethargy produced by the smoking of mariajuana [sic]."

On November 3, 1934, a 40-year-old dishwasher named Eddie Laska committed one of the most bizarre suicides New York has ever seen. Laska jumped from the Manhattan end of the Brooklyn Bridge but missed the water. Instead, he hit a tow rope connecting a tug to a barge. The rope gave a little then snapped taut, flinging Laska's body 30 feet in the air. The dishwasher landed stone dead on the deck of the barge.

The still-warm body of Brownsville gangster Frank "Little Frankie" Teitlebaum was tossed from a speeding car under the bridge's Manhattan approach at 9:15 p.m. on the evening of October 11, 1935. Teitlebaum's murder was thought to be retaliation for the murder of Joseph Amberg, with whom Teitlebaum had been feuding, two weeks earlier. In fact, the hit was ordered by Meyer Lansky and Benjamin "Bugsy" Siegel—who were moving in on the Brownsville rackets—and carried out by Murder, Incorporated.

On the evening of July 23, 1937, George Sauter, a 46-year-old salesman from Dyker Heights, was driving over the bridge with his wife Lena. Halfway across, Sauter stopped the car suddenly, turned to Lena and casually remarked that "I think I have a flat tire." As angry horns blazed all around him, he calmly left his car, hurriedly ran to the outer rail, and jumped off the bridge. His body was never found.[29]

CHAPTER FIVE

Evolution and Explosion (1946–1982)

Abstract art dominated post-war American painting and helped make New York the global capital of art. Likewise, its burgeoning influence contributed to an evolving trend in representations of the Brooklyn Bridge. As Feininger showed, the bridge was an exceptional civic achievement—a teaming roadway and an extraordinary public space—but also a potent work of art. Beginning in the modernist era, and reaching its high point at the middle-century, representations of the span often ignored the foot-traffic that gave life to the bridge and focused instead on the structure: on the towers and the network of cables. Their approach mirrored that of the influential New Critics who believed art, and especially poetry, should be judged in and of itself, without reference to external context. Such artists as Georgia O'Keeffe, Howard Cook, Ellsworth Kelly, and Robert Indiana followed this lead. They depicted the span as a pure shape or an aesthetic ideal. Lifted above the messy business of urban life, their bridge became a perfect, self-contained art object, an American version of Keats's "well-wrought urn."

For the Record: Documentary Photography after World War II

Where some artists chose to work in the realms of aesthetic abstraction, others opted for a documentary approach. After the Farm Security Administration (FSA) was closed down, its director, Roy Stryker, signed on with the Standard Oil Company of New Jersey (SONJ) and helped produce the largest private collection of documentary photographs ever assembled in the U.S. Standard Oil got into the photography business for one simple reason: public relations. In 1942, during the height of the Second World War, SONJ was caught doing business with a prominent Germany company and its public image crumbled. Regarded with great suspicion by the American people, SONJ decided to tone down its big business image and try to "show the genuine face" of its

Arthur Max Cohen, *(Untitled) Brooklyn Bridge*, ca. 1945–1950.
Color screenprint: 55.6 × 47.4 cm (21 ⅞ × 18 ¹¹⁄₁₆ inches). Gift of Dr. Irving Burton (1996/2.24).
Courtesy of the University of Michigan Museum of Art.

American operations. As photographer Harold Corsini put it: SONJ wanted "to explain that [it] was a nice company and one that lots of people made their livings from." Just as the FSA had raised public awareness and sympathy for the rural poor a decade earlier, so SONJ hoped a similar approach might help improve its own public profile, which is why it tapped Stryker to lead their efforts.[1]

Under Stryker's direction, the SONJ photo file evolved into much more than a PR campaign. He enlisted FSA veterans Esther Bubley, John Vachon, Gordon Parks, Russell Lee, and John Collier, and took a broad approach to his mandate. He would document not only oil wells and refineries, and the towns they supported, but the ways in which "oil seeped into every joint" of American life. One of Stryker's most beloved projects was called "Harbor Story," which sought to document all aspects of the (oil-fueled) New York port and harbor system. With so many of Stryker's photographers living in New York, the project was undertaken piecemeal. When photographers were home between projects or waiting for assignments, they were asked to spend a few days on the harbor project. The result was a mammoth, amorphous, rambling hulk of a file that was never formed or finished.

Most of Stryker's photographers worked on "Harbor Story" at one time or another and many found themselves drawn to the Brooklyn Bridge while scouting the region. As the novel-

Howard Cook, *Brooklyn Bridge*, 1949.
Lithograph on paper: 13 ⅞ × 8 inches. Gift of Barbara Latham. Courtesy of the Smithsonian American Art Museum, Washington, DC/Art Resource, NY.

ist Ernest Poole realized back in 1915, "the sweeping arch of that Great Bridge" was a permanent fixture in the "restless, heaving, changing" life of the New York harbor.[2] The bridge and the harbor were complementary parts of the same scene, with one framing and presiding over the other. Many SONJ photographers understood this as instinctively as Poole had, and none more so than Esther Bubley, one of the most accomplished photo-journalists of the twentieth century. Of all the SONJ photographers,

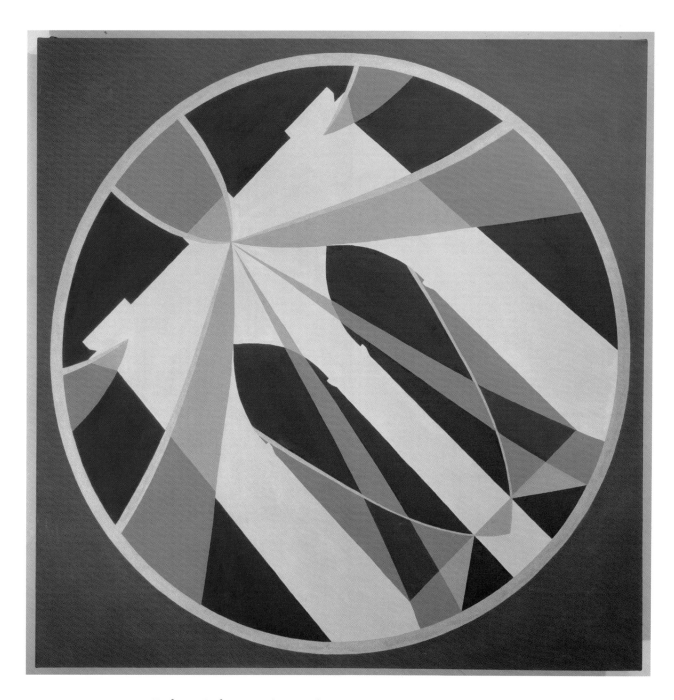

Robert Indiana, *Silver Bridge*, 1964–1998.
Oil on canvas: 67 ½ × 67 ½ inches. Private collection. Courtesy of Simon Salama-Caro
© 2007 Morgan Art Foundation Limited/Artists Rights Society, New York.

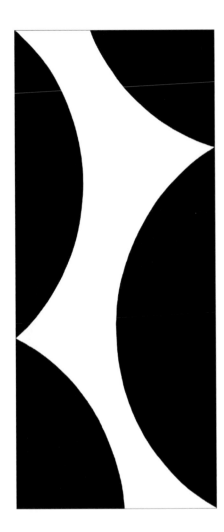

Ellsworth Kelly, *Brooklyn Bridge IV*, 1956–1958.
Oil on canvas: 30 × 13 inches (76.2 × 33.0 cm).
Private collection. EK 174 © Ellsworth Kelly.

Esther Bubley, "Rope,
Brooklyn Bridge," 1946.
(SONJ 42690).
Courtesy of the Standard Oil (New
Jersey) Collection, Photograph Archives,
University of Louisville. Photo courtesy
of the Estate of Esther Bubley.

Esther Bubley, "Two Painters, Brooklyn
Bridge," 1946.
(SONJ 43316).
Courtesy of the Standard Oil (New Jersey) Collection,
Photograph Archives, University of Louisville.
Photo courtesy of the Estate of Esther Bubley.

Esther Bubley, "Painters Climbing Brooklyn
Bridge," 1946.
(SONJ 43320).
Courtesy of the Standard Oil (New Jersey) Collection,
Photograph Archives, University of Louisville.
Photo courtesy of the Estate of Esther Bubley.

Bubley lingered longest around the bridge and looked the hardest. She shot the bridge
from near and far: from beneath the span staring out at the tug boats that plied the
East River and from Fulton Market looking up at the bridge through the traffic-jams
that clogged South Street. On the bridge, Bubley gazed out at the skyline and down
at the cars that rumbled towards Brooklyn. Like many before her, and many to come,
Bubley was fascinated by the painters who made their living on the bridge. The natural
descendents of the riggers who'd fixed the cables in place 70 years earlier, these city
workers clambered all over the bridge with seeming impunity. They walked the large
support cables, shimmied along the intricate cable work, and spent long days on narrow
wooden platforms suspended high above the East River. Like the construction workers
celebrated by Lewis Hine, these are modern aerial heroes: ordinary men doing extraordinary work.

While Bubley was walking the bridge transfixed by the painters high above, Arthur
Leipzig was up there with them, scared stiff by all accounts. A young photographer
at the time, Leipzig had just started working for International News Photos when, in
October 1946, he was sent on assignment to photograph the painters on the bridge.

Arthur Leipzig, "Painters on Brooklyn Bridge," 1946.
© Arthur Leipzig.

Arthur Leipzig, "Painters on Brooklyn Bridge," 1946.
© Arthur Leipzig.

Henri Cartier-Bresson, "Brooklyn Bridge," 1946.
© Magnum Photos.

Henri Cartier-Bresson,
"Below the Brooklyn Bridge," 1946.
© Magnum Photos.

Leipzig arrived at the bridge at 7:30 a.m. on the designated day "feeling very anxious" and was immediately led up the bridge by the painters' foreman. "The first thing you have to know when you climb a bridge," advised the foreman, "is *never* look down," which (of course) is exactly what Leipzig did. With his eyes fixated on the roadway beneath, and with the sure belief that "with one misstep" he would plunge to his death, Leipzig persevered up the bridge. To cover his fear, Leipzig stopped every now and then and took a picture. His confidence renewed, he went on. Slowly. [3]

Despite what must have been a terrifying ordeal, Leipzig completed his assignment and returned to terra firma with some of the most exhilarating images ever taken of the bridge. He captured the Manhattan skyline from the top of the Brooklyn tower, the jaunty gait of workmen stepping lively up the bridge's main cables, painters hoisting

their rope-and-pulley scaffolds high above the East River, and the rail tracks and cargo bays that once defined the industrial landscape of DUMBO. Leipzig's perspective was not unique—photographers had been scaling the bridge's towers since the mid-1870s—but the style and clarity he brought to the assignment were. He blended the documentary aesthetic of the 1930s with the bold compositional approach of the 1920s to produce a vibrant new chapter in the bridge's visual history. His approach—one might almost call it daring—would not be equaled until Burham Dogançay, the Turkish–American photographer, scaled the bridge with some ironworker friends in 1986.

Bubley and Leipzig helped set the standard for twentieth-century photo-journalism. The French photographer Henri Cartier-Bresson helped redefine the entire medium. And, coincidentally, he also took a walk over the bridge, just a few short months before Bubley and Leipzig. Cartier-Bresson went there with his camera and with bridge aficionado Alfred Kazin.

Kazin and Cartier-Bresson were brought together by *Harper's Bazaar*, which wanted the two men to collaborate on an article about the bridge. The U.S. wasn't new to Cartier-Bresson, who'd visited in 1935, but the bridge was. Even though he'd spent time with Paul Strand—who'd taken photographs from the bridge in 1916 and included the span as a key image in his 1921 film *Manahatta*—and shared gallery space with Walker Evans, Cartier-Bresson had somehow failed to find his way to the bridge in the 1930s. Yet when he finally got there in 1946, he was amazed. Cartier-Bresson loved the bridge, especially the central walkway. "It breathes!" he purred, "see how it breathes!"[4] Cartier-Bresson took plenty of pictures of the bridge, ten of which ran alongside Kazin's short tribute.

Cartier-Bresson's published photographs ran the gamut of life on and around the bridge: a husband and wife pose theatrically for the photographer, a courting couple strolls unawares over the span, a young man and his dog forage around the bridge's base, a couple of middle-aged men argue right in front of the photographer, hands on hips, a tramp stands beneath the Water Street approach and stares hard at Cartier-Bresson, elsewhere men shovel coffee beans before carting them off to who-knows-where. Cartier-Bresson was not the first photographer to click a few rolls of film while strolling along the bridge, but he was the first to focus so intently on the people he found there. If the walkway gave the bridge its breath, Cartier-Bresson's photographs gave it life, in all its myriad forms.[5]

FACING PAGE

Eric Hartmann, "Man in Street Under the Brooklyn Bridge," 1955.
© Magnum Photos.

Eric Hartmann, "Abandoned Car Next to Brooklyn Bridge," 1955.
© Magnum Photos.

Cartier-Bresson helped found the Magnum photo agency a year after he met up with Kazin, and (quite by chance) Magnum photographers have a long history with the Brooklyn Bridge. Thomas Hoepker, Ferdinando Scianna, Inge Morath, and Bruce Davidson have all taken photo series of the span, although the most enduring was undertaken by a bored young photographer on a Sunday afternoon in 1955.

Eric Hartmann came to the U.S. in 1938 as a 16-year-old refugee from Nazi Germany. His family settled in Albany, but he was soon on his way back to Europe as an American solider. He settled in New York after the war and apprenticed as a photographer. By the early 1950s he was freelancing for such illustrious magazines as *Fortune* and *Life*, and in 1952, he was invited to join Magnum, an association that lasted up to his death in 1999. Hartmann was known for big, sprawling subjects: documenting the American grain harvest, wintertime in the frozen Midwest, and the construction of the St. Lawrence Seaway system. But his first museum exhibition was a small, highly personal series

Eric Hartmann, "Street Beneath the Brooklyn Bridge," 1955.
© Magnum Photos.

called "Sunday with the Bridge" (1955). It premiered in 1956 at the Museum of the City
of New York and ran later that year at the Brooklyn Museum.[6]

"Sunday with the Bridge" is exactly what it says it is—an amiable amble around the
structure on a fine Sunday afternoon—and an interesting counterpoint to Cartier-
Bresson's bridge photographs. Unlike Cartier-Bresson, Hartmann took no photographs
on the bridge itself, yet always the span is there in the background, a constant escort to
the photographer's roaming. The key words to Hartmann's photographs are near, beneath,
under, and below. "Sunday with the Bridge" explores the area around the bridge on both
sides of the East River. Like much of the art of the 1930s, Hartmann's bridge exists as a
backdrop to the lives lived in its shadow and the streets and regions over which it looms.
Yet, taken together, the series provides a fascinating sense of the bridge's context—where
it stands—and the people that swarm around its base. In this respect, "Sunday with the
Bridge" is similar to Rudy Burckhardt's documentary short *Under the Brooklyn Bridge* (1953),

Rudy Burkhardt, "A View From
Brooklyn II," 1953.
© 2007 Estate of Rudy Burckhardt/Artists Rights
Society (ARS), New York.

Eric Hartmann, "Father and Children
Below the Brooklyn Bridge," 1955.
© Magnum Photos.

FACING PAGE

William Gedney, "Cable with Arch and
other Cables in Background," ca. 1955.
© Rare Book, Manuscript, and Special Collections Library,
Duke University.

the Swiss filmmaker's compelling, impressionistic account of life around the base of the span. Both Hartmann and Burckhardt shot young boys diving headfirst into the East River during the bright glare of daylight and the deserted regions around Fulton Landing at twilight. Both also examined the human traffic that trudged home passed the structure, the dreary vista under the bridge's dark approaches, and the people who enjoyed their time off around the span (a father reading his newspaper as his children sit nearby and young girls playing around the recently constructed Governor Alfred E. Smith Houses for Hartmann; demolition workers eating their lunch for Burckhardt). Hartmann added breadth and context to Cartier-Bresson's approach, and, with Burckhardt, helped illuminate the hidden life of those for whom the bridge was a constant presence.

Exploration was the key to William Gedney's photographs of the bridge taken between 1955 and 1962, a series he hoped to collect and publish in book form. Gedney

William Gedney, "Tower and Arch;
Cables in Foreground," ca. 1955.
© Rare Book, Manuscript, and Special Collections Library,
Duke University.

William Gedney,
"Brooklyn Bridge," ca. 1958–1962.
© Rare Book, Manuscript, and Special Collections Library,
Duke University.

didn't get to publish his book, and neither was he able to publish any of the other eight book projects he prepared. Despite limited success—Gedney's work was admired by Walker Evans, Diane Arbus, John Szarkowski (the long-time director of photography at New York's Museum of Modern Art), and Lee Friedlander—Gedney remains one of the most under-appreciated American photographers of the past 50 years. He enjoyed only one solo exhibition during his lifetime, and in 1987 was denied tenure by the Pratt Institute, his *alma mater*, after having taught there since 1969. Two years later Gedney died of complications resulting from AIDS.[7]

Comprising 15 photographs, spread over 25 pages, Gedney's bridge project is a remarkable attempt to approximate the experience of walking the span after dark. None of the photographs gaze out *from* the bridge: they all look *at* the bridge, ensuring

Richard Bergere (American, 1912–), *Twilight Over Brooklyn Bridge*, 1946.
Lithograph. Image: 23.1 × 32.1 cm; sheet: 30.7 × 44 cm. Fine Arts Museums of San Francisco,
Achenbach Foundation for Graphic Arts, 1963.30.24998.

our experience of the structure is the only focus. With our eyes trained on the bridge
we begin our journey. From the squat old warehouses that sit by the Brooklyn tower,
we ascend to the walkway and rumble on through the lingering gloom. We pass through
the bridge's intricate cable structure, pause at the great towers, and continue on. As we
move, we examine the span as a physical object. Many of Gedney's photographs invite
the viewer to reach out and touch the rough granite of the bridge's towers, the tensile
strength of the cable stays or the smooth solidity of the main support cables. Gedney's
photographs are among the first to acknowledge the tactile nature of the bridge's unique
architecture and serve as a fitting tribute to an essentially hand-made icon.

All of Gedney's images are taken at night, yet the bridge—silent, deserted, and somewhat desolate—is enlivened by the play of light on its own proud form. The softened

glare of electric lights marks out the superstructure while moonlight pours over the upper reaches of the bridge. The effect is both dramatic and subtle. In some images, the bold outlines of the bridge stand free and clear, in others, it is more intangible: the wires jumbled, the towers seen as partial shapes, both often reduced to mere silhouettes. Repeatedly, it takes us a minute or so to realize we are looking at the Brooklyn Bridge, but when we finally see through the darkness, we glimpse a fresh new approach to the bridge, one that melds the documentary tradition with the concerns of abstract art. Long hidden in a box in Brooklyn, Gedney's photo project has only recently emerged as a solution to the puzzle that dogged American art for decades.

Gedney spent most of his adult life in Brooklyn, and the borough's most famous icon clearly made a deep impression on the young photographer, as it did with Bubley, Cartier-Bresson, Hartmann, and Burckhardt. These post-war documentarians held a mirror to the great modernist painters of 30 years earlier, and, in so doing, proved themselves the heirs to Struss, Marin, Stella, and Evans. They brought a more inclusive, oftentimes grittier approach to the bridge, but, like their predecessors, they found something in the structure that spoke to (and of) the city. Each saw a very different city, certainly, but one whose essential energy could be found in and around the Brooklyn Bridge.

Changing New York

As abstract art and documentary photography played out a tug-of-war, the bridge struggled to find its place in a new historical moment. Abbott, it seems, had been right, although a little premature. New York was changing. And fast.

New York's post-war growth challenged the bridge on two fronts. With a healthy economy, thousands of returning GIs, and a flood of new migrants, the city's real estate market took off. Low-scale housing was torn down all over New York to make room for massive apartment buildings and giant new commercial towers. Between 1945 and 1970, the city's physical landscape was remade with radical abandon, and, as the skyline grew taller and taller, the bridge began to look smaller and smaller. It no longer dominated the downtown skyline as it had for so long. Overtopped and overtaken, the bridge seemed old-fashioned—quaint even—and squat next to the sleek new glass-and-steel wonders rising all over Manhattan.

Swiss architect Le Corbusier captured the change while reserving a little charity: "Brooklyn Bridge, which is old (elevateds, cars, trucks, pedestrians all have special lanes), is as strong and rugged as a gladiator, while George Washington Bridge, built yesterday, smiles like a young athlete." On the bridge, "the sky before you bristles with the skyscrapers of Wall Street," wrote the architect, while "a violent feeling takes hold of you: the feeling of unanimity. There should be sensations of contriteness, of troubled judgment and taste, reservations, doubt, cacophony. But no! There is dominating force:

Nat Lowell, *Brooklyn Bridge*, 1947.
Etching and drypoint, 11 ½ × 15 inches. Albright-Knox Art Gallery, Buffalo, New York.
Gift of Frederic P. Norton, 1999.

unity; a subjugating element, magnitude," he continued approvingly. Le Corbusier walked the span not to contemplate the bridge, but to gaze in awe at its surrounding successors.[8] A little later, in 1966, Russian poet Andrei Voznesenski was less charitable. Comparing the Roeblings' bridge to Eero Saarinen's new Trans World Airlines building at JFK Airport, he wrote: "Brooklyn Bridge, rearing its idiot stone, cannot consort / with this monument of the era."[9] Amid the city's onward march into the twentieth century, the span's revolutionary power was on the wane. Once upon a time people had stood on the bridge and seen the future. Now they saw only the past. Decidedly, the old gladiator was losing its fight against the young athletes swarming all around it.

New eras present new problems, and by the mid-1940s, the bridge seemed outdated, not just aesthetically but structurally. With a little help from Robert Moses and the flourishing economy, the age of the automobile had arrived in New York. The boom in auto-traffic was all very well and good, but cars need roads, and lots of cars need lots of big, wide roads. Clearly, the city's infrastructure would have to be modernized to account for this new reality. The old would have to be made new, or replaced. In this

Jet Lowe, "Details of Underside of Deck," 1982.
From the Historic American Engineering Record, National Parks Service,
Department of the Interior. Courtesy of the Library of Congress.

context, the Brooklyn Bridge, of course, seemed ancient. Built for horse and buggy, and
well before the commercial production of cars, the span was grounded in public transit,
not private traffic. It supported only a single-lane highway in each direction through the
first half of the twentieth century. This capacity was doubled when the city removed the
trolley lines in 1944, but it was not enough. Something else was needed.

John A. Ward, an influential real estate broker, thought the city should just tear the
damn thing down, and the Manhattan Bridge too: "these two transportation arteries
between lower Manhattan and downtown Brooklyn are obsolete and should be replaced
with tunnels." Ward thought bridges were outmoded, a military liability (bomb the
bridge: divide the city), and a cause of social evil, helping to sustain "one of the most
insidious means of creating slums."[10] If the span's approaches continued to darken and
divide the waterfront neighborhoods, the area would forever languish.

Ward was a bit of a kook, but his ideas had traction. Frederick Zurmuhlen, the Commissioner of Public Works, published a reply even though, like most public officials, he

Jet Lowe, "Base of Brooklyn Tower," 1982.
From the Historic American Engineering Record, National Parks Service,
Department of the Interior. Courtesy of the Library of Congress.

rarely responded to public debate.[11] Surprisingly, Zurmuhlen's rejoinder turned on the cost of constructing additional tunnels, not on the historic nature of the bridge. It was not that the bridge was sacrosanct; Ward's plan was just too expensive. And anyway, the city had decided what to do with the Brooklyn Bridge: it was getting a spiffy new makeover to accommodate all those extra cars zooming around New York.

In 1948, the city announced that, in two years' time, the bridge would be closed for remodeling. The project would be put in the hands of the noted bridge engineer David Steinman. Steinman seemed like the perfect choice: he loved the Brooklyn Bridge. Like Al Smith, he'd grown up beneath the span in lower Manhattan, and its presence had inspired him to become an engineer. Professionally, he'd trained with master bridge-man Gustav Lindenthal (as did Othmar Ammann) and subsequently built bridges all over the world. With his reputation established, he returned to the bridge. He wrote a biography of the Roeblings and composed reams of poetry in its honor. Granted, his poems were awful, but they were at least earnest. At the ceremony to announce his commission, Steinman assured the press: "although we plan to convert the present two-lane auto roadway … into a six-lane modern concrete highway … the appearance of the bridge will not be changed. To me, Brooklyn Bridge is sacred."[12] As an engineer and a devotee, he seemed like a safe pair of hands. Well, almost.

The year 1948 wasn't Steinman's first go-around with the bridge. In 1934, he had drawn up plans to convert the span into a modern aerial highway and submitted them to the city's Commissioner of Plants and Structures. Thankfully, they didn't pass, although this had more to do with money than aesthetics. This earlier plan had involved removing the entire roadway, and then rebuilding it with two decks. The new bridge would contain twelve ten-foot-wide traffic lanes, but no trolleys, trains, or pedestrian access. It also proposed to do away with the diagonal cable-stays that lent the bridge its web-like beauty. The towers would stay and the rest would be scrapped, including its precious central walkway.[13] This earlier proposal might have raised alarm bells in City Hall 14 years later, but it didn't. Nevertheless, the question reverberated around New York: what would Steinman do when he finally got his hands on the bridge?

Anonymous, "Bridge Alterations," n.d.
Courtesy of the Brooklyn Collection, Brooklyn Public Library.

Steinman's new plan called for a number of significant changes, the most serious of which concerned the bridge's lower deck. Since 1883, the bridge's outer roadway had ended at an eight and a half foot railing truss, above which there was nothing but open sky. Steinman, however, planned to enclose the roadway with 18-foot tall continuous trusses, effectively boxing in the entire highway. At this point alarm bells did ring, if not around City Hall, then around the offices of several civic watchdogs. Francis Keally, president of the Municipal Arts Society, was outraged: "should this proposed change be carried out as planned, the beautiful silhouette of this world-renowned structure will be nothing but a memory," he wrote in an open letter to New York Mayor William O'Dwyer. The Brooklyn Bridge, he continued, was "an esthetic thing that only a designer has real feeling about." Steinman wasn't a designer, but an engineer, and if he were to change Robeling's design, it would be "as if some artist were to change the feet of a Rembrandt painting." If the proposed alterations were carried out, Keally concluded, "motorists driving across the bridge to glimpse the city's skyline will see nothing but steel. Traffic," he lamented, "has become more important than beauty."[14]

Godfrey Frankel, "Abandoned Chairs, Brooklyn Bridge," 1947.
Gelatin silver print on paper: 9 ¾ × 7 ¾ inches.
Museum purchase. Courtesy of the Smithsonian American Art Museum, Washington, DC/Art Resource, NY.

Zurmuhlen refuted Keally's objections; O'Dwyer ignored them. Neither of which made the problem go way. In November 1949, Zurmuhlen appeared before the city's Art Commission to give an "informal" description of the "renovation." After the meeting, he told the assembled press that the commission was "pleased with the plans," but William Delano, director of the Art Commission, was more cautious: the commission wanted more information and a more formal process. Given that "the bridge was one of the city's prized artistic possessions," Delano believed "the commission should have an opportunity to make certain that any alterations would not change its design." Unfortunately, the city's lawyers disagreed, and they blocked the request. The alterations, they argued, did not fall within the commission's jurisdiction. Officially, they were "repair," not construction, and it was within the city's mandate to repair public structures as it saw fit. Likewise, the bridge was not a formal "monument"—it had not been erected to any special person or group—and thus deserved no special consideration.[15]

The legal verdict freed the renovation project. There would be no official review, and Steinman would have free rein over the bridge. Despite his pretensions to poetry, Steinman was an engineer, not an artist. And he was a very good one. In engineering terms, his changes made a lot of sense. They increased the bridge's load-bearing capacity, saving it from obsolescence. New York of the 1950s, after all, was a far cry from New York of the 1880s. If the bridge was to continue in operation *and* serve the city's escalating arterial needs, something had to be done. It would *have* to change.

The bridge was finally reopened at a grand "unveiling" ceremony—titled "New/Old Brooklyn Bridge"—on May 3, 1954. Clearly the organizers intended "new" to mean refreshed and reenergized, but many interpreted the word otherwise. "New" meant different, altered, changed: no longer the same. And as city officials lined up to give speeches and praise, some New Yorkers began to grumble. In rebuilding the walkway, Steinman had removed the ornate ironwork that ran the length of the bridge, replacing it with cheap modern railings. As for the new roadway, the massive steel truss girders did indeed impede the view, and not only from the highway but from the walkway too. The addition of so much extra weight also caused further problems: it flattened the bridge, removing its elegant, arching form. Where the bridge had once soared, it now slumped. As Keally had warned, the bridge's "inviolate curve" (as Hart Crane had called it) was now "nothing but a memory."

This issue of remodeling spoke to the bridge's aesthetic dimension. To the editors of the *Architectural Forum*, Steinman was a civic criminal: he'd taken Roebling's soaring nineteenth-century magnificence and replaced it with his own pedestrian twentieth-century utility. Now, after Steinman, the bridge just didn't *look* as glorious or as graceful as it once had. Writing in 1958, Pete Coutros confirmed that the older it gets, "the less it resembles the bridge thrown open in 1883." Many years later, Alfred Kazin was more direct: "genuine aficionados [including presumably Kazin himself] have never ceased to deplore" what Steinman did to the bridge.[16]

Conservation, Comics, and Culture

Steinman's alterations were part of the city's massive post-war overhaul, but they also provoked the nation's emerging preservation movement. In 1964, the grand old Pennsylvania Station was torn down and many in the city were aghast. Jacqueline Kennedy-Onassis captured the mood a year later while campaigning to save New York's Grand Central Station: "is it not cruel to let our city die by degrees, stripped of all her proud monuments, until there will be nothing left of all her history and beauty to inspire our children?"[17] Mayor Robert Wagner certainly thought so, and in 1965 he created the

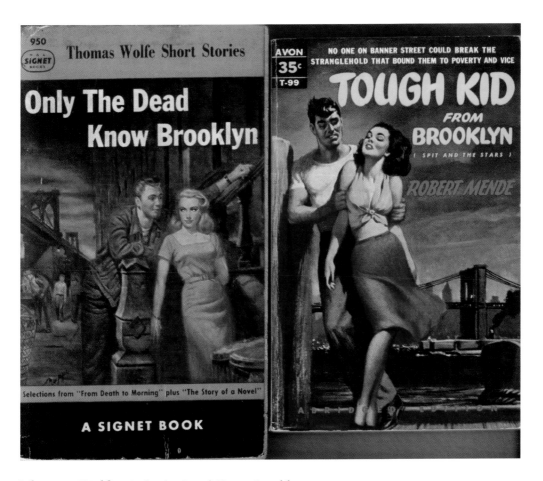

Thomas Wolfe, *Only the Dead Know Brooklyn*, 1947
and Robert Mende, *Tough Kid from Brooklyn*, 1949.
From the author's collection.

New York Landmarks Preservation Commission. Within weeks the newly created commission was holding hearings about the Brooklyn Bridge.

The bridge became an official landmark on August 24, 1967. In its report, the commission praised the span as "a milestone in the history of American engineering" and "the most picturesque of all the bridges spanning the rivers and harbors of New York." "In legend and story, in painting and photo, in poetry and prose," it continued, "the Brooklyn Bridge has inspired and evoked more praise and comment than any other bridge in America."[18] The formal designation enshrined the bridge within New York's pantheon of pre-eminent icons and confirmed its place as a sacred cultural symbol. This new sensibility was reflected in the culture at large.

The bridge exploded throughout American culture in the post-war years. The advertising industry revived the bridge as a marketing icon and used it to sell coffee, cars, colas, and a host of others products. The publishing industry also began to use

NOVEMBER 1951 · 35 CENTS

Astounding
SCIENCE FICTION

Street & Smith's
ASTOUNDING

SCIENCE FICTION | Making Worlds Collide, by R. S. Richardson

Astounding Science Fiction, November 1951.
From the author's collection.

the bridge to sell magazines and books. Mass-market paperbacks arrived in the U.S. in the late 1930s and took off after the Second World War, with a little help from the occasional dramatic cover shot. The bridge appeared quite naturally on the covers of books by Henry Miller (*Plexus* (1953), *Nights of Love and Laughter* (1955)), Thomas Wolfe (*Only the Dead Know Brooklyn* (1947), *From Death to Morning* (1963)), Albert Idell (*Bridge to Brooklyn* (1944)), and Hart Crane, authors who wrote specifically about the span. But, in a tradition that continues today, the bridge also found a home on the covers of many a Brooklyn-based novel. Ruth Fenisong's *The Butler Died in Brooklyn* (1943), Irving Shulman's *The Amboy Dukes: A Novel of Wayward Youth in Brooklyn* (1948), and Robert Mende's *Tough Kid from Brooklyn* (1949) all featured the bridge on their covers but not in their stories. Thanks to its dramatic night-time setting, and with a nod perhaps to Weegee, the bridge also became a staple on the covers of crime novels, even those, like Raymond Chandler's *The Long Goodbye* (1954), that were set on the other side of the continent.

The same easy associations between the bridge and anything Brooklyn also permeated the world of film posters. Advertisements for *Cowboy from Brooklyn* (1938), *Brooklyn Orchid* (1942), *Two Mugs from Brooklyn* (1942), *Blonde from Brooklyn* (1945), and *Port of New York* (1949), for example, all featured the bridge even though the span itself plays no part in the films.

The bridge's sheer visual appeal lent itself to a mass of new cultural forms, including comic books, where it had enjoyed a sporadic presence for years. Between 1905 and 1911, comic strip artist Windsor McCay included the bridge in many episodes of "Dreams of a Rarebit Fiend" (serialized in the *New York Evening Telegram*) and "Nemo in Slumberland" (which ran in the *New York Herald* and the *New York American*). In 1906, Bowery Billy, a poor young waif made good on the streets of New York, chased a bunch of ruffians over the bridge in *Bowery Billy's Runabout Race; or, The Brigands of Brooklyn Bridge*. Eight years later, Old and Young King Brady, the detective heroes of *Secret Service*

Port of New York, 1949.
Film poster. From the author's collection.

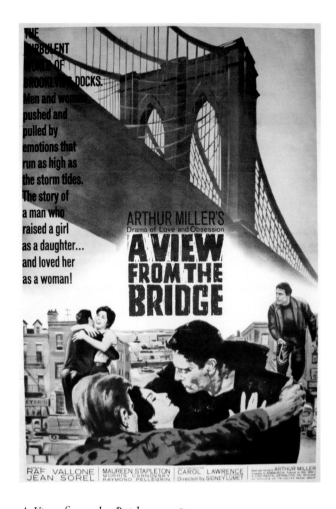

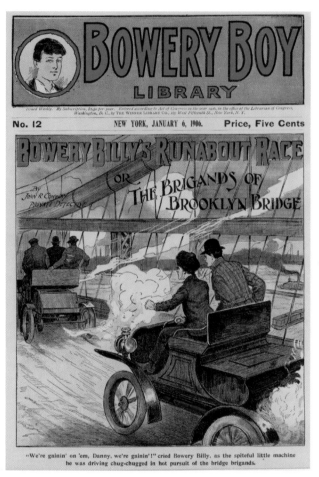

A View from the Bridge, 1962.
Film poster. From the author's collection.

Bowery Billy's Runabout Race; or, the Brigands of Brooklyn Bridge, January 6, 1906.
Courtesy of Street and Smith Archive, Special Collections Research Center, Syracuse University Library.

magazine, found themselves embroiled in "Found in the River; or, The Bradys and the Brooklyn Bridge Mystery."[19] Captain Marvel flew around the bridge—as did Superman in the 1978 film—on the cover of *Whiz Comics* in April 1949, the same month *Real Clue Crime Stories* ran a little cartoon strip about a cad—complete with obligatory twirly moustache—selling the bridge to an unsuspecting dupe.[20] From 1940 to 1952 the bridge made a number of appearances in Will Eisner's *The Spirit*. Slowly, the bridge was edging its way into the comic-book world. It would arrive in the 1970s.

In April 1978, *Batman* comic opened with an image of the caped crusader perched on the "fog-shrouded bridge" by moonlight, waiting for a boat in the river below. Two years later, Captain America ran over the span sounding less like a superhero and more like a real estate broker: "Moving to Brooklyn Heights was one of the smartest things

Dong Kingman, *Bridge and White Building*, 1951.
Courtesy of the Charles H. MacNider Art Museum, Mason City, Iowa.

I've ever done! Not only is it a good neighborhood … but its proximity to the bridge provides easy access to Manhattan!"[21]

More than any other superhero, however, the bridge has become identified with Spider-Man. In 1973, the span became immortalized in comic-book lore when it played host to the death of Gwen Stacy, Peter Parker's first love. Eventually that is. The first printing identified the bridge as the George Washington, a mistake that was corrected in subsequent reprints. The significance of Stacy's death—thrown from the bridge by the Green Goblin—lay in the concept of fallibility. For the first time in comic-book history, a superhero was unable to save his beloved. The comic-reading public was shocked.

The bridge wasn't new to Spider-Man in 1973—he'd battled Mysterio on the span almost ten years earlier—and it wouldn't become old either. Trying to recapture the

John Whorf, *View of New York from Brooklyn Heights (River of Gold)*, 1957.
Watercolor and gouache on paper: 30 × 40 inches. Private collection, courtesy of Berry-Hill Galleries.

success of the Gwen Stacy issue, Marvel had Spider-Man battle all sorts of evil types on the bridge in subsequent issues: the Tarantula in 1975, Platoon in 1994, and, perhaps most ludicrously, Stacy's twin children in 2003. Other Marvel series have also tried to cash in on the bridge. In 2003, Magnito, arch-enemy of the X-Men, blew up the bridge, killing 2,000 New Yorkers—Brian Wood did the same thing in 2006 in his futuristic comic-book series *DMZ*—although two years later, in the movie *The Fantastic Four*, the Thing turned things around and saved the bridge.[22]

FACING PAGE
Stow Wengenroth, *Manhattan Gateway*, 1948.
Courtesy of the Library of Congress.

Stow Wengenroth, *Brooklyn Bridge in Winter*, 1959.
Lithograph on paper: 10 ½ × 15 ⅞ inches. Bequest of Frank McClure.
Courtesy of the Smithsonian American Art Museum,
Washington, DC/Art Resource, NY.

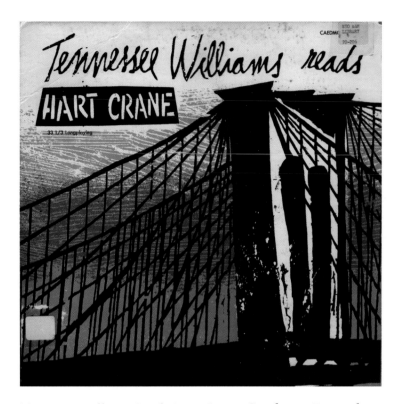

Tennessee Williams Reads Hart Crane, Caedmon Records, 1965.
From the author's collection. Cover image: Antonio Frasconi, *Brooklyn Bridge,* 1959
© Antonio Frasconi/Licensed by VAGA, New York, NY.

While superheroes were scampering around the bridge, the span flourished in the fine arts. Despite the pervasive influence of abstract art, many continued to paint the bridge. Chinese-American Dong Kingman lived on State Street in Brooklyn Heights for much of the 1950s and on Sundays would often walk down to the bridge with his son. He would paint there for hours while Dong Jr. ran around playing. Kingman produced over ten paintings of the bridge, as well as a mural of the span for Lingnan's Chinese restaurant. As payment, Kingman received $1,000 in restaurant credit. Danish-American Johann Berthelsen painted the bridge a number of times from the 1940s to the 1960s, as did New England watercolorist John Whorf. Stow Wengenroth, who spent most of his career in New England, likewise managed to find his way to the bridge from time to time, producing four glorious lithographs of the span between 1948 and 1960. Elsewhere in the graphic arts, Uruguayan immigrant Antonio Frasconi produced a number of woodcuts in 1959 based on Hart Crane's poetry, having previously depicted the bridge towering over the Fulton Fish Market. In 1971, Gordon Matta-Clark spent some time beneath the Brooklyn and Manhattan bridges turning a bunch of abandoned cars into homeless shelters. He called the installation "Jacks" and capped off the event by roasting a pig on a spit and passing around free sandwiches. Four years later, fellow public artist Red Grooms

Antonio Frasconi, *Fulton Market, Dawn*, 1953.
© Antonio Frasconi/Licensed by VAGA, New York, NY.

unveiled *Ruckus Manhattan*, his bizarre, sculptural "city within a city," in which he included a weirdly contorted, and wonderfully whimsical, large-scale model of the bridge.[23]

In literature, the bridge found its usual assortment of devotees, especially among poets. Beat writers Allen Ginsberg, Jack Kerouac, Lawrence Ferlinghetti, and Gregory Corso all wrote verse about the bridge. In 1955, Edwin Morgan called it "the pledge and audacity / Of a century." A decade later, long-time Brooklynite Marianne Moore described it as the "implacable enemy of the mind's deformity, / of man's uncompunctious greed / his crass love of crass priority," while praising its "enfranchising cable, silvered by the seas." Fellow poet and good friend Elizabeth Bishop subsequently implored Moore to "please come flying … over the Brooklyn Bridge." William Meredith wrote of the "growing need to be moving around to see it, / To prevent its freezing, as with sculpture and metaphor"; cultural critic Kenneth Burke preferred the stationary approach, spending the winter of 1968–1969 staring out at the bridge while holed up in the St. George's Hotel in Brooklyn Heights, eventually producing "Eye-Crossing—From Brooklyn to Manhattan," his long, complex ode to Crane, Whitman, and the East River.[24] Spanning the age of the beats to the post-9/11 world, Harvey Shapiro has found a place for the bridge in almost every one of his twelve poetry collections. His achievement is as large as his love of the bridge.

The Road to Oz: The Brooklyn Bridge on the Silver Screen

Films flourished above all other art forms in post-war America, and the bridge prospered with them, lengthening and strengthening its place as a cinema icon on movie screens all over the world.

The life of the bridge in the movies had begun in the late nineteenth century when the fledging art of motion pictures was born. In 1899, the American Mutoscope and Biograph Company took a camera up to the top of the bridge's New York tower and shot a motion-picture panorama of lower Manhattan. The same year, Thomas Edison placed a camera on a Brooklyn-to-Manhattan elevated railroad and captured the journey. Edwin S. Porter was a cameraman for Edison at the time, but he soon graduated to film director. And in 1906, he managed to film a man in a bed flying over the Brooklyn Bridge.

Theodore Hancock, *Brooklyn Bridge*, 1961.
From the author's collection.

FACING PAGE

"Mio and Miriamne Climbing up from the Morass Which Has Engulfed Them"
Winterset, 1936. Film still. From the author's collection.

In 1903, Porter made cinema history with *The Great Train Robbery*, and three years later turned Windsor McCay's comic strip into the surrealist film fantasy *Dreams of a Rarebit Fiend*. *Rarebit Fiend* opens with a gluttonous dandy stuffing his face with food and drink before staggering home to bed. While sleeping, the "fiend" endures terrible nightmares: little pixies emerge to batter his head with hammers and shovels; his bed starts to buck and bounce around the room before spinning off out the window like a whirling dervish. High over Manhattan, the glutton loses his balance as he flies past the Brooklyn Bridge, and he ends up gripping onto the bedstead for dear life. Eventually, both bed and rider return home, and the dandy wakes having learned a traumatic lesson, or at least hopefully. [25]

Rarebit Fiend, of course, was all trick photography, stock footage, and studio shots. On-location shooting would not take off in New York until the 1920s, and its first great age would pass pretty quickly after studios headed west to the cheaper movie lots of

Tarzan's New York Adventure, 1944.
Lobby card.
From the author's collection.

Hollywood. Paul Strand and Charles Scheeler's *Manahatta* (1921) was filmed on the streets of New York, as was the conclusion of Harold Lloyd's *Speedy* (1928), in which Lloyd careens about DUMBO in the shadow of the Brooklyn Bridge in a runaway horse-drawn trolley before crashing into the el tacks that ran by the bridge, an accident that was eventually written into the film. The bridge also appeared in Josef von Sternberg's *The Docks of New York* (1928), and in Rouben Mamoulian's *Applause* (1929) Joan Peters enjoys the view from the bridge—"Even Brooklyn looks pretty!"—while strolling hand-in-hand with Henry Wadsworth. In 1924, New York Police Commissioner Richard E. Enright had the bridge roped off for an entire day so George Seitz could shoot scenes for *Into the Net*, a detective movie based on a story by, you guessed it, Police Commissioner Enright.[26]

The bridge continued to appear in movies after the film industry headed west, but it was usually rebuilt "Hollywood-Style" in California or glimpsed through back-projection. Although the bridge is the key to *The Bowery* (1933), Raoul Walsh's fanciful retelling of the Brodie legend, it appears only briefly in the movie, and the leap, performed heroically by George Raft, was probably no more than a few feet, or however high the Hollywood set was. In *Every Day's a Holiday* (1937), set in 1899 New York and photographed coincidentally by Karl Struss, Mae West makes her living selling the Brooklyn Bridge. In West's first appearance in the film, she rides a horse and carriage over a re-created Brooklyn Bridge—complete with cobblestones!—built from scratch on the Paramount lot. A year earlier, in 1936, RKO studios built a stage set of the bridge's walkway and the area surrounding the span for the movie version of Maxwell Anderson's *Winterset*. All labyrinthine alleys and dark shadows, the whole area is darkly menacing, as is the shot of the bridge during the opening credits.

In 1940, Twentieth Century Fox announced that Henry Fonda and Tyrone Power would star in *Brooklyn Bridge*, a biopic about the Roeblings. The film was never made, despite F. Scott Fitzgerald's work on the script (or perhaps

It Happened in Brooklyn, 1947.
Magazine advertisement.
From the author's collection.

On the Town, 1949.
Film still © Hulton Archive.
Courtesy of Getty Images.

Kenneth Snelson, "Brooklyn Bridge," 1980.
Silver print: 15 ½ × 91 inches © Kenneth Snelson.

because of it, given how lousy Fitzgerald's Hollywood work was).[27] Four years later—while, as luck would have it, Fitzgerald's wife Zelda was busy with her brush and easel painting a picture of the span—someone threw a dummy (in the shape of Johnny Weissmuller) off the bridge, and initiated the return of on-location filming to the Brooklyn Bridge. *Tarzan's New York Adventure* (1944) was one of the first movies to feature an extended action sequence filmed almost entirely on the bridge, and a ridiculous bit of fun to boot. As was Hollywood's way at the time, however, none of the principal actors were involved in the shooting. While the bridge was closed off and stuntmen clambered up the cables and over the towers, Weissmuller and company sat round a pool in California.

The bridge was no distant icon for Jersey-boy Frank Sinatra, who, before he became Mr. New York, was Mr. Brooklyn (Bridge). In *It Happened in Brooklyn* from 1947, Sinatra played a homesick Brooklynite stationed in Germany at the close of the Second World War, so homesick in fact, that he carries a photo of the bridge in his wallet. "Yeah, that's my pinup girl," he tells his fellow soldiers, "aint she a beauty?" Apparently not—the soldiers are understandably less than impressed—but as soon as Sinatra returns to U.S. soil he hops in a cab and heads to the bridge, where he ambles along the boardwalk, happy as a clam, singing: "What a lovely view from / Heaven looks at you from / The Brooklyn Bridge."

Sinatra was back singing and dancing on the bridge two years later in *On the Town*. Most of the movie was filmed in LA, but, at the insistence of Gene Kelly, some scenes were shot on-location in New York, most memorably the opening "New York, New York" number where Kelly, Sinatra, and Jules Munshin frolic over the bridge and around the city.

The bridge, of course, is no stranger to song and dance. In the bizarre crime-musical *Never Steal Anything Small* (1959), James Cagney plays a ruthless, all-singing, all-dancing mob boss who campaigns (and sings) for union votes beneath the bridge. A few years

later, in 1963, country singer Bobby Bare wrote a song about buying the bridge for two dollars, two cigarettes, and an autographed photo of Elvis Presley.

Subsequently, the bridge has appeared in countless films, its use shifting from establishing shot, to complex symbol, to trysting place, to dramatic stage, to yellow brick road. It has played host to rabbits (*Bowery Bugs*, 1949) and werewolves (*Wolfen*, 1981), Dorothy, the Tin Man, the Scarecrow, and the Lion entering the emerald city of Oz (*The Whiz*, 1978) and scared CIA agents fleeing for their lives (*Three Days of the Condor*, 1975), jazz musicians (*Mo' Better Blues*, 1990) and time travelers (*Kate and Leopold*, 2001), disaffected stoners (*Virginal Young Blondes*, 2004) and horny porn-stars (*Sexual Freedom in Brooklyn*, 1971), neo-Nazis (*Marathon Man*, 1976) and a modern-day John the Baptist (*Godspell*, 1973). Godzilla was brought to her knees on the bridge in 1998; 45 years earlier the Beast from 20,000 Fathoms crept past the structure on its way to terrorize New York. In 1992, the bridge was closed down for six full nights—much to the annoyance of local residents—so Bruce Willis could be pulled over the bridge by an ambulance (only to emerge, oddly, out of the Brooklyn–Battery Tunnel) in the awful *Hudson Hawk*. In *The Siege* (1998), Willis was back in charge of the bridge, albeit as a fictional army general presiding over the imposition of martial law.

The Siege brought something new and horrifying—albeit purely logical—to Roebling's masterpiece. It took the bridge, wrapped it in razor wire, peopled it with a thousand soldiers, and made of it a barrier, a tightly controlled checkpoint between a military dictatorship in Manhattan and internment camps in Brooklyn. This was the rational flipside to the bridge's long symbolic tradition: if it can represent open movement, it can also, in the wrong hands, represent confinement. In perilous times, of course, the symbols of freedom can quickly come to serve totalitarian tendencies. As the film's tagline spelled out: "Freedom is History," when a reactionary nation fears for its life.

There was no escaping Brooklyn in *The Siege*, although that wasn't always the case: disco king John Travolta, for example, managed it quite famously in 1977. The Brooklyn Bridge frames the action in *Saturday Night Fever*, from the film's opening shot to Travolta's eventual move to Manhattan. It symbolizes the troubled young Brooklynite's transformation: from his adolescent past in a provincial borough to his adult future in cosmopolitan Manhattan. The Verazano Bridge, by contrast, the movie's other obsession, leads only to futility in Bay Ridge or a watery death. At the end of *Sophie's Choice* (1982), Stingo, played by Peter MacNicol, also leaves Brooklyn over the bridge in one of the most poignant moments in recent cinema.

An aspiring writer, Stingo first visits the bridge with his two best friends—Nathan Landau (Kevin Kline), a good-natured but occasionally violent paranoid-schizophrenic, and Sophie Zawistowski (Meryl Streep), a Polish Holocaust survivor traumatized by the murder of her two children at Auschwitz—to celebrate the writing of his first novel.

N. Jay Jaffee, "Brooklyn Bridge," 1981.
Courtesy of the Museum of the City of New York. Gift of Pamela Walter Hackeling (91.54.1).

Nathan believes the book will make Stingo a literary star, and, as they walk the bridge at midnight, he offers a toast, champagne flutes and all:

> On this bridge. Where so many great American writers had stood and reached out for words to give American its voice. Looking towards the land that gave us Whitman, who from its Eastern edge dreamt his country's future and gave it words. O'er this span of which Thomas Wolfe and Hart Crane wrote, we welcome Stingo into that pantheon of the Gods where words are all we know of mortality.

On the surface, the moment is full of great joy—an initiation and a confirmation—but its implications are bittersweet. Nathan has taken Stingo to the bridge to show him the path he must take, but they won't walk over together. The path is Stingo's alone, for neither Nathan nor Sophie can follow. They are too damaged, too haunted by pain and suffering to cross. They have no future over the bridge, only a quick, painless end in a boarding house in Brooklyn. The great gothic towers are Stingo's entrance to the world, but he must walk through them alone, leaving his best friends behind.

CHAPTER SIX

Commemoration and the Contemporary Era (1983–2008)

On May 24, 1983 the Brooklyn Bridge celebrated its one hundredth birthday. And it was helped along by some friends, a horde of journalists, countless well-wishers, thousands of entrepreneurs, and several million Americans. By the end of the day, the bridge had been bought, sold, fêted, traipsed over, praised, photographed, and roundly petted by all and sundry. It was, by any measure, quite a day.

The Centennial

The celebration began early. At 5 a.m., the FDR Drive was shut down and cleared while preparations took place on either shore. An hour or two later, 18,000 marchers—about 17,980 more than marched over the span in 1883—began to gather at Brooklyn Borough Hall. At 9:30 a.m., all ready and assembled, they set off. They marched down Cadman Plaza, over the bridge, down Broadway, and ended up at the Battery. Crowds lined every inch of the route, cheering wildly. Many of the marchers wore period costume, as, apparently, did some of the crowd. Men donned morning coats and striped trousers; women wore whalebone corsets, hoop skirts, and carried parasols. Floats accompanied the marchers bearing makeshift Brooklyn Bridges, as did clowns, jugglers, and an all-female barbershop quartet. Horse-drawn delivery wagons clip-clopped alongside young men in boaters encased in large cardboard bridge customs.

President Ronald Reagan and Governor Mario Cuomo sent their regrets, but Mayor Ed Koch—who once made the faux pas of suggesting the city sell advertising space on the bridge's towers, before retracting the statement a day later saying he was only joking—and Brooklyn Borough president Howard Golden were everywhere, speechifying, offering platitudes, and commendation to anyone who would listen.

William Gedney, "Lee Friedlander Shooting the Centennial Parade
for the Brooklyn Bridge," 1983.
© Rare Book, Manuscript, and Special Collections Library, Duke University.

Down below, the River Café hosted a family reunion for 150 descendants of John Roebling, and out on the bay 86 vessels clogged the East River while fireboats launched streams of red, white, and blue water 75 feet into the air. One man, wearing a top hat and tails, managed to gate-crash the party, zooming about the flotilla on a motorized surfboard. No one seemed to mind. Up at the far reaches of Manhattan, the city draped a massive U.S. flag from the George Washington Bridge to greet anyone arriving via the Hudson.

After everyone had eaten and drunk their fill, bought their souvenirs, and been very, very merry, they made their way to the East River for the day's main event. At 9:25 p.m.,

FACING PAGE

Bruce Cratsley, "Brooklyn Bridge, Centennial Fireworks," 1983.
Gelatin silver print. Image/sheet: 15 ⅛ × 14 ¾ inches (38.5 × 37.6 cm); board: 24 × 20 inches.
Brooklyn Museum, Gift of Billy Leight, 1996.167.

Andy Warhol, *Brooklyn Bridge*, 1983.
© 2007 Andy Warhol Foundation for the Visual Arts/ARS, New York.

over two million people crowded along the shorelines to watch the largest fireworks display in the nation's history. Staged by the world-famous Grucci family of Long Island, the display featured 9,600 individual fireworks shot from the towers, the roadway, and three nearby barges, culminating in a 3,600 shell "mind-blaster finale" (as the *Daily News* put it). For over half an hour, the assembled masses were transfixed: oohing and ahhing with each new wave of explosions. One man was so captivated that he walked off the back of his cabin cruiser and into the East River. Luckily, a nearby police boat wasn't so engrossed and he was soon fished out.[1]

The bridge's birthday bash was more than just a day, it was an entire summer of events. The Brooklyn Museum of Art held a massive exhibition on the art and history of the bridge, and smaller exhibitions were held at the New-York Historical Society, the Municipal Archives, and the Museum of the City of New York, as well as at the Library of Congress and the Smithsonian Institution in Washington, DC. The New York Academy of Sciences held a two-day conference that explored the bridge from all angles, and throughout the spring and summer a sound and laser show played on the span at night. By all accounts, if you didn't like the Brooklyn Bridge, you were in for a tough summer. The damned thing was everywhere.

Mainly, the bridge was on souvenirs, advertisements, magazine covers, and TV, and, by the end of the year, the centennial had generated enough cultural junk to fill your average Wal-Mart. T-shirts, key chains, posters, beach towels, caps, umbrellas, coasters, pennants, paperweights, ashtrays, mugs, glasses, badges, and medals were all emblazoned with the official centennial logo and shipped out to stores. Tiffany's, which designed the hand-engraved invitations to the bridge's opening in 1883, issued a sterling silver sugar spoon, a money clip, and a small enamel box, all bearing an image of the bridge. Macy's and Abram Strauss put together a line of "Bridge-a-Brac," the U.S. Postal Service put the bridge on its first-class stamps, and Sherry-Lehmann sold a "Great Bridge White Wine," which wasn't too tasty but did quite well all the same.

The outpouring of love (and the production of stuff) was matched by an outpouring of art and opinion. As the city geared up to celebrate the bridge's first hundred years, artists of all stripes busied themselves in their studios, preparing for a possible bonanza. Andy Warhol designed the official centennial poster, which the public didn't take to. Lacking the pop of his earlier Pop Art, Warhol's bridge seemed a bit too gritty and uninspiring for a celebration. Far more popular were the photographs of Joel Greenberg and Alfred Eisenstaedt, who captured the bridge in all its monumental glory. Hank Virgona created a wonderful series of watercolors and etchings, which were quickly snapped up by bridge lovers. John Shaw produced a striking, slightly abstracted linoleum cut of the span, and Florence Neal captured the centennial fireworks in a block print (as Jed Devine and Bruce Cratsley did to great effect in photography). Mark di Suvero also took a slightly abstract approach, taking time off from sculpture to produce *Roebling's Arch* (1983), his

Hank Virgona, Study for "Brooklyn Bridge (Variant)", 1983.
© Hank Virgona/licensed by VAGA, New York, NY.

bright yellow lithograph of the bridge. Arthur Cohen and Howard Koslow both produced a series of popular etchings, and Bronx-born Stuart Klipper brought his panoramic eye, now most often aimed at the Antarctic frontier, to the bridge's walkway.

As for opinion, everyone, it seems, had something to say about Roebling's great bridge. Many—surprisingly many, as if everyone was working from the same crib sheet—began their tributes in the same way. An immigrant ship, full of soon-to-be new Americans, sails into New York. The first thing they glimpse is the lady with the torch, then the skyline, then, hey presto: the Brooklyn Bridge. For Bill Prochnaw, the bridge was "an American epic about hardworking newcomers who had nowhere to go but up"; for Brooklyn Borough President Howard Golden, "the bridge is a symbol of the trials and tribulations that immigrants faced when they came here." Exactly how it symbolized the trials and tribulation of immigrants, he never said (after all John Roebling arrived in the U.S. as a fully trained engineer and with enough money to buy several thousand acres of land in Western Pennsylvania), but such associations came free

John P. Shaw, *Brooklyn Bridge*, 1983.
Edition: 1/35. Linoleum cut. Image: 7 ⅞ × 10 inches (20 × 25.4 cm);
sheet: 19 ¹¹/₁₆ × 25 ⅞ inches (50 × 65.7 cm). Brooklyn Museum, purchased
with funds given by the Louis Comfort Tiffany Foundation, 85.47.

and easy. Comedian Alan King called the bridge "my own Yellow Brick Road." "When
I was a kid in a poor neighborhood in Williamsburg," he continued, "the bridge always
symbolized whether or not you'd be able to get out of that poverty," which seems like
an odd sort of statement given that one can't actually see the Brooklyn Bridge from
Williamsburg.[2] Such quibbles were of no account, of course. The bridge was there to be
celebrated, and all summer wild pontifications rained down relentlessly on the span.

Amid the bromides, outrageous and otherwise, some voices shone through the haze
with honest clarity. Bill Reel took a long, hard look at all the famous ex-Brooklynites
now lining up to praise the bridge and the borough and found fault with their rosy nostalgia. On the one hand, Brooklyn was a wonderful place, on the other, all the assembled dignitaries got out as fast as they could and never went back. Brooklyn no longer
belonged to these people, Reel decided, but to those now living there, those who might
end up famous. "Brooklyn is always coming and going. That's what the Brooklyn Bridge
stands for," Reel concluded with an easy shrug, and *sans* bullhorn.

Ferdinando Scianna, "East River: Manhattan Bridge and
Brooklyn Bridge in the Fog," 1986.
© Magnum Photos.

While many gazed from afar at the bridge's magnificent form, art critic Martin Filler saw it as "a vital fact of everyday life," an essential working part of the city's infrastructure. What Filler prized was not beauty as such, but beauty tied to function. The Brooklyn Bridge was "the world's one great anthropocentric bridge": beautiful when you use it, but less so when merely gawked at. Filler also felt that the bridge was the perfect symbol of its age, of the "dichotomy between romanticism and materialism," a theme also echoed by *The Boston Globe*: "it embodies the visionary *and* the pecuniary: those simultaneous urges in our national character to build a city on a hill—and then subdivide it for a quick profit."[3]

Praise was clearly the order of the day, but some begged to differ, and the nation's pecuniary bent lay at the heart of these complaints. The *Christian Science Monitor* deplored the "history as fireworks approach"—"a few minutes of noise and flash and then darkness again"—and the anniversary's rampant commercialization; Richard Eder lambasted the champagne and smoked salmon "street fairs" that took up much of the prime viewing space at $500 a head. Worried about the span's upkeep, Jimmy Breslin thought "the bridge [now] reflects a city that has so confused glory with making money that it allows a priceless monument to rot." Still, Breslin was not all doom and gloom. The bridge, he remarked with obvious pride, was "the only large span in the world that really belongs to people," which, when you think about it, is a pretty good reason for a summer-long celebration involving over two million people.[4]

Making, Marching, and Mayhem: After the Centennial

Already an icon of great stature, the bridge's centennial sanctified the span into the pantheon of American excellence. And in many respects, the process freed the bridge from the confines of history and argument; no longer a novelty, a modernist emblem, a lost original, an aged relic, or a cause, the span became, well, whatever one wanted it to be.

As a result, the contemporary era has turned out to be the most eclectic in the bridge's history. Writers, activists, artists, urban planners, entrepreneurs, educators, and often people who should know better, have gone at the bridge from all angles, helping to fashion a more expansive, fun, and generous legacy. In 1980, Alan Rose released "Build Your Own Brooklyn Bridge," a self-assembly cardboard replica of the span. Thanks to Rose, children everywhere (and certain future authors of books about the bridge) were able to labor away with scissors, glue, thread, and great patience to produce their very own scale model of the span. Unfortunately, and very impractically (considering the confines of most New York apartments), the finished item clocked in at over eight feet in length. Such concerns were of no account to others, and the building of Brooklyn Bridges has taken place all over the U.S. Legions of school teachers have set their students to constructing models of the bridge, bakers have made cakes in the shape of the span, Legoland in California built a Brooklyn Bridge out of its trademark plastic blocks, and twice, in 1995 and again in 2005, the New York Botanical Gardens built a Brooklyn Bridge out of bark, twigs, and other vegetable matter for its Holiday Train Show. One can visit a model of the Brooklyn Bridge under the bright lights of the Las Vegas strip, outside the New York New York hotel and casino, in the rural confines of the Roeblings' hometown of Saxonburg, Pennsylvania, and as far away as Israel.

While many Americans were building their own Brooklyn Bridges, New Yorkers were rediscovering their waterfront. The River Café opened its doors in 1977, just a few months before Olga Bloom parked her 102-year-old ferry boat by the span and started to entertain the local longshoremen with live lunch-time chamber music. Bloom's eccentricity would evolve into Bargemusic, one of the world's unique musical experiences. Soon after Bloom arrived, the city, in an attempt to counter almost a hundred years of neglect and bring people back to the shore, began to renovate Fulton

Trish Mayo, "Botanical Gardens, Brooklyn Bridge," 2005.
Courtesy of the artist.

BELOW
Bruce Davidson, "A View of the Brooklyn Bridge from a Tugboat," 1996.
© Magnum Photos.

FACING PAGE
Peter de Sève, *Liberty*, 1998.
© Peter de Sève.

Landing on the Brooklyn side and the South Street Seaport in Manhattan. In 1978, the Empire–Fulton Ferry State Park, a nine-acre patch of grass between the Manhattan and Brooklyn bridges, was opened. A year later, David Walentas bought two million square feet of abandoned industrial real estate and began his decades-long fight to establish DUMBO as a premier urban neighborhood. He succeeded spectacularly, of course, as has Brooklyn generally since the bridge's centennial. The (re)gentrification of brownstone Brooklyn helped re-established the bridge as a prime, if somewhat inappropriate, symbol of Brooklyn. On magazine covers, life-style guides, and real estate brochures and websites, the bridge has come to symbolize a new way of life in the past few years—the gateway not to adventure and ambition in Manhattan, but to the tree-lined streets and French bistros of an upwardly mobile Brooklyn—one far removed from the dead-end disaffection of *Saturday Night Fever*.

Marches and protests over the bridge have remained standard fare, as have ludicrous stunts and spectacular stupidity. Anyone walking over the bridge at about two o'clock on the afternoon January 30, 2005, for example, would have witnessed hordes of weirdly dressed lunatics (all pulling decorated shopping carts) careening up the bridge, like a pack of stampeding wildebeest. The city's annual Idiot-a-Rod was up and running. The same journey almost a year later might have been just as puzzling, when 500 people, all dressed as Santa, made their way over the bridge for the city's annual Santacon festivities.

The prize for the most creative oddball, however, goes to Raymond Masa, a paraplegic who, in 1988, lowered himself (in his wheelchair) on a rope from the bridge while clutching a variety of fireworks and samurai swords. Masa hung 75 feet below the bridge for over an hour before he was persuaded to lower himself still further to a waiting police boat. Masa performed the feat in an effort to inspire other paraplegics. He was arrested for disorderly conduct and the illegal possession of fireworks and knives.[5]

Hidden Treasures: Inside the Bridge

While millions were marching, strolling, or careening over the bridge, some were rummaging around its insides. In 1983, Creative Time—the public art organization that brought Red Grooms's *Ruckus Manhattan* to the streets of New York—started "Art in the Anchorage," an annual program of arts, readings, music, dance, and, on one occasion a mock circus, held beneath the enormous barreled ceiling of the bridge's Brooklyn anchorage. Art in the Anchorage was one of the most compelling and dynamic, not to mention fun, legacies to emerge from the bridge's centennial. In scheduling its annual jamboree, Creative Time defined the idea of art broadly, showcasing artists of all descriptions and working across almost all forms of media. For the program's tenth anniversary in 1993, the entire space was given over to renowned choreographer

Elizabeth Streb, who decided to ditch the mores of traditional theater and experiment with a vertical stage. Streb built a 40-foot high wall in the anchorage and installed a complex harness system that allowed her performers to walk, swing, and dance their way up and down the bright yellow partition and out over the audience. Rehearsals for the show were held most afternoons, and the doors were always open to the public. What they saw was the slow development of the dancer as superhero.

In 1995, Creative Time built a twelve-foot half-pipe and invited the city to come to watch skateboarders fly through the air. Four years later, it held a fashion show (of sorts) directed by some of the world's most avant-garde designers. In between, in 1996, it expanded its operations to include Music in the Anchorage, a series of summer concerts, musical hybrids, and dance parties that featured, amongst others, DJ Spooky, the McCollough Sons of Thunder, Mogwai, Mos Def, Sonic Youth, Soul Coughing, the SRC All-City Gospel Chorale, and John Zorn. The introduction of musical performance underscored the evolving nature of the summer festival. Art in the Anchorage began with art inspired by the bridge's unique interior space, but developed to include a vast tapestry of social and aesthetic concerns: the impact of technology on the environment, the issue of homelessness, the physiological experience of light and sound, the interaction between music, film and performance, and the political dimensions of public health. Creative Time worked with local residents, activist groups, community choirs, schools, settlement houses, and the disabled. For almost 20 years, Art in the Anchorage was one of the city's most imaginative and inclusive events. That it is no longer a part of the city's cultural fabric owes more to new realities than innate popularity.

Horst Hamann, "Brooklyn Bridge, East Tower," 1996.
From *New York Vertical* (teNeues)
© Horst Hamann (www.horsthamann.com).

Marty Heitner, "Karin Giusti's *Over Brooklyn Bridge*"
From Art in the Anchorage, 1995
© Marty Heitner.

The 9/11 attacks put an end to Art in the Anchorage. Fearing for the bridge's safety, the city shut down, locked up, and mothballed the space. Creative Time moved on, of course, helping to create "Tribute in Light," the city's most affecting response to its loss. But its absence at the bridge remains a great shame, as is the closing of the anchorage generally. When the city cancelled the annual art program, it deprived New Yorkers of entry to one of the city's most historic and memorable spaces. That the bridge's interiors still lie dormant—both unused and untended—does no credit to New York. It is an exceptional waste of a magnificent place.

FACING PAGE
Charlie Samuels, "Erwin Redl's *Matrix IV*"
From Art in the Anchorage, 2001
© Charlie Samuels (www.charliesamuels.com).

Robin Holland, "Jane Greengold's
Agatha Muldoon"
From Art in the Anchorage, 1983 © Robin Holland.

Creative Time was not the only group to explore the bridge's secret heart in the past quarter-century. Photographers Stanley Greenberg and Barbara Mensch both took their cameras into the bridge's Manhattan anchorage and emerged with startling images of the span's cavernous interior: the now-deserted old wine cellars and storage vaults that bustled with activity over a hundred years ago. Mensch went there with the city's permission, but later took a friend—author Phillip Lopate—along for the ride. In *Waterfront* (2004), Lopate described their illicit journey past the piles of garbage and the chain-link fence that guards (or supposedly guards) the bridge, through an obscure metal door that leads into the span's interior. Lopate described the bridge's core—three floors tall, and in a state of "total abandonment"—as "fantastically beautiful" yet equally "sad." That a "national monument" could fall into such disrepair was a great shock to the author.[6]

Periodically, city workers have also had reason to delve inside the bridge—usually for routine maintenance—and in 2006 they made the national news. On the morning of March 21, a large stockpile of Cold War "supplies" were found in one of the bridge's long-forgotten storage rooms. Dating from 1957, when the Soviet Union launched its first satellite, to the height of the Cuban Missile Crisis in 1962, the supplies (some were labeled "to be opened after attacks by the enemy") consisted of water drums, blankets, medical supplies, and over 350,000 "Civil Defense All-Purpose Survival Crackers," possibly the most brilliantly named snack-food in the world. When queried, the city was at a total loss to explain the presence of the supplies, or why they had been stored in the bridge. After all, if it took the city 50 years to find its own provisions, then there'd be little hope for the population at large. And anyway, if an author and photographer could slip into the vaults undetected, albeit many years later, one can only imagine how the (above ground) space would function as a fallout shelter. Frightened New Yorkers would be dropping like flies, one imagines, before anyone could think to say "pass the crackers."[7]

Stanley Greenberg, "Former Wine Cellar, Brooklyn Bridge," 1992.
Gelatin silver print. Image: 10 ½ × 13 ½ inches; sheet 11 × 13 ¾ inches.
Brooklyn Museum, Gift of the artist, 1994.86.

Photographers: Contemporary Artists Return to the Past

Amid the rapid changes in digital technology, many photographers returned to the rich techniques of the past. Jerry Spagnoli helped spearhead the return of the daguerreotype, influencing and teaching, amongst others, Chuck Close. Spagnoli's daguerreotypes of the bridge perfectly convey what he calls the "realistic" yet "idiosyncratic … subjective and illusive" nature of the medium. As with many of Spagnoli's New York daguerreotypes, a silent calmness reigns over his images of the bridge, when one might expect a rushing cacophony. The effect is like wearing earplugs on a crowded city street.[8] Spagnoli's labor-intensive commitment to the daguerreotype has been equaled by Tom Baril's dedication to a host of print-making techniques: collodian, gum bichromate, and photogravure. Baril began his career as a print-maker for Robert Mapplethorpe but soon branched out as an independent photographer, eventually producing a number of exquisite hand-pulled photogravures of the bridge.

Jerry Spagnoli, "Brooklyn Bridge," 2006.
© Jerry Spagnoli.

Spagnoli and Baril are defined by their artisanal respect for the photographic craft. Their work is complex, difficult, and involved; their prints are pure elegance. By contrast, the photographs of Dona McAdams and Michel Bayard are pure simplicity, although no less elegant. McAdams and Bayard both reached back to the very beginnings of photographic history—the pin-hole camera—in their efforts to capture the bridge. McAdams's pin-hole image from 1983 combines the medium's slow shutter speed with the diagonal lines of the bridge's cable-stays to create an exhilarating sense of speed. As with John Marin's great bridge images, the viewer seems to be hurtling across the bridge. Bayard's pin-hole images are marked by distortion and originality. Using cameras made from film canisters, dog-food cans, and old Altoids tins, Bayard's photographs transform the straight and rigid into sweeping, fluid curves, the effects of

Tom Baril, "Brooklyn Bridge, 96," 1996.
© Tom Baril.

Tom Baril, "Brooklyn Bridge, 99 (w/clamp)"
1999.
© Tom Baril.

Dona Ann McAdams, "Pinhole of Brooklyn Bridge," 1983.
© Dona Ann McAdams.

which can be either soothing or startling. His "Brooklyn Bridge #3" (2003), for example, seems equal parts Brooklyn Bridge and Galloping Gertie, the Tacoma Narrows suspension bridge that spent several days twisting and turning in high winds before collapsing on November 7, 1940.

The pin-hole camera may be photography's most basic device, but few cameras are as primitive as the Holga, the cheap Chinese box camera manufactured in the 1980s. Composed of a shoddy, decidedly un-light-tight body, and a cheap plastic meniscus lens, the Holga is a piece of crap. The user has no means of adjusting the shutter speed, the aperture, or the focus. Neither is there any link between the shutter and the winding mechanism. One just turns the knob and hopes that the film has advanced sufficiently. The

Michael Bayard, "Brooklyn Bridge #3 Done with Film Canister," 2003.
Courtesy of the artist.

Holga is so bad, in fact, so light porous and so unbelievably tawdry, so prone to multiple exposures, that it now ranks as a true cult object among many photographers. The reasons are simple: the blurs, light leaks, vignetting, and overlapping exposures that plague the camera produce fascinating, dreamlike images that are unique in photography.

Michael Iacovone bought a Holga camera in 2001 and has since spent hours and hours trudging over the bridge. The fruits of these walks, fortunately, are some of the most original and striking images of the span in contemporary photography. Iacovone's photographic process mirrors and inverts the sense of the bridge itself. The multiple exposures reflect how the cables divide the city into precise yet ever-changing sections and segments. In this respect, Iacovone's photographs are similar to those of Thomas Kellner.

Michael Iacovone, "I Followed This Guy Across the Bridge (Paula's Bridge)," 2005.
Courtesy of the artist (www.mikedax.com).

Michael Iacovone, "Brooklyn Bridge (Cloudy Day)," 2006.
Courtesy of the artist (www.mikedax.com).

Thomas Kellner, "Skyline at Brooklyn Bridge," 2003.
Courtesy of the artist (www.tkellner.com).

Through photography, both redefine the sense of space that itself defines the bridge. And this effect is not simply found or discovered but well-planned. Kellner's prints take the montage principle—favored, for example by David Hockney in his 1982 image of the bridge—to its logical extreme: the precisely ordered contact sheet, wherein every individual photograph occupies a specific place in an ongoing landscape. Get one wrong, and the entire print ends up in the bin. Against Kellner's prints—clean and clear despite their staccato aesthetic—Iacovone's images appear as a chaotic vision. They take the bridge's orderly symmetry and muss it up. Yet these images, busy as they are with the bridge, are as meticulously planned as Kellner's. Iacovone uses random number sequences to dictate when to stop, when to depress the shutter, and how far to advance the film. The photographer's actions are decided upon, in effect, before his camera is even out of his bag. While Iacovone's medium is wonderfully messy, his process is as precise as the lines that define the bridge. Or the laws that control a camera, even one as primitive as a Holga.

From Reverence to Ruin: Painters

Iacovone, Baril, Bayard, and Kellner all prove that the bridge series is alive and well in the contemporary era, as do Burhan Dogançay, Bill Murphy, Emily Trueblood, and a host of others. The emergence of the Internet also played its part. Such websites as flickr.com and photo.net have vastly expanded the size and scope of the bridge's visual history—as has youtube.com for amateur filmmakers—allowing photographers of all levels and persuasions to find an audience for their work. A search for the Brooklyn Bridge on flickr, for example, currently returns over 45,000 images, many of which fall comfortably into the realms of fresh, fascinating, or just plain fun.

In the fine arts, Bascove has spent much of the past 15 years painting the bridges of New York, producing many different versions of the Brooklyn Bridge. Her canvases have re-energized and transformed our understanding of the city's rugged industrial landscape. Painted in warm, bold lines, and with a sensuous attention to geometric form, Bascove's canvases re-imagine the city as a voluptuous siren. And, by imbuing the city's muscular limbs with such feminine grace, Bascove has managed to out-Georgia O'Keeffe Georgia O'Keeffe. No easy task.

Recently, Brooklyn store-front artist and streetscape jester Jonathan Blum put ostriches, camels, dogs, sheep, pigs, cows, and other assorted barnyard friends on the bridge, then, for some reason, put fruit on their heads. His prints sold like hotcakes, and, to date, Blum and P.T. Barnum are the only two people to decide that putting a camel on the Brooklyn Bridge is a good idea. Jen Ferguson is no stranger to animals—or weird street folk either—but, like Blum, she reserves a certain respect for Brooklyn's grand old bridge. Working out of her studio in DUMBO, Ferguson has painted the bridge almost 15 times in the past ten years. Most of Ferguson's outsized images are autumnal in tone—her palate all browns, reds, yellows, and oranges—and enigmatic in feel. The bridge itself is both solid and decrepit. The towers stand tall and iconic, all the more so given the sheer size of Ferguson's canvases, while the cables melt and the roadway breaks. Parts of the bridge seem to vanish, very suddenly, as if the structure were disintegrating before our very eyes. Yet the overall tone keeps the painting in balance: the warmth of the colors counteracts the structure's evident decay. Standing before *Big Bridge* (2006), for example, or *The Brooklyn Side* (1999), is like drinking a mug of hot chocolate while contemplating the end of the world.

Ferguson's images take the bridge to the verge of ruin, but stop short of full devastation. Others, however, have been more direct. H.G. Wells blew up the Brooklyn Bridge in his novel *The War in the Air* (1908), as did O. Louis Guglielmi in his painting *Mental Geography* (1938), Marvel Comics in its series *Ultimate War* (2003), and the special effects team on the recent movie *I Am Legend* (2007). Elsewhere, the bridge has been reduced to rubble through earthquakes (the movie *Aftershock: Earthquake in New York* (1999)), tidal

Bascove, *Brooklyn Bridge III*, 2001.
Private collection © Bascove.

Rose Alber, *Brooklyn Bridge, Red and Blue*, 1995/96.
Courtesy of the artist.

Jonathan Blum, *Dog with Cherries on the Brooklyn Bridge*, 2005.
Monoprint. Courtesy of the artist (www.jonathanblumportraits.com).

Jen Ferguson, *Blue Moon*, 2004.
Courtesy of the artist (www.artinchaos.com).

Jen Ferguson, *Big Bridge*, 2006.
Courtesy of the artist (www.artinchaos.com).

"The Two Monuments in the River"
From J.A. Mitchell, *The Last American*, 1889.
From the author's collection.

waves (Chesley Bonestell's cover art for *Astounding Science Fiction* (1951) and the movie *Deep Impact* (1998)), or through pure science fiction (the recent American film version of *Godzilla* (1998)). The most popular scenario for the bridge's ruin is the natural erosion of time. In 1873, while the bridge was barely begun, *Appletons' Journal* cast its eye upon New York's future. Should a lonely wanderer stumble upon the city "there might be enough of the piers of the Brooklyn Bridge left for him to sit upon amid the desolation, but it is doubtful whether his eye would be gratified with the sight of a standing column or a wall." Ten years later, Montgomery Schuyler took a similar tack, supposing that "the web of woven steel that now hangs between the stark masses of the towers may have disappeared, its slender filaments rusted into nothingness under the slow corrosion of the centuries. Its builders and the generation for which they wrought may have been as long forgotten as are now the builders of the Pyramids." In his 1889 utopian novel *The Last American*, J.A. Mitchell had the Persian navy sail into a deserted New York harbor in the year 2951. What they find are "two colossal structures, rising high in the air and standing like twin brothers, as if to guard the deserted streets below." As to the origins and purpose of these "two monuments in the river," the Persians haven't got the slightest idea.9

"New Zealanders on the Brooklyn Bridge"

Life, May 25, 1916.

From the author's collection.

Eco-artist Alexis Rockman went much further than Mitchell. Commissioned by the Brooklyn Museum of Art to paint a mural to mark the opening of the museum's new entrance, Rockman delivered *Manifest Destiny* (2002–2004), a massive landscape of the Brooklyn waterfront as it might appear in the year 5004. For those looking for a glimpse of the future, the news, according to Rockman, isn't good. Global warming has caused the East River to rise by 82 feet; toxic barrels of filth float downstream as an impressive panoply of marine life frolics beneath a post-apocalyptic glow. All the achievements of technological progress—underground tunnels, skyscrapers, factories, sports stadiums, the Brooklyn Bridge: all the concrete symbols of America's belief in its own Manifest Destiny—lie in ruins. Nature has mutated, adapted, and survived—flourished even—while humanity has withered and died. Man is the author of this scene, but no longer survives to bear witness to what he has wrought. For Rockman, the endpoint of Manifest Destiny is not the winning of the West but our own ruination.

Alexis Rockman, *Manifest Destiny*, 2002–2004.
© 2007 Alexis Rockman/Artists Rights Society (ARS), New York.

Bombs and Blowtorches

Ironically, perhaps, while Rockman was painting his bedraggled, tumble-down Brooklyn Bridge, a man was plotting to destroy the span. Well, sort of. On June 20, 2003, U.S. Attorney General John Ashcroft announced a great victory for the forces of freedom: that Iyman Faris, a 34-year-old truck driver from Columbus, Ohio, had been arrested several months earlier, held in a secret detention center, denied a lawyer, tried before a closed court, and found guilty of providing "material support" to terrorists. Al Qaeda, it seems, were "deeply interested" in bringing down "the bridge in the *Godzilla* movie" using "gas cutters" (blowtorches) to sever the span's main cables. In Faris, they found a ready ally, and in 2002 the truck driver sallied forth to research the plan. He inquired of an American friend where he might buy a blowtorch and studied the bridge's structural design in an Internet café in Karachi, before deciding that "the weather is too hot." This was Faris's code phrase for "security is too tight," although it might also have meant "this plan is silly."

Many in the U.S. were shocked and stunned by Faris's nefarious plot, and editorials flowed freely about the wonders of the newly created Department of Homeland Security. Conversely, civil rights activists were indignant about the "capture" and secret trial of an American citizen. (Jimmy Breslin likened the incident to "the internment camps of World War II and the practices of the secret police in the 'Old Soviet Union.'") As it turned out, Faris was actually an FBI double-agent, which for some reason didn't stop him from receiving a 20-year jail sentence.[10]

The Brooklyn Bridge, regrettably, is no stranger to bomb scares and terrorist threats. In 1916, hundreds of extra police officers were dispatched to the bridge "to keep a sharp watch against the tossing of an explosive" onto the U.S.S. Washington as it made its way to the Brooklyn Navy Yards. Initially, neither the police department nor the navy would comment on the affair, although it was later discovered that Secretary of the Navy Josephus Daniels had received two letters warning how "some crank or conspirator" might drop "a can of nitroglycerine" down the funnel of the passing warship.[11]

Several months later, America's perceived vulnerability to attack motivated Lloyd Thompson into a bizarre series of stunts. In what he termed a "preparedness lesson," Thompson boarded a plane at Governor's Island, flew to Brooklyn, soared over the bridge, South Ferry, and the Battery, all the while dropping time-fuse bombs designed to exploded harmlessly 1,500 feet over their "targets." Thompson came a cropper at the Woolworth Building, when, after having set the fuse, one of the explosives stubbornly refused to fall. The bomb exploded under Thompson's right wing but didn't bring him down, and he eventually limped back to base.[12]

Bomb threats resurfaced in 1922, when a man purporting to be the infamous Wall Street bomber of 1920 wrote to Brooklyn Borough President Edward Riegelmann to say that he intended to blow up Borough Hall "and kill everyone in the building. May be

Sara K. Schwittek, "World Trade Center Burns
After Being Hit by Plane," 2001
© REUTERS/Sara K. Schwittek.

after I will cut Brooklyn Bridge in two pieces. I love to kill," he added.[13] The man turned out to be a disgruntled but harmless sign painter by the name of Julius Reynolds.

On July 18, 1931, 117 police officers and 60 detectives were sent out to patrol the bridge after the police commissioner received a bomb threat. "Every car passing over the Brooklyn Bridge tomorrow morning at the Brooklyn end is going to be bombed, and there is no maybe about it," warned the saboteur.[14] Nothing came of the threat.

On August 2, 1979, an emergency call was put through to the police department's bomb section, and within minutes agents were rushing off to the Brooklyn Bridge. A "very sophisticated" radio-controlled homemade bomb, housed in a five-gallon paint-can, had been discovered by maintenance workers atop the bridge's Manhattan tower. Experts scaled the bridge, disarmed the bomb, and walked it down one of the main suspender cables. Exactly what it was intended for, and who had put it there, remained a mystery.[15] But not for long.

The following day, SoHo artist John Halpern—who'd been arrested three months earlier for trying to start a fire atop one of the bridge's towers—held a press conference

Peter de Sève, *Trunk Party*, 2004
© Peter de Sève.

to announce that he was responsible for the "bomb." A friend had taken the device up to the tower the night before it was discovered. Halpern had then tried to detonate it, but the tower proved too high and the radio signal too weak. The paint-can, though, was not a bomb, the artist continued, but an "environmental sculpture," an "aesthetic statement" about the state of the U.S. economy. According to Halpern, the device wasn't designed to injure anyone: its potency lay purely it its symbolism.

Not given to aesthetic statements and complex symbolisms, the police clapped Halpern in irons and carted him off to the cells, before releasing him shortly afterwards on bail.[16] Halpern's case dragged on for two years, however, before Manhattan D.A. Robert Morganthau requested that the charges be dropped. Halpern's bomb, it turned out, just wasn't a bomb—the contents of the can were nothing more than fireworks-grade explosives—and no expert would testify otherwise. The issue of whether experts could be found to testify that it was art, unfortunately, was not addressed.

No one has really tried to blow up the bridge, of course, although the subject was studied by the Office of Civil and Defense Mobilization in 1959 at the height of the Cold War ("two large hydrogen bombs dropped near the Brooklyn Bridge on a typical mid-October day," they concluded, "would kill at least 6,098,000 persons in the New York area"). And Faris wouldn't have brought it down either, despite what certain officials were saying; at least, not on his own, and not with a blowtorch. One police official thought the operation "may have saved the Brooklyn Bridge," another that they were "still not sure … whether he really could have accomplished this or not." But this was rubbish. Even at 120 years old, the bridge is a sturdy structure, built to last and with fail-safes. Should any (or all) of its main cables fail, the bridge would stay standing as the weight would be transferred to the diagonal cables that radiate out from the towers. And anyway, it would take over two days of continual work for one man wielding a blowtorch to cut through the four main cables. New Yorkers are certainly notorious for not getting involved in street incidents, preferring to keep their eyes down and their legs moving forward, yet one doubts that Faris could have fired up his blowtorch and sat whittling away at the main cables for two days straight without anyone raising the alarm.[17] Yes, the weather was too hot, but the plan was also very stupid.

The more interesting question concerns Faris's orders: to bring down "the bridge in the *Godzilla* movie." A common complaint these days is that children find their history in films not in books. Well so, it seems, do certain international terrorists. In fact, the whole incident conjures up a bizarre image of deadly international assassins more famil-iar with Hollywood movies than the national landmarks of their most hated foe. Not to mention the question of when, exactly, did the leading lights of Al Qaeda gather around a TV in a cave in Afghanistan to watch Matthew Broderick speeding over the Brooklyn Bridge in a taxi cab with Godzilla in hot pursuit. Bin Laden and his ilk might well hate the United States, but they do seem to watch its movies, which might just represent a bigger victory against international terrorism than catching and jailing Iyman Faris.

Seth Wenig, "Commuters Pack the Brooklyn Bridge," 2005.
© REUTERS/Seth Wenig.

Looking Forward: The Bridge's Future

So where does the bridge go from here? Well, Sheffield, in the north of England apparently. As I write, plans to build a replica of the Brooklyn Bridge across the River Don, about 35 miles south of my hometown, have just been approved by the city council. Running from the Kelham Island Industrial Museum to the Brooklyn Works apartment complex, the pedestrian bridge is designed to commemorate the strong trading links (in the nineteenth century) between the UK's Steel City and the City of Homes and Churches. And to cash in, no doubt, on the bridge's fame and the borough's new-found chic.[18]

As for Brooklyn itself (the American version), plans for Brooklyn Bridge Park continue to work their way through the legislature. With an expected completion date of 2012, the park will extend Empire–Fulton State Park a further mile down the waterfront to Atlantic Avenue, and contain lawns, beaches, playgrounds, and, to the chagrin of many locals, a luxury hotel, and high-end housing. The plan promises to continue the work of the past 30 years, revamping and revitalizing the waterfront, and providing Brooklynites with a fantastic new place to hang out. If, that is, the park doesn't turn into a private playground for wealthy residents or block out the view from the Brooklyn Heights Promenade. Given the current clamor for prime Brooklyn real estate, one can only hope that Brooklyn Bridge Park does indeed turn out to be the Prospect Park of the twenty-first century (as its sponsors maintain), and not a pernicious land-grab.

One also hopes that the Department of Transportation will be true to its own promises. In August 2006, the *New York Sun* ran an article, a series of photographs, and an editorial attacking the city's indolent maintenance program. The Brooklyn Bridge, claimed the *Sun*, was rusting away to the point of "serious deterioration," all-the-while looking uglier and more ramshackle by the day. When reached for comment, the Department of Transportation admitted that the bridge was only in "fair" condition but also that a $236 million renovation project was slated to begin in 2009. The project would see improvements to the bridge's decks, approaches, and ramps, along with a spiffy new paint job.[19] If we are lucky, maybe a shiny new Brooklyn Bridge will await the completion of Brooklyn's gleaming new waterfront park.

One thing is for sure, however: that writers will continue to write of it, artists will continue to make art of it, filmmakers will continue to make films on and around it, and the world will continue to walk over it. Cyclists will no doubt continue to shout at bewildered pedestrians who have unwittingly strayed across the white dividing line and Brooklyn Borough President Marty Markowitz will continue to pop up on the bridge every now and then to preach about the glories of his hometown, and remind us all that the Brooklyn Bridge remains one of New York's great stages, fit for all the world's Barnums and Brodies, a place for pomp, politics, promotion, and pure pleasure. Long may it all happily continue.

Notes

Prologue: Crank, Crackpot, and Creative
Genius—Plans to Bridge the East River
(1800–1867)

1. Quoted in Edwin G. Burrows and Mike Wallace,
    Gotham: A History of New York City to 1898 (New York:
    Oxford University Press, 1999), 419–422.

2. See Henry R. Stiles, "Brooklyn Ferries and Ferry
    Rights," in *The Civil, Political, Professional and Ecclesias-
    tical History, and Commercial and Industrial Record of the
    County of Kings and the City of Brooklyn, New York from
    1683 to 1884*, 2 vols., ed. Henry R. Stiles (New York:
    Munsell, 1884), I: 425–446.

3. Quoted in Henry Stiles, *A History of the City of Brooklyn,
    Including the Old Town and Village of Brooklyn, the Town
    of Bushwick, and the Village and City of Williamsburgh*, 3
    vols. (1867–70; Bowie, MD: Heritage Books, 1993),
    II: 383–384.

4. *New-York Evening Post*, February 18, 1802: 2.

5. *Daily Advertiser*, February 19, 1802: 3.

6. *Mercantile Advertiser*, February 19, 1802: 2.

7. See *Daily Advertiser*, February 20, 1802: 2; February
    22, 1802: 3; February 23, 1802: 2; March 15, 1802:
    2. Also see *Daily Advertiser*, March 10, 1802: 2 and
    March 12, 1802: 2.

8. For information on Stevens's plans to lay a two-way
    vehicular tunnel on (not under) the Hudson river bed,
    and for further details about his bridge proposals see
    Archibald Douglas Turnbull, *John Stevens: An American
    Record* (New York: Century, 1928), 216–225.

9. See *Journal of the Senate of the State of New York*, 30th
    Session, 1807, 62, 75.

10. The petition was published in the *American Citizen*, the
    Public Advertiser, the New York *Evening Post*, the *Albany
    Register* and the *Albany Gazette* and ran, at the behest
    of the state Senate, for two months. Also see *New
    York Gazette and General Advertiser*, January 16, 1808:
    2; *American Citizen*, January 27, 1808: 3; *Public Adver-
    tiser*, January 28, 1808: 2. For a general summary
    of the opposition, see Turnbull, 219–222. A Citizen
    expounded on the "ruinous consequences" of "land
    speculation" at great length in a further letter: "Does
    not this present proposition of erecting bridges over
    the north [Hudson] and east rivers smell strongly of
    land speculation? Are not the few men, who are most
    assiduous, and who have left no stone unturned, to
    effect the purpose, the sole proprietors of the land
    upon which the abutments are to be raised?" Unfor-
    tunately, the answer was yes: Stevens owned most of
    Hoboken. See the *Public Advertiser*, February 6, 1808:
    2. Also, see *Journal of the Senate of the State of New York*,
    31st Session, 1808, 26, 33–34, 49.

11. John Q. Wilson quoted in Alice Crary Sutcliffe, *Robert
    Fulton and the "Clermont"* (New York: Century, 1909),
    247.

12. See *Evening Post*, April 29, 1807: 2. Shortly after
    his open letter, Pope took out space in numerous
    newspapers to advertise his bridge. See *Mercantile
    Advertiser*, June 16, 1807: 1, for example. See I.N.
    Phelps Stokes, *The Iconography of New-York Island,
    1498–1909*, 6 vols. (New York: Robert H. Dodd,
    1915), V: 1506. The most interesting assessment of
    Pope's book, and in many respects its most generous,
    remains Alan Trachtenberg, *Brooklyn Bridge: Fact and
    Symbol*, 2nd edition (Chicago: University of Chicago
    Press, 1979), 24–29.

13. Pope's book appears to have generated only a single
    review, a thoroughly hostile rebuke printed in *The

General Repository and Review. After rubbishing the entire treatise, the reviewer concluded with a stinging reference to Pope's poetry: "for ourselves we set about as high a value on his inventive powers in poetry as in bridge building." See *The General Repository and Review*, 2:1 (July 1812), 141–163.

14. See Thomas Pope, *A Treatise on Bridge Architecture* (New York: A. Niven, 1811), frontispiece and 281.

15. See *Aurora and General Advertiser*, February 10, 1812: 1 and February 14, 1812: 2.

16. See Charles Barnard, "The Brooklyn Bridge," *St. Nicholas*, 10:9 (July 1883), 699–700 and www.smallspiralnotebook.com/interviews/2006/09/aaron_hamburger_interviews_emi.shtml

17. Brian J. Cudahy, *Over and Back: The History of Ferryboats in New York Harbor* (New York: Fordham University Press, 1990), 34–37. As late as 1829, the *New-York Mirror* could write: in a "former period, the scheme [to bridge the East River] seemed connected with some semblance of propriety, inasmuch as there was very frequent delay and difficulty, and sometimes serious danger, in crossing the river. Since the establishment of steamboats, this objection has been completely removed. A passage is now effected in much less time than it could be on foot over a bridge." See *New-York Mirror*, November 14, 1829: 7.

18. *New-York American*, August 22, 1825: 2.

19. *New-York Gazette and General Advertiser*, August 24, 1825: 3.

20. See L.T.C. Rolt, *Isambard Kingdom Brunel: A Biography* (1957; London: Book Club Associates, 1972), 20–37; *Brooklyn Daily Advertiser*, January 22, 1846: 3; Nathaniel Hawthorne, "Up the Thames," *The Atlantic Monthly*, 11:7 (May 1863), 599–602. Visiting London during the American Civil War, Hawthorne himself raised the issue of a tunnel beneath the Hudson River as a somewhat lighthearted yet surprisingly vicious solution to ongoing conflict: "Could I have looked forward a few years, I might have regretted that American enterprise had not provided a similar tunnel, under the Hudson . . . It would be delightful to clap up all the enemies of our peace and Union in the dark together, and . . . when the turmoil shall be all over, the Wrong washed away in blood (since that must needs be the cleansing fluid), and the Right firmly rooted in the soil which that blood will have enriched, they might crawl forth again and catch a single glimpse at their redeemed country, and feel it to be a better land than they deserve, and die!" See ibid., 602.

21. *Long-Island Star*, October 27, 1849, quoted in Jacob Judd, "The History of Brooklyn, 1834–1855: Political and Administrative Aspects" (PhD Dissertation, New York University, 1959), 188.

22. See "Sendzimir's Submarine Thoroughfare" *Scientific American*, April 4, 1857: 233 and "Holcomb's Submarine Carriage Way," *Scientific American*, June 6, 1857: 305. Both Sendzimir's and Holcomb's plans were revived and reprinted a decade later by *Scientific American* in response to both the Brooklyn Bridge and the construction of the Whitehall Pneumatic Tube Railway across the Thames in London. For the magazine's editors, Roebling's bridge was too expensive and too injurious to the surrounding area (the approaches would stretch deep into both cities, obliterating many houses and businesses), whereas a tunnel, built on the "submerged" principle, would prove both cheap and convenient. Unfortunately, *Scientific American* had too much faith in the British. London's pneumatic tube was abandoned a year later. See "Crossing the East River," *Scientific American*, June 22, 1867: 396. Two subsequent proposals were also issued in the late 1850s. See "Becker's Plan for Connecting New York and Brooklyn," *Scientific American*, June 26, 1858: 336 and *American Railroad Times*, February 19, 1859: 2.

23. *New-York Gazette & General Advertiser*, November 5, 1829: 2.

24. *New-York Mirror*, November 14, 1829: 7. The *Saturday Evening Post* was also virulently against the scheme. See *Saturday Evening Post*, November 14, 1829: 1.

25. *Long-Island Star*, February 13, 1834 quoted in David McCullough, *The Great Bridge: The Epic Story of the Building of the Brooklyn Bridge* (New York: Simon and Schuster, 1972), 113 and *Long-Island Star*, November 5, 1835 quoted in Judd, "The History of Brooklyn," 188.

26. See *American Railroad Journal*, January 10, 1835: 4–5 and January 17, 1835: 19–20.

27. See Hamilton Schuyler, *The Roeblings: A Century of Engineers, Bridge-Builders and Industrialists* (Princeton: Princeton University Press, 1931), 131; Harold Coffin Syrett, *The City of Brooklyn, 1865–1898: A Political History* (New York: Columbia University Press, 1944), 146; *The Family Magazine*, May 1, 1838: 41–3.

28. See Benjamin Latrobe, "Report and Estimate on the New York–Long Island Bridge," in *Benjamin Henry Latrobe* by Talbot Hamlin (New York: Oxford University Press, 1955), 578–582. Latrobe's report reached the following conclusions: first, that such a bridge was structurally feasible; second, that no municipal government or private organization would be able to afford it.

29. See *New York Tribune*, November 3, 1849: 2 and November 10, 1849: 2. Unfortunately, Ellet's stock as a bridge-builder would fall over the next five years: he lost his contract to construct the Niagara

Gorge Bridge in December 1848 and, on May 16, 1854, his beloved Wheeling Bridge was swept away by a storm.

30. Walt Whitman, "Letters From a Travelling Bachelor, Number X," *New York Sunday Dispatch*, December 23, 1849 reprinted in Joseph Jay Rubin, *The Historic Whitman* (University Park: Pennsylvania State University Press, 1973), 347–352.

31. See Judd, "The History of Brooklyn," 189.

32. John A. Roebling, "Memoir of the Niagara Falls Suspension and Niagara Falls International Bridge," in *Papers and Practical Illustrations of Public Works of Recent Construction, Both British and American* (London: John Weale, 1856), 3.

33. See Roebling Collection, Rensselaer Polytechnic Institute, Box 6, Blackwell's Island Bridge (1856–57) Folder.

34. Quoted in McCullough, *The Great Bridge*, 24.

35. See John A. Roebling, "Bridge Over the East River Between New-York and Brooklyn," New York *Tribune*, March 27, 1857: 5.

36. *Circular*, March 5, 1857: 27.

37. See *Architects' and Mechanics' Journal*, March 31, 1860: 5 and April 14, 1860: 13–14.

38. See "Proposed American Suspension Bridge," *The Engineer*, February 19, 1864: 107.

39. The fullest account of the machinations behind the creation of the bridge is McCullough, *The Great Bridge*, 122–143.

40. See *Scientific America*, December 20, 1856: 120; *Brooklyn Daily Eagle*, January 28, 1867: 2; *Annual Report of the American Institute of the City of New York, for the Year 1866–67* (Albany: Van Benthuysen, 1867), 893–907; Barbara Head Millstein, "Crossing the River: The Alternatives," in *The Great East River Bridge, 1883–1983* (New York: Harry H. Abrams, 1983), 146; *Brooklyn Daily Union*, January 7, 1869: 2.

41. McCullough, *The Great Bridge*, 120.

42. John A. Roebling, *Report of John A. Roebling, C.E., to the President and Directors of the New York Bridge Company on the Proposed East River Bridge* (Brooklyn: Daily Eagle Print, 1867), 3–4.

Chapter One: Construction, Completion, and Panic (1867–1883)

1. See Washington A. Roebling, "Life of John A. Roebling, C.E., By His Oldest Son Washington A. Roebling" (1897–1907) MS, Roebling Collection, Rutgers University, 45. Also see Donald Sayenga, "Pittsburg Aquaduct: Reconstruction of the Pittsburg Aquaduct by John A. Roebling," *Canal History and Proceedings*, XIV (1995), 75–6.

2. See *The Railway Times*, July 31, 1869: 243.

3. See Washington A. Roebling, "Life of John A. Roebling, C.E.," 278–280.

4. See ibid. and McCullough, *The Great Bridge*, 93.

5. See *Brooklyn Daily Eagle*, July 8, 1869: 2 and July 23, 1869: 3.

6. See *Brooklyn Daily Eagle*, July 22, 1869: 2 and *New-York and Brooklyn Bridge: Proceedings, 1867–1884* (Brooklyn: n.p., 1885), 327–328.

7. See *Scientific American*, November 12, 1870: 307. Also see *Frank Leslie's Illustrated Newspaper*, October, 15, 1870: 77; *New York Commercial Advertiser*, May 29, 1872: 3.

8. See *Harper's Weekly*, March 19, 1870: 181; *Railway Times*, May 7, 1870: 148; *Scientific American*, July 9, 1870: 15–6; Thomas W. Knox, *Underground; or, Life Below the Surface* (Hartford, CT: J.B. Burr Publishing, 1875), 416–425.

9. See Washington A. Roebling, "The East River Bridge: Chief Engineer's Report," *Railway Times*, August 3, 1872: 243.

10. E.F. Farrington, *Concise Description of the East River Bridge* (New York: C.D. Wynkoop, 1881), 17.

11. *Railway Times*, October 15, 1870: 335.

12. *Harper's Weekly*, December 17, 1870: 812.

13. See *Youth's Companion*, August 29, 1872: 279; *Scientific American*, November 2, 1872: 272; *Brooklyn Daily Eagle*, May 3, 1872: 4.

14. Washington A. Roebling, "The East River Bridge: Chief Engineer's Report," *Railway Times*, August 10, 1872: 253.

15. Ibid., 252–253.

16. *Boston Daily Globe*, September 23, 1882: 4.

17. *New York Times*, July 8, 1871: 1.

18. See "The Rink Committee—Address to the Citizens," in *New York Times*, November 30, 1871: 2.

19. See *New York Times*, April 10, 1872: 2; *Brooklyn Daily Eagle*, April 10, 1872: 2.

20. *Brooklyn Daily Eagle*, April 10, 1872: 2. As it turns out, this agreement also included the stipulation that Kingsley be paid $130,000 for some of his stock. See *New-York and Brooklyn Bridge: Proceedings, 1867–1884*, 109.

21. *Brooklyn Daily Eagle*, April 13, 1872: 5; April 16, 1872: 2; April 25, 1872: 4.

22. See *Frank Leslie's Illustrated Weekly*, July 5, 1873.

23. The *New York Times* reprinted much of Tweed's testimony in full. See September 19, 1877: 1; September 22, 1877: 1 and 4; October 7, 1877: 1–2.

24. See *New York Times*, September 19, 1877: 1 and October 7, 1877: 2.

25. *New York Times*, October 7, 1877: 2.

26. *New York Times*, September 19, 1877: 1.

27. Walt Whitman, "Manhattan from the Bay," in *Specimen Days & Collect* (1883: New York: Dover, 1995), 116.

28. See *New York Herald*, August 15, 1876: 2; *New York Tribune*, August 15, 1876: 2; *New York Times*, August 15, 1876: 1.

29. Farrington, *Concise Description of the East River Bridge*, 36.

30. *Brooklyn Daily Eagle*, August 28, 1876: 4.

31. *New York Times*, August 27, 1876: 1.

32. See Ernest Poole, "Cowboys of the Sky," *Everybody's Magazine*, 19:19 (November 1908), 641–653. Poole coined the phrase to describe the construction workers who helped build New York's early twentieth-century skyscrapers, the "rough pioneers … pushing each year their frontier line up towards the clouds."

33. *New York Tribune*, August 28, 1876: 2.

34. All quotes from the *New York Times*, June 15, 1878: 8. Also see *New York Herald*, June 15, 1878: 2 and *New York World*, June 16, 1878: 4.

35. See *New York Times*, June 15, 1878: 8; Farrington, *Concise Description of the East River Bridge*, 48.

36. See *New-York and Brooklyn Bridge: Proceedings, 1867–1884*, 132–138.

37. Hewitt's role in the wire fraud is fully documented in Trachtenberg, *The Brooklyn Bridge: Fact and Symbol*, 104–109. For a broad, although somewhat biased, overview of the history of the scandals that plagued the bridge's construction see *New York World*, September 18 through September 25, 1882.

38. Henry Adams, *The Education of Henry Adams* (1918: Harmondsworth, UK: Penguin, 1995), 282.

39. See David McCullough, *The Great Bridge*, 443–446; *New York Times*, January 6, 1880: 8 and April 1, 1893: 8.

40. *Brooklyn Union*, January 18, 1877: 2. For further rumors see *New York Sun*, July 31, 1882: 2.

41. Emily Warren Roebling to John A. Roebling II, June 20, 1898, Roebling Collection, Special Collections and Archives, Rensselaer Polytechnic Institute. Also see Marilyn E. Weigold, *Silent Builder: Emily Warren Roebling and the Brooklyn Bridge* (Port Washington, NY: Associated Faculty Press, 1984).

42. *Report of the Special Committee of the Common Council of the City of Brooklyn upon the Celebration of the Opening of the New York and Brooklyn Bridge* (Brooklyn: Eagle Book and Job Printing, 1883), 4.

43. William Glazier, *Peculiarities of American Cities* (Philadelphia, 1886), 315.

44. *Opening Ceremonies of the New York and Brooklyn Bridge, May 24, 1883* (Brooklyn: Brooklyn Eagle Job Printing, 1883), 53, 89, 91.

45. See ibid., 45; *The W.P.A. Guide to New York City: The Federal Writers' Project Guide to 1930s New York* (1939: New York: Pantheon Books, 1982), 441; "Crossing the River," *Scientific American*, June 22, 1857: 396.

46. Joseph Mitchell, "Up in the Old Hotel," in *The Bottom of the Harbor* (London: Jonathan Cape (2000)), 33.

47. Farrington, *Concise Description of the East River Bridge*, 62.

48. See *New York Herald*, May 26, 1883: 3 and May 28, 1883: 5; *New York Sun*, May 26, 1883: 3.

49. See *The Daily Graphic*, May 31, 1883: 630; *Puck*, July 4, 1883: 285.

50. See *New York Tribune*, June 1, 1883: 1; *New York Times*, May 31, 1883: 1 and June 1, 1883: 4.

51. *Brooklyn Daily Eagle*, May 31, 1883: 1.

52. *National Police Gazette*, June 16, 1883: 6.

53. *Brooklyn Daily Eagle*, May 31, 1883: 1; *National Police Gazette*, June 16, 1883: 6.

54. See *New York Times*, June 5, 1883: 8; *Brooklyn Daily Eagle*, June 2, 1883: 2 and June 5, 1883: 1, 2.

Chapter Two: Spectacle and Show (1883–1911)

1. See *National Police Gazette*, June 23, 1883: 7, 13; December 29, 1883: 8; May 3, 1884: 12; February 14, 1885: 1; May 19, 1883: 8; May 26, 1883: 8; May 11, 1895: 1–2. In nineteenth-century slang, a "masher" was a man who forced himself on women.

2. *Brooklyn Daily Eagle*, May 18, 1884: 12.

3. *New York Times*, May 18, 1884: 2.

4. Barnum never admitted this, of course; instead passing off his stunt as an attempt to put to rest any "lurking suspicion[s] … as to the vaunted solidity of the big bridge." See *Iron Age*, May 22, 1884: 23.

5. *Brooklyn Daily Eagle*, October 10, 1877: 2.

6. *Puck*, June 5, 1878: 10.

7. *National Police Gazette*, December 17, 1881: 2.

8. *Brooklyn Daily Eagle*, July 20, 1883: 4.

9. *National Police Gazette*, May 6, 1882: 14.

10. *New York Times*, June 1, 1882: 8.

11. *Brooklyn Daily Eagle*, May 17, 1885: 16.

12. Events surrounding Odlum's leap are drawn from *New York Times*, May 20, 1885: 1 and May 21, 1885: 2; William Inglis, "On the Story: Random Notes from the Notebook of a New York Newspaper Reporter; Robert Emmet Odlum, Who Jumped into Oblivion," *Harper's Weekly*, June 10, 1911: 9.

13. Ibid.: 9.

14. Boyton was an inventor and an adventurer. He fought in the Mexican Revolution, the American Civil War (1864), the Franco–Prussian War (1870–71) and the Peru–Chile War (1881). He was the first man to swim the English Channel in 1875, although not unassisted. He is mainly remembered for inventing a strange rubber swimming suit. Made of vulcanized rubber, the all-over body suit had numerous internal compartments that, when filled with air, allowed the wearer to float for long periods of time. Armed with a canoe paddle, Boyton spent many years propelling himself in his suit around the waterways of America

and Europe in an effort to attract investors. He even spent some time trying to persuade Mark Twain to publish a memoir of his travels. He eventually acquired the nickname "the fearless frogman."

15. *New York Times*, May 22, 1885: 4.

16. See Catherine Odlum, *The Life and Adventures of Prof. Robert Emmet Odlum* (Washington, DC: Gray & Clarkson, 1885); *New York Times*, May 20, 1885: 1.

17. "Picturesque People: Steve Brodie," *Peterson Magazine*, 10:8 (August 1895), 857.

18. Charles Dickens, *American Notes for General Circulation*, eds. Arnold Goldman and John Whitley (1842; Harmondworth, UK: Penguin, 1985), 136.

19. "Out Among the Bootblacks," *New York Times*, August 17, 1879: 5.

20. Alvin F. Harlow, *Old Bowery Days: The Chronicle of a Famous Street* (New York: A. Appleton & Co, 1931), 417.

21. See *Boston Advertiser*, June 1, 1885: 2.

22. *Paterson Daily Press*, May 20, 1885, quoted in Paul E. Johnson, *Sam Patch, the Famous Jumper* (New York: Hill & Wang, 2003), 55.

23. Luc Sante, *Low Life: Lures and Snares of Old New York* (New York: Farrar Straus Giroux, 1991), 122.

24. "It Was Not Brodie After All," *New York Times*, September 30, 1888: 16.

25. *Chicago Daily Tribune*, September 10, 1889: 8.

26. See Sante, *Low Life*, 123 and "A Leap from the Bridge," *New York Times*, July 24, 1886: 1.

27. See John Hanners, "The Man Who Jumped off the Brooklyn Bridge: Steve Brodie (1858–1901) and the Public/Private Persona," *Mid-Atlantic Almanac*, 1:5 (1995), 88–95.

28. Alvin Harlow, *Old Bowery Days*, 419–420.

29. See ibid., 424.

30. *Kelly* opened on Broadway on February 7, 1965 and closed after a single performance. It cost $650,000 to produce. See *New York Times*, February 8, 1965: 28 and February 9, 1965: 42.

31. "Brodie's Rival," *Brooklyn Daily Eagle*, August 28, 1886: 4.

32. See *New York Times*, October 21, 1886: 1; November 9, 1886: 1; January 28, 1887: 1; February 19, 1887: 7; August 8, 1888: 5.

33. *New York Herald*, April 28, 1887: 3; *National Police Gazette*, August 20, 1887: 3; *Brooklyn Daily Eagle*, April 24, 1889: 6; *New York Times*, June 19, 1893: 1.

34. *Brooklyn Daily Eagle*, August 30, 1895: 1.

35. See *New York Tribune*, September 8, 1895: 2.

36. See Montgomery Schuyler, "The Bridge as a Monument," *Harper's Weekly*, May 26, 1883: 326.

37. See John A. Roebling, *Report of John A. Roebling, C.E., to the President and Directors of the New York Bridge Company, on the Proposed East River Bridge* (Brooklyn: Daily Eagle Print, 1867), 18, 45.

38. *Brooklyn Daily Eagle*, May 21, 1883: 2.

39. See McCullough, *The Great Bridge*, 545; *New York Times*, May 25, 1889: 8.

40. *New York Times*, June 27, 1883: 5.

41. *New York Times*, December 6, 1885: 1 and December 21, 1889: 1.

42. *New York Journal and Advertiser*, August 5, 1898: 1; *Harper's Weekly*, August 3, 1901: 779.

43. See "Brooklyn Bridge Observatories," *Frank Leslie's Illustrated Newspaper*, January 30, 1886: 396.

44. *New York Times*, October 2, 1889: 8.

45. "To Improve the Great Brooklyn Bridge," *Harper's Weekly*, March 25, 1893: 275; "New Plans to Prevent Overcrowding at the Brooklyn Bridge During Rush Hour," *Harper's Weekly*, September 23, 1905: 1378–9; "A Study of the Brooklyn Bridge Problem," *Scientific American*, March 18, 1905: 222.

46. *Harper's Weekly*, March 2, 1907: 308; "Brooklyn Planning Section," *Brooklyn Daily Eagle*, April 12, 1912.

47. *New York Times*, September 10, 1889: 2.

48. *Maritime Reporter*, April 10, 1886: 34.

49. *New York Times*, October 11, 1892: 3.

50. *New York Times*, September 26, 1909: 1; *Harper's Weekly*, October 2, 1909: 10.

Chapter Three: Modernism Takes Command (1912–1929)

1. Henry James, *The American Scene*, ed. John F. Sears (1907: New York: Penguin, 1994), 60.

2. Ibid., 11 and 61.

3. Ibid., 59–61.

4. H.G. Wells, *The Future in America: A Search After Realities* (1906: London: Granville Press, 1987), 27–29.

5. Ibid., 28–30.

6. See *Henry James and H.G. Wells: A Record of their Friendship, their Debate on the Art of Fiction, and their Quarrel*, eds. Leon Edel and Gordon N. Ray (London: Rupert Hart-Davis, 1958), 113–117.

7. See *Alvin Langdon Coburn and H.G. Wells: The Photographer and the Novelist* (Urbana–Champaign, IL: Krannert Art Museum at the University of Illinois, 1997).

8. See Mike Weaver, *Alvin Langdon Coburn, Symbolist Photographer, 1882–1966: Beyond the Craft* (New York: Aperture Foundation, 1986), 6–18.

9. Alvin Langdon Coburn, "Artists of the Lens: The International Exhibition of Pictorial Photography in Buffalo," *Harper's Weekly*, November 26, 1910: 11.

10. David E. Nye, *American Technological Sublime* (Cambridge, MA: MIT Press, 1994), 87.

11. See Bonnie Yochelson, "Karl Struss' New York," in *New York to Hollywood: The Photography of Karl Struss*, by

Barbara McCandless, Bonnie Yochelson and Richard Koszarski (Albuquerque: University of New Mexico Press, 1995), 91–92.

12. Jonathan Lethem, *Fortress of Solitude* (New York: Doubleday, 2003), 78.

13. Quoted in Sheldon Reich, "John Marin: Paintings of New York, 1912," *The American Art Journal*, 1:1 (1969), 43. As Ruth Fine notes, Marin's "subject … is energy, not atmosphere." See Ruth E. Fine, *John Marin* (New York: Abbeville Press, 1990), 129.

14. Max Weber, "On the Brooklyn Bridge," in *Max Weber: The Cubist Decade, 1910–1920* (Atlanta, GA: High Museum of Art, 1991), 96.

15. *James Daugherty Newsletter*, 6 (December 2000), 1–2; Robert W. Snyder and Rebecca Zurier, "Picturing the City," in *Metropolitan Lives: The Ashcan Artists and Their New York*, by Rebecca Zurier, Robert W. Snyder and Virginia M. Mecklenburg (New York: Norton, 1995), 85.

16. Joseph Stella, "New York," in Barbara Haskell, *Joseph Stella* (New York: Harry Abrams, 1994), 219. On the contradictions inherent in Stella's painting of the bridge see Richard Haw, *The Brooklyn Bridge: A Cultural History* (New Brunswick, NJ: Rutgers University Press, 2005), 75–82.

17. Alan Trachtenberg, "Cultural Revisions in the Twenties: Brooklyn Bridge as 'Usable Past,'" in *The American Self: Myth, Ideology, and Popular Culture*, ed. Sam B. Girgus (Albuquerque: University of New Mexico Press, 1981), 64–68.

18. Lola Ridge, "Brooklyn Bridge," in *The Ghetto and Other Poems* (New York: B.W. Huebsch, 1918), 87.

19. Charles Reznikoff, *Rhythms* (New York: Charles Reznikoff, 1918), 15.

20. Waldo Frank, *The Unwelcome Man* (Boston: Little, Brown, 1917), 168–169.

21. See Joseph Stella, "The Brooklyn Bridge (a page of my life)," in Haskell, *Joseph Stella*, 206–207.

22. See Neil Cornwell, "Introduction," in Vladimir Mayakovsky, *My Discovery of America*, trans. Neil Cornwell (London: Hesperus Press, 2005), xiii.

23. See Peter Conrad, *The Art of the City: Views and Versions of New York* (New York: Oxford University Press, 1984), 223–225.

24. Colum McCann, "Foreword," in Mayakovsky, *My Discovery of America*, vii.

25. Thomas Wolfe, "No Door," in *The Complete Short Stories of Thomas Wolfe*, ed. Francis E. Skipp (New York: Collier, 1987), 69.

26. John Dos Passos, *Manhattan Transfer* (1925: Harmondsworth, UK: Penguin, 1986), 118–119.

27. Ibid., 119.

28. Benjamin De Casseres, *Mirrors of New York* (New York: Joseph Lawren, 1925), 218–221.

Chapter Four: Depression and Recovery (1929–1945)

1. See Carl Good, "A Chronicle of the Poetic Non-Encounter in the Americas," *CR: The New Centennial Review*, 3:1 (Spring 2003), 225–255.

2. Federico García Lorca "Lecture: A Poet in New York," in Federico García Lorca, *Poet in New York*, ed. Christopher Maurer, trans. Greg Simon and Steven F. White (Harmondsworth, UK: Penguin, 1989), 190.

3. *O My Land, My Friends: The Selected Letters of Hart Crane*, eds. Langdon Hammer and Brom Weber (New York: Four Walls Eight Windows, 1997), 131.

4. Ibid., 258–259.

5. See Trachtenberg, *Brooklyn Bridge: Fact and Symbol*, 167–70.

6. Lorca, *Poet in New York*, 11, 73, 131, 161.

7. See Lorca, "Sleepless City (Brooklyn Bridge Nocturne)," in *Poet in New York*, 67–71; Conrad Aiken, "The Poet in New York and Other Poems," *The New Republic*, 103 (1940), 309.

8. See Henry Miller, "The Brooklyn Bridge," in Henry Miller *The Cosmological Eye* (1939: New York: New Directions, 1961), 346–356.

9. Van Wyck Brooks, "On Creating a Usable Past," in *Van Wyck Brooks: The Early Years*, ed. Claire Sprague (1968: Boston: Northeastern University Press, 1993), 219–220. On Whitman and the bridge see Richard Haw, "American History/American Memory: Reevaluating Walt Whitman's Relationship to the Brooklyn Bridge," *Journal of American Studies*, 39 (2004), 1–22.

10. Alfred Kazin, *A Walker in the City* (1951: New York: Harcourt, Brace, Jovanovich, 1979), 105–108.

11. See Charles Baudelaire, "Crowds," in *Baudelaire, Vol II: The Poems in Prose and La Fanfarlo*, ed. and trans. Francis Scarfe (London: Anvil Press, 1989), 59.

12. See Trachtenberg, *Brooklyn Bridge: Fact and Symbol*, 185–193; Gordon K. Grigsby, "The Photographs in the First Edition of *The Bridge*," *Texas Studies in Language and Literature* 4 (1962), 4–11.

13. *Walker Evans at Work* (London: Thames and Hudson, 1984), 42. This volume reprints most of Evans's photographs of the Brooklyn Bridge.

14. On New Deal art see Marlene Park and Gerald E. Markowitz, *New Deal for Art: The Government Art Projects of the 1930s with Examples from New York City and State* (Hamilton, NY: Gallery Association of New York State, 1977); Richard D. McKinzie, *The New Deal for Artists* (Princeton, NJ: Princeton University Press, 1973).

15. Thomas Hart Benton, *An Artist in America* (1937: Kansas City, MO: University of Kansas City Press, 1951), 316; William Stott, *Documentary Expression and Thirties America* (Chicago, IL: University of Chicago Press, 1973 (1986)).

16. McKinzie, *The New Deal for Artists*, 93.

17. Quoted in Peter Conrad, *The Art of the City*, 130.

18. See Bonnie Yochelson, *Berenice Abbott: Changing New York, The Complete WPA Project* (New York: The Museum of the City of New York, 1997).

19. See *New York Times*, December 22, 1934: 14; March 4, 1953: 19; August 14, 1935: 2.

20. See *New York Times*, March 6, 1944: 21; June 5, 1944: 21.

21. See McKinzie, *The New Deal for Artists*, 124.

22. See Rebecca E. Lawton, *Heroic America: James Dougherty's Mural Drawings from the 1930s* (Poughkeepsie, NY: The Frances Lehman Loeb Art Center, Vassar College, 1998), 38–40.

23. Alexander Alland, "Approach to Manhattan," Art Commission of the City of New York, Archives, 1554 CJ.

24. See Bonnie Yochelson, *The Committed Eye: Alexander Alland's Photographs* (New York: Museum of the City of New York, 1991), 6–7.

25. See Park and Markowitz, *New Deal for Art*, 51–52 and www.columbia.edu/cu/iraas/wpa/murals/pursuit.html

26. The most complete history of the Brooklyn Borough Hall murals is Leonard Benardo and Jennifer Weiss, "The Other Battle of Brooklyn," *New York Times*, April 9, 2006, XIV: 1, 8.

27. John von Hartz, "Introduction," in Andreas Feininger, *New York in the Forties* (New York: Dover, 1978), 2.

28. See Miles Orvell, "Weegee's Voyeurism and Mastery of Urban Disorder," in *After the Machine: Visual Arts and the Erasing of Cultural Boundaries* by Miles Orvell (Jackson, MS: University of Mississippi Press, 1995), 71–96.

29. See *New York Times*, July 19, 1931: 6; June 24, 1932: 21; October 18, 1934: 4; November 4, 1934: N6; October 12, 1935: 36; July 24, 1937: 3.

Chapter Five: Evolution and Explosion (1946–1982)

1. See Steven W. Plattner, *Roy Stryker: U.S.A., 1943–1950* (Austin: University of Texas Press, 1983), 11–25.

2. Ernest Poole, *The Harbor* (New York: Thomas Nelson, 1915), 13–15.

3. See Arthur Leipzig, *Growing Up in New York* (Boston: David R. Godine, 1995), no pagination.

4. Alfred Kazin, *Writing Was Everything* (Cambridge, MA: Harvard University Press, 1995), 119.

5. See Alfred Kazin and Henri Cartier-Bresson, "Brooklyn Bridge," *Harper's Bazaar*, 79 (1946), 397.

6. www.magnumphotos.com/Archive/C.aspx?VP=XSpecific_MAG.Biography_VPage&AID=2K7O3R13Z6VT

7. See Margaret Sartor and Geoff Dyer eds., *What Was True: The Photographs and Notebooks of William Gedney* (New York: W.W. Norton, 2000). Gedney's photo archive can be accessed at: scriptorium.lib.duke.edu/gedney/

8. Le Corbusier, *When the Cathedrals Were White*, trans. Francis E. Hyslop, Jr. (1947: New York: McGraw-Hill, 1964), 76–78.

9. Andrei Voznesenski, "New York Airport at Night," in *Antiworlds and The Fifth Ace*, eds. Patricia Blake and Max Hayward, trans. William Jay Smith (New York: Basic Books, 1966), 149.

10. Robert A. Ward, "Removing East River Bridges," *New York Times*, August 25, 1953: 20.

11. Frederick H. Zurmuhlen, "Cost of River Tunnels Estimated," *New York Times*, September 1, 1953: 22.

12. "Artist-in-Bridges to Realize Dream by Modernizing Old Brooklyn Span," *New York Times*, September 20, 1948: 27.

13. See Alfred Albelli, "Is the Brooklyn Bridge Falling Down?" *Modern Mechanix and Inventions*, 14:2 (June 1935), 64–65, 130.

14. "Brooklyn Bridge Plan Condemned as Ruining Beauty of Silhouette," *New York Times*, August 15, 1949: 19.

15. "Art Examination of Bridge Curbed," *New York Times*, November 15, 1949: 27.

16. See "What Happened to Brooklyn Bridge," *Architectural Forum* 102 (1955), 122–124, 76, 180, 184; Pete Coutros, "Suspended Animation: Brooklyn Bridge Will be 75 Years Old on Saturday but She Wears the Span of Years Well," *Sunday News*, May 18, 1958: 11; Alfred Kazin and David Finn, *Our New York: A Personal Vision in Words and Pictures* (New York: Harper & Row, 1989), 84.

17. See John Belle and Maxinne Rhea Leighton, *Grand Central: Gateway to a Million Lives* (New York: W.W. Norton, 1999), 3.

18. See Landmarks Preservation Commission, August 24, 1967, No. 1, LP–0098.

19. See *Brooklyn Bridge Bulletin*, 3 (May 1983), 24–25 and 4 (March 1984), 5; *Bowery Billy's Runabout Race; or, The Brigands of Brooklyn Bridge* (New York: Winner Library Co., 1906); "Found in the River; or, The Bradys and the Brooklyn Bridge Mystery," *Secret Service*, May 29, 1914: 1–18.

20. See *Whiz Comics*, 108 (April 1949); "For Sale ... The Brooklyn Bridge," *Real Clue Crime Stories*, 4:2 (April 1949), no pagination.

21. See *Batman*, 39: 298 (April 1978), 1–2; *Captain America*, 247 (July 1980), 1–2.

22. See *The Amazing Spider-Man*, 13 (June 1964); *The Amazing Spider-Man*, 121 (June 1973); *Ultimate War*, 1:1 (February 2003); *DMZ*, 11 (November 2006).

23. See *Avalanche*, 2 (Fall 1971) and 3 (Winter 1971), no pagination; Judd Tully, *Red Grooms and Ruckus Manhattan* (New York: George Braziller, 1977).

24. See Allen Ginsberg, "Howl," "Waking in New York," "Today," and "Hospital Window" in *Collected Poems, 1947–1980* (New York: Harper & Row, 1984), 126–127, 129, 339–342, 345–347, 634; Jack Kerouac, "Hymn," in *Poems All Sizes* (San Francisco: City Lights, 1992), 151–152 and "The Brooklyn Bridge Blues," *Kerouac—Kicks Joy Darkness*, Rykodisc RCD 10329; Lawrence Ferlinghetti, "#89," in *A Far Rockaway of the Heart* (New York: New Directions, 1997), 107; Gregory Corso, "The Last Warmth of Arnold," in *Gasoline* (San Francisco: City Lights, 1958), 20–21; Edwin Morgan, "The Cape of Good Hope," in *Collected Poems* (Manchester, UK: Carcanet Press, 1990), 72; Marianne Moore, "Granite and Steel," in *Complete Poems* (London: Faber, 1968), 205; Elizabeth Bishop, "Invitation to Miss Marianne Moore," in *The Complete Poems, 1927–1979* (New York: Farrar, Straus and Giroux, 1983), 82–83; William Meredith, "A View of the Brooklyn Bridge," in *Earth Walk: New and Selected Poems* (New York: Knopf, 1970), 53; Kenneth Burke, "Eye-Crossing—From Brooklyn to Manhattan," in *Directions in Literary Criticism: Contemporary Approaches to Literature*, eds. Stanley Weintraub and Philip Young (University Park: Pennsylvania State University Press, 1973), 228–251.

25. See http://video.google.com/videoplay?docid=-238327798630047498 or www.youtube.com/watch?v=TF7dex_5AZA

26. See James Sanders, *Celluloid Skyline: New York and the Movies* (New York: Knopf, 2001), 37–38.

27. See *New York Times*, June 1, 1940: 17; F. Scott Fitzgerald, "An Opinion on *Brooklyn Bridge*" F. Scott Fitzgerald Papers, Department of Rare Books and Special Collections, Princeton University, Box 29b.

Chapter Six: Commemoration and the Contemporary Era (1983–2008)

1. See *New York Times*, *New York Post* and *Daily News*, May 23, 1983; May 24, 1983 and May 25, 1983.

2. See Bill Prochnaw, "New Yorkers Throw a Bridge Party," *Washington Post*, May 25, 1983: A2 and *Daily News*, May 25, 1983: 31. Also see Pete Hamill, "Bridge of Dreams," *New York*, May 30, 1983: 30 and George F. Will, "Brooklyn Bridge: Form and Function," *Detroit News*, May 22, 1983: A19.

3. Bill Reel, "The Brooklyn Bridge is an Exit," *San Francisco Sunday Examiner and Chronicle*, May 29, 1983: B11; Martin Filler, "The Brooklyn Bridge at 100," *Art in America*, 71 (1983), 142–144; "The American Bridge," *Boston Sunday Globe*, May 22, 1983: A22.

4. Melvin Maddocks, "Selling the Brooklyn Bridge," *Christian Science Monitor*, June 2, 1983: 22; Richard Eder, "Brooklyn Bridge Spans a Century," *Los Angeles Times*, June 5, 1983: Calendar, 6; Jimmy Breslin, "The Bridge," *House and Garden*, 152 (June 1983), 150.

5. "Man in a Wheelchair Dangles from Bridge," *New York Times*, August 2, 1988: B3.

6. See Phillip Lopate, *Waterfront: A Journey Around Manhattan* (Crown: New York, 2004), 256–261.

7. See www.cnn.com/2006/US/03/21/coldwar.trove/index.html and Sewell Chan, "Inside the Brooklyn Bridge, a Whiff of the Cold War," *New York Times*, March 21, 2006: B2.

8. See Anthony Lasala, "Jerry Spagnoli and the Mysterious World of the Daguerreotype," January 10, 2007, *Photo District News Online*, www.pdnonline.com/pdn/spotlight/article_display.jsp?vnu_content_id=1003531185

9. See "Minor Mention," *Appletons' Journal* 9 (1873), 571; Schuyler, "The Bridge as a Monument," 332–334 and J.A. Mitchell, *The Last American: A Fragment from the Journal of Khan-Li, Prince of Dimph-Yoo-Chur and Admiral of the Persian Navy* (New York: Frederick A. Stokes Co., 1889), 20.

10. Eric Lichtblau, "US Cites Al Qaeda in Plot to Destroy Brooklyn Bridge," *New York Times*, June 23, 2003: 1; "Al Qaeda in America: The Enemy Within," *Newsweek*, June 23, 2003: 3; Jimmy Breslin, "A Fate Sealed Under Secrecy," *Newsday*, June 22, 2003: 2; David Rennie, "Captured al-Qa'eda Man was FBI Spy," *Daily Telegraph* (London), June 23, 2003: 12.

11. *New York Times*, February 7, 1916: 1 and February 8, 1916: 3.

12. *New York Times*, April 20, 1916: 11.

13. *New York Times*, November 22, 1922: 20 and November 24, 1922: 9.

14. *New York Times*, July 19, 1931: 6.

15. *New York Times*, August 3, 1979: B1.

16. See *New York Times*, August 5, 1979: 22, August 16, 1979: B2 and June 1, 1981: B2.

17. See *New York Times*, June 27, 1959: 3 and June 20, 2003: 12.

18. See *The Star* (Sheffield), February 21, 2007.

19. See *New York Sun*, August 29, 2006: 1, 4.

Index